WHERE TYRANNY BEGINS

ALSO BY DAVID ROHDE

*In Deep: The FBI, the CIA, and the Truth
about America's "Deep State"*

*Beyond War: Reimagining American Influence
in a New Middle East*

A Rope and a Prayer: The Story of a Kidnapping
(with Kristen Mulvihill)

*Endgame: The Betrayal and Fall of Srebrenica, Europe's
Worst Massacre since World War II*

WHERE TYRANNY BEGINS

*The Justice Department,
the FBI, and the
War on Democracy*

DAVID ROHDE

W. W. NORTON & COMPANY

Independent Publishers Since 1923

For information about permission to reproduce selections from this book,
write to Permissions, W. W. Norton & Company, Inc.,
500 Fifth Avenue, New York, NY 10110

For information about special discounts for bulk purchases,
please contact W. W. Norton Special Sales at
specialsales@wwnorton.com or 800-233-4830

Manufacturing by Lakeside Book Company
Book design by Lovedog Studio
Production manager: Anna Oler

ISBN 978-0-393-88196-7

W. W. Norton & Company, Inc.
500 Fifth Avenue, New York, N.Y. 10110
www.wwnorton.com

W. W. Norton & Company Ltd.
15 Carlisle Street, London W1D 3BS

10 9 8 7 6 5 4 3 2 1

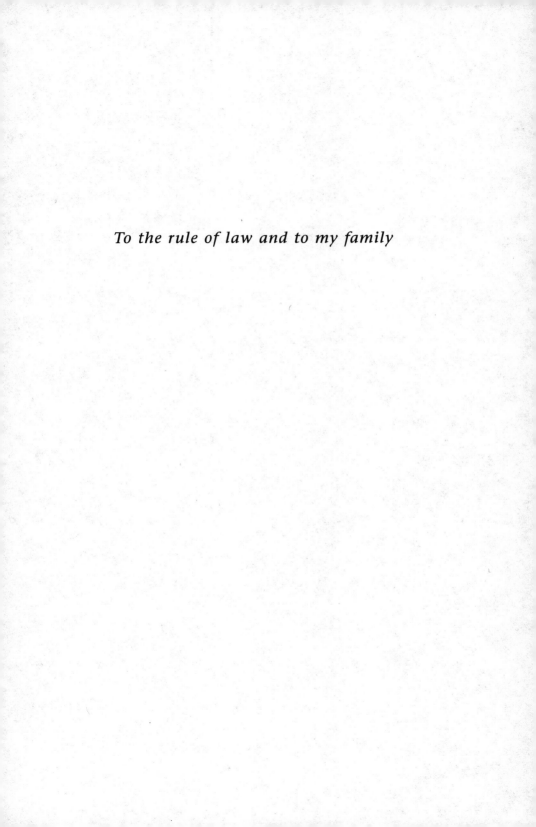

To the rule of law and to my family

"Where-ever law ends, tyranny begins."

—JOHN LOCKE, 1689

CONTENTS

PART II

BIDEN

AUTHOR'S NOTE

THE VAST MAJORITY OF THE PEOPLE I INTERVIEWED FOR this book asked to remain anonymous. That is not unusual for employees of the Justice Department and the FBI, where discretion is prized for legitimate reasons. Over time, though, it became clear that one emotion was driving many of the requests: fear.

This book is both an investigation and a psychological study. It exposes and explores how Donald Trump successfully used online denigration, the rampant spread of conspiracy theories, and threats of violence to discredit, divide, and intimidate FBI and DOJ officials.

The difficulty I found in getting people to speak publicly increased my already deep respect for the journalists who have covered the DOJ and FBI in the Trump and Biden years. Their extraordinary work is cited in endnotes, but I want to also acknowledge it here and thank them. Their reporting is the foundation of this book.

Former Attorney General William Barr declined multiple interview requests. I have included brief passages from his memoir to convey his views of events that this book describes and cited his memoir in the endnotes. Most of all, I thank the DOJ and FBI officials who overcame their fear and did speak with me. This book would not have been possible without their courage.

Prologue:

A COME-TO-JESUS MEETING

O N AUGUST 1, 2022, SENIOR JUSTICE DEPARTMENT AND FBI officials gathered on the seventh floor of the FBI head-quarters in Washington, DC, for a historic meeting. They exchanged pleasantries, shook hands, and took seats in Room 7427, the FBI general counsel's conference room, a nondescript gathering place with a long rectangular table surrounded by no-frills office chairs. Each official—all of them men—wore a suit, tie, and dress shirt, mandatory attire on the storied floor that houses the office of the FBI director and his top advisors.

The senior DOJ officials had left their headquarters, an elegant mix of Classical and Art Deco architecture, and met their bureau colleagues across Pennsylvania Avenue in the FBI headquarters, a brutalist structure considered one of the ugliest buildings in Washington. Their goal was to have what one participant later called a "come to Jesus" meeting.

For months, prosecutors from the DOJ's national security division and the leaders of the FBI's Washington field office had argued over an ongoing criminal probe. Tension and debate between prosecutors and agents during an investigation is routine, and often welcomed. But this case had taken on an extraordinary level of intensity, pressure, and acrimony due to the potential defendant: former president Donald Trump.

The relationship between the DOJ and the FBI, the country's two most powerful federal law enforcement agencies, had ebbed and

The lesson of J. Edgar Hoover's forty-eight-year tenure as FBI director was clear: the bureau could be a powerful political weapon. (EVERETT COLLECTION / BRIDGEMAN IMAGES)

flowed in their century-long joint existence. Located a few blocks from the White House, the Justice Department, led by the attorney general, both predates and oversees the FBI. The department's Latin motto, *Qui Pro Domina Justitia Sequitur,* or "who prosecutes on behalf of justice," describes its mission to apply the law equally, without fear or favor, to all Americans. That has not always been true.

During the Cold War, FBI Director J. Edgar Hoover had repeatedly bypassed the attorney general and unilaterally conducted law enforcement operations designed to infiltrate, disrupt, and discredit political leaders and organizations that Hoover deemed subversive. Hoover's perceived enemies ranged from Martin Luther King Jr., who the FBI director viewed as a Communist, to the right-wing John Birch Society. Hoover also secretly provided the eight presidents he served—four Republicans and four Democrats—with dirt on their political rivals.

Justice Department officials committed abuses as well. In 1919 and 1920, Attorney General A. Mitchell Palmer, with Hoover's help, rounded up thousands of immigrants, falsely declared them dangerous radicals, and deported hundreds of them, in the hopes of boosting his own planned presidential campaign. In the early 1970s, John Mitchell, Richard Nixon's attorney general, used the Justice Department to target Nixon's perceived political enemies, from opponents of the Vietnam War, to Black nationalist groups, to officials suspected of leaking politically damaging information about the president.

After the Watergate scandal and the historic Church Committee congressional investigation exposed decades of abuses by the FBI and CIA, sweeping reforms were enacted in the late 1970s to prevent presidents, attorneys general, and FBI directors from using the DOJ and FBI for improper political or personal gain.

Those reforms also reinforced the dual, and contradictory, duties of the attorney general and the FBI director. Both leaders were expected to enact the broad policies of the president, such as cracking down on violent crime or strictly enforcing environmental laws. At the same time, they were expected to investigate, in a fair and nonpartisan manner, potential crimes or corruption by presidents and their aides. The tension between those two missions—serving a president and investigating one—exploded during the Trump and Biden years.

WHEN THE DOJ AND FBI officials met in the FBI headquarters, they were deadlocked over how to retrieve what they believed were dozens of top secret documents that Trump had taken from the White House to Mar-a-Lago.

While they disagreed over how to retrieve the documents, DOJ and FBI officials shared the same feeling about the case: dread. They had initially assumed that Trump would simply hand over the materials. When he didn't, they saw no good options. "You know what the reaction was in the department? We were like, 'Oh shit, we don't want any part of this. The real enemies are Russia and China,'" recalled a former senior FBI official involved in the case who asked not to be named.

Steven D'Antuono, the head of the bureau's Washington field office, feared that the documents dispute would further erode public faith in the FBI. "I was worried about it increasing distrust in us," D'Antuono said in an interview.

Trump's firing of James Comey, as well as Special Counsel John Durham's probe of the FBI's Trump-Russia investigation and bipartisan criticism of the Hillary Clinton email investigation, had taken a toll. Growing numbers of FBI agents saw politically charged cases as career-enders that could result in public vilification, the loss of their pensions, and, given Trump's vows of revenge, criminal prosecution.

"We all thought this posed a risk to us both professionally and personally," said the former senior FBI official. "I can't impress upon you the pressure. We're all living through the special counsel investigation of Trump and the Hillary Clinton email investigation, and Durham. . . . We're trying to make the best decisions we can with all the emotions swirling."

The intense pressure fueled distrust. Several FBI agents in the Washington field office suspected that one of the lead Justice Department prosecutors, Jay Bratt, was politically biased against Trump. According to public records, Bratt had donated $600 to a former DOJ colleague's unsuccessful Democratic primary campaign for the US Senate in Oregon in 2007, $150 to the Oregon Senate Democratic Campaign Committee that same year, and $500 to the Democratic National Committee in 1993 and 1994.

In a less divisive era in American politics, such donations might have drawn less attention. It was generally accepted that career DOJ and FBI officials could put their personal politics aside and investigate any elected official, Republican or Democrat, in a fair and fact-based manner. In the Trump era, bias was assumed, encouraged, and expected. Nonpartisan public service was dismissed as naïve.

Steven D'Antuono recalled being concerned about the approach of the DOJ team investigating Trump, which Bratt led. "Jay was being a little overly aggressive," D'Antuono said in an interview. "The aggressiveness that was there, from day one."

D'Antuono said that other factors could have fueled their behavior. "This is a huge case. It's the former president," D'Antuono said. "Was some of it due to ambition? Jay has been an attorney for a long time. This is the case of the century."

Justice Department officials flatly dismissed D'Antuono's claim that Bratt was somehow biased against Trump. They said that Bratt pursued all cases aggressively, noting that he had a long history of investigating the handling of classified documents by Democrats, including Hillary Clinton. In the Trump case, they added, Bratt had tried for months to reach a resolution with the former president that would not involve a search of Mar-a-Lago.

A senior DOJ official with knowledge of Bratt's work said in an interview that he had never seen him show political bias. "It would be hard for me to overstate how much I disagree with that characterization," said the official, who asked not to be named. "He is one of the finest career prosecutors I've worked with. I've never seen a hint of bias."

Justice Department officials feared that foreign adversaries might try to gain access to the classified documents in Mar-a-Lago. Matthew Olsen, the head of the DOJ's National Security Division, which investigates leaks of classified information, had brought a draft search warrant to the meeting at the FBI. If they could persuade a federal judge to sign off on the warrant, FBI agents could immediately enter Mar-a-Lago without Trump's permission and retrieve the documents.

D'Antuono said he and other FBI agents were determined to recover the classified documents, but not in a way that they saw as needlessly provocative. D'Antuono worried that a search would bolster years of exaggerated claims from Trump that the FBI was politically persecuting him. Hyper-partisanship, conspiracy theories, and distrust threatened to paralyze the investigation.

The most senior Justice Department official at the meeting was Olsen. A graduate of the University of Virginia and Harvard Law School, Olsen had worked as a federal prosecutor in Washington, as general counsel of the National Security Agency, and as director of the National Counterterrorism Center during the Obama adminis-

Stephen D'Antuono, the head of the FBI's Washington field office, feared that DOJ officials were biased against Trump. (SARAH SILBIGER / POOL / EPA-EFE / SHUTTERSTOCK)

tration. FBI officials viewed Olsen as aggressive but fair. Bratt, also a Harvard Law School graduate, was seen as more pugnacious. George Toscas, a career DOJ lawyer and top counterintelligence official, joined the meeting by phone.

The FBI team was led by Jason Jones, the FBI's general counsel. A Cornell Law School graduate, Jones had been a federal prosecutor in New York and a DOJ official before working at the same Atlanta law firm as FBI Director Christopher Wray. Alan Kohler, a New Jersey native who graduated from Rutgers with a master's degree in engineering, headed the agency's Counterintelligence Division. D'Antuono, a Rhode Island native and a graduate of the University of Rhode Island, had worked as a CPA before rising through the bureau ranks to become head of the FBI's Washington field office.

The officials hailed from different parts of an increasingly stratified America, economically, politically, and culturally. And they found themselves at the center of a historic, six-year-long power struggle between Trump-led Republicans and Biden-led Democrats that was the worst political and legal crisis in the United States since the abuses of Hoover and Watergate. At the same time, millions of Americans deeply distrusted the FBI and DOJ thanks to cable news and social media becoming consequence-free cesspools of hyper-partisanship, grievance, and conspiracy theories. The bias of the officials in the room, though, was toward defending their institution and enforcing the law equally, not either political party.

Bratt argued that Trump's defiance of a subpoena they had obtained in May was clear. On June 3, Bratt and two FBI agents had visited Mar-a-Lago and met in person with Trump's lawyers. The former president's attorneys handed over another thirty-eight documents that contained classification markings and gave them a signed certification stating that a "diligent search" had been conducted and that "any and all" documents responsive to the subpoena had been provided. Trump himself had greeted Bratt and the FBI agents and promised to cooperate, saying he was "an open book."

Soon after Bratt and the FBI agents left Mar-a-Lago, they received a tip from a source. Days before Bratt and the agents arrived, staffers had moved boxes out of the Mar-a-Lago storage room where Trump kept documents from his presidency. To confirm the claim, they subpoenaed footage from surveillance cameras near the storage room.

In July, the FBI officials received surveillance camera footage that stunned them. Employees had removed as many as thirty boxes of documents from the storage room just before Bratt and the FBI agents arrived. Whoever had told them to move the boxes could be charged with obstructing a federal investigation.

The surveillance videos prompted Jones, the FBI general counsel, and Kohler, the FBI's head of counterintelligence, to change their position. After opposing an FBI search, they now supported one.

As the meeting dragged on, Kohler asked some of his FBI colleagues to consider the damage that would be done to the FBI's reputation if they didn't treat the Trump case as they had similar cases. Since 2017, the FBI had investigated hundreds of cases of classified information being reportedly mishandled. During that period, the bureau conducted more than eighty searches to recover classified documents.

In an ongoing case in Kansas City, DOJ prosecutors were seeking several years in federal prison for an FBI analyst, Kendra Kingsbury, who had improperly taken 386 classified documents from her office to her home, in violation of federal law.

But D'Antuono and several of his subordinates were unpersuaded that the search needed to be done immediately. D'Antuono felt that the documents were secure, noting that Secret Service agents were present at the resort. He wanted Olsen to call Trump's lawyer, Evan Corcoran, and ask him to convince his client to agree to a consensual search. "I think he would've worked with us," D'Antuono recalled, referring to Corcoran. Regarding Trump, he said, "We search his place and we're walking right into his MO. You got to know the behavior of the person you're dealing with."

Justice Department officials shared the FBI's concerns about stoking conspiracy theories about both organizations, but argued that a clear track record existed that Trump was not cooperating. Prosecutors felt they had a duty to investigate a former president no more aggressively or less aggressively than any American. In an earlier email exchange, Toscas, the DOJ counterintelligence official, had written to FBI officials, "We don't care about optics."

As the meeting continued, the discussion grew increasingly heated. Bratt raised his voice several times. When D'Antuono asked if prosecutors now considered Trump the subject of the investigation, Bratt shot back, "What does that matter?" but didn't answer the question. D'Antuono knew that Trump was not listed as a subject in the FBI's case file. Everybody was arguing, recalled one participant, and FBI officials from the Washington field office were in open conflict with Bratt.

D'Antuono dug in, convinced that a private, consensual search could end the standoff. "If it was a consent search, I don't know if he would have broadcast that we were there," he said. "We would've gotten the records." D'Antuono said he would have his agents search Mar-a-Lago only if ordered to do so by his FBI superiors. "I was trying to be a different voice in the room. Why do we have to be aggressive?

We have an attorney in this case," he said, adding, "If it didn't work with Corcoran then fine. We would serve the search warrant and go in. No harm no foul."

While DOJ officials feared that Trump might move the documents again, D'Antuono felt there was no need to rush. The FBI also had a plan in place for how to respond if it appeared that documents were being removed from the property. "In my opinion, there was no harm in doing it that way," D'Antuono said.

At the center of the disagreement were perceptions of Trump. Like the country, the investigators were deeply divided over the former president. D'Antuono and some of his subordinates felt that Trump did not want the documents dispute made public. When Bratt and two FBI agents visited Mar-a-Lago on June 3, Trump had kept the meeting secret and had not posted about it on social media. They saw Trump as buffoonish and most likely motivated by a desire to show off the classified documents.

Justice Department officials and some FBI officials believed that Trump's continued possession of the documents was a direct threat to national security. They worried that China, Russia, or another foreign rival could infiltrate Mar-a-Lago and gain access to the documents. Not acting quickly could expose US secrets, spies, or spying methods.

After roughly an hour, the meeting concluded with no agreement. Kohler and Jones, the FBI general counsel, were unable to change the views of D'Antuono and other agents in the Washington field office. D'Antuono would have to be ordered to conduct the search by FBI Director Chris Wray or Deputy FBI Director Paul Abbate.

After the DOJ officials left, the FBI officials spoke alone. D'Antuono and others from the Washington field office expressed a new concern. They noted that the draft search warrant included a potential criminal charge against Trump that they did not recall seeing before: Section 2071 of Title 18. The law made it illegal for an individual who possesses government documents to "willfully and unlawfully" conceal, remove, mutilate, obliterate, falsify, or destroy them. If a person is convicted of the charge, they shall "be disqualified from holding" any federal office. "The barring from office charge," D'An-tuono recalled. "People saw that charge as 'Aha, is that DOJ's effort to get Trump?'"

Other FBI officials disagreed about Bratt and did not consider him politically biased. Instead, they feared that Trump's years of attacks were now impacting the decision-making of current FBI agents. "They had a lot of co-workers who were impacted by Crossfire Hurri-cane," said the former official, using the Trump-Russia investigation's code name. "The lesson some in the FBI took away was: Stay away from politically charged cases—they can ruin your career."

The following day, tensions between DOJ and FBI officials flared again. Toscas, the DOJ official who had been on the phone during the meeting, scolded D'Antuono in an email for resisting the search. "You are way out of line on substance and form," Toscas wrote. "You and your leadership seem to have gone from cautious to fearful."

D'Antuono, who felt he had been called a coward, was irate. He believed he was simply being logical and methodical. "I take it to heart to do the right thing in the right way for the right reasons," he said. "They put such urgency into getting into Mar-a-Lago, for the circumstances, it just didn't smell right, it didn't feel right."

The scorched-earth political wars of the Trump era exacerbated tensions among law enforcement officials. "The cultural maelstrom, we were all part of it," recalled the former senior FBI official. "You know that whatever decision you make you're going to be crucified. You either do the search and get crucified by the Republicans. If you don't it, the Democrats crucify you."

The following day, an official known to few Americans ended the debate over Mar-a-Lago. FBI Deputy Director Paul Abbate, who outranked D'Antuono, agreed that the bureau had taken the steps it needed to execute the search.

On August 8, agents dressed in polo shirts and khakis—not jack-ets emblazoned with "FBI"—entered Mar-a-Lago and recovered one hundred classified documents that Trump had retained. After the FBI agents left Mar-a-Lago, D'Antuono, who had been monitoring

Paul Abbate, the deputy FBI Director and an obscure figure to most Americans, approved agents' search of Mar-a-Lago. (CJ GUNTHER / EPA-EFE / SHUTTERSTOCK)

the search from his office in Washington, was initially relieved. To his surprise, the agents' arrival and departure from the resort had not leaked to the press.

That ended just before 7:00 p.m. In an error- and exaggeration-laced 340-word statement, Trump disclosed the search, declared it illegal, and falsely claimed that FBI agents had "occupied" his residence and resort. "These are dark times for our Nation, as my beautiful home, Mar-a-Lago in Palm Beach, Florida, is currently under siege, raided, and occupied by a large group of FBI agents," Trump wrote.

Republicans immediately called for the investigation, and potential impeachment, of Attorney General Merrick Garland. "Attorney General Garland: preserve your documents and clear your calendar," House Republican leader Kevin McCarthy tweeted. The Republican National Committee solicited money off of the search. "In an UNPRECEDENTED move Joe Biden's Department of Justice RAIDS President Trump's home at Mar-a-Lago," the committee said in a "BREAKING NEWS" message on its website. "Donate ANY AMOUNT RIGHT NOW to show your support for the GOP."

————

SUSPICION OF THE SEARCH emerged inside the FBI as well. FBI officials from dozens of the bureau's fifty-six field offices demanded answers from their superiors. They called colleagues in Washington and asked why the search had been conducted. Some even asked about a conspiracy theory circulating online that evidence had been planted by the FBI in the former president's home.

Instead of responding to the public and private attacks, FBI and DOJ officials, citing a long-standing policy of not commenting on ongoing criminal investigations, initially said little about why they had conducted the search.

Three days later, an armed forty-two-year-old man wearing body armor tried to force his way into the FBI field office in Cincinnati. In a subsequent standoff, police shot him dead. Individuals also attempted to breach three additional FBI field offices, but the bureau kept the incidents secret. On a social media site frequented by anti-Semites and white supremacists, users said they were readying for armed revolution.

Attorney General Merrick Garland held a press conference, took responsibility for the search and condemned the attacks on FBI personnel. "I will not stand by silently when their integrity is unfairly attacked," he said. "Every day, they protect the American people from violent crime, terrorism, and other threats."

Garland, though, declined to share any further details about why the FBI had searched Mar-a-Lago. "This is all I can say right now," he said. "More information will be made available in the appropriate way and at the appropriate time."

Frustration simmered in corners of the FBI. Some supervisors and agents felt that the DOJ and FBI's policy of not publicly commenting on investigations was ill-suited for the Trump era. While prosecutors and agents dutifully waited to present their evidence in court, the DOJ and FBI were discredited by pro-Trump politicians, cable news pundits, and social media personalities. "'Trust me' doesn't cut it," said the former senior FBI official, who came to realize the DOJ and

FBI needed to explain their actions more openly to the public. "No one wanted this. Everyone wanted it to go away," the official recalled. "There were reasonable disagreements about the path forward, but the path we followed was the right one given how we usually handle these cases and the facts before us."

The Mar-a-Lago search was a microcosm of a broader dynamic. In four years as president and three years as an ex-president, Trump had successfully used conspiracy theories, co-option, and threats to bend DOJ and FBI officials to his will to a greater extent than publicly known. Those who dared to defy him had their reputations damaged and their careers derailed.

One former senior DOJ official said that Trump's goal during and after his presidency was clear. "I think he is intentionally trying to weaken public confidence in the Justice Department and federal law enforcement in order to keep himself from going to jail," the official said. "He tries to degrade any institution that acts as a check on his power. He degrades them systematically. It's all part of a whole, leading him to try to be able to get away with whatever he wants."

To a greater extent than any president in US history, Trump had successfully discredited the DOJ and FBI in the eyes of large groups of American voters. After special counsel Robert Hur cited Biden's poor memory as a reason he should not be prosecuted for retaining classified documents, Hur was denounced by Biden and Democrats as partisan. In an age of hyper-partisanship, it was proving impossible for the country's most powerful federal law enforcement agencies to criminally investigate Trump or Biden and maintain broad public support.

In private, exasperated DOJ and FBI officials complained that law enforcement institutions were being asked to settle the country's political disputes, a task normally reserved for voters, elections, and Congress. They said law enforcement agencies were not created for, nor equipped to ease, the country's polarization.

During and after Trump's presidency, both political parties came to view the DOJ and FBI as potential political weapons. Democrats who believed Trump was a dictator in waiting and Republicans who believed Biden had stolen the 2020 election saw the FBI, the DOJ, and judges as politically biased. After five decades, the post-Watergate reforms that were designed to prevent the use of the DOJ and FBI for political meddling began to unravel.

At the same time, belief in a founding principle of American democracy—"equal justice under law"—was under assault. The four words carved above the entrance to the US Supreme Court Building summarize it. All Americans should be treated equally by the courts, the Justice Department, and federal and local law enforcement agencies.

As allegations of political bias by the DOJ and FBI became central issues in the 2024 presidential campaign, two forms of public reaction—violence and apathy—posed the gravest threats to American democracy. A five-word warning written by the English philosopher John Locke in 1689 anticipated the stakes for America's twenty-first-century political, cultural, and factual divide: "Wherever law ends, tyranny begins."

Part I

TRUMP

CHAPTER 1

LOL
NOTHING MATTERS
LAWYERING

SIX DAYS AFTER DONALD TRUMP TOOK OFFICE AS PRESI-
dent, he defied the Justice Department. In an immediate test
of whether the department would enable or constrain the new president, Trump signed an executive order without asking DOJ lawyers
to carefully vet it.

In a Friday afternoon ceremony at the Pentagon, Trump signed
Executive Order 13679: "Protecting the Nation from Foreign Terrorist Entry into the United States." The order shocked civil liberties
groups and the Washington establishment in its xenophobic sweep.
With a stroke of a pen, Trump banned foreign nationals from seven
predominantly Muslim nations from entering the United States for
ninety days. He barred refugees—worldwide—from arriving in the
United States for 120 days and blocked all Syrian refugees from entering the country indefinitely.

Democrats and civil liberties groups dismissed the ban as dangerous, demagogic, and unconstitutional. They said that Trump was
exaggerating the security threat posed by refugees, claiming sweeping new presidential powers, and attempting to legitimize and legal-
ize the Islamophobia and xenophobia that he had run on in 2016.
Within hours, the American Civil Liberties Union filed lawsuits
arguing that the order violated the constitutional right of freedom
of religion and myriad federal laws banning discrimination based on
religion, race, or ethnicity. Within days, federal judges blocked parts
of the order. Trump's legal gambit appeared to have failed.

The order, though, exposed how ill-equipped the Justice Department was to respond to Trump's disregard for basic facts, post-Watergate norms, and the rule of law. For the next four years, Trump's seeming indifference to public shaming would allow him to undermine the department in myriad ways. Initially, career DOJ lawyers saw his unabashed attempts to gain personal and political power as errors that stemmed from his lack of government experience. Many could not yet imagine a president who would blithely undermine the Justice Department and all that it stood for.

On its face, Trump's travel ban was legally deficient in glaring ways. It seemed to violate the Constitution by discriminating on the basis of religion, particularly as he had made a campaign vow to keep all Muslims from entering the United States. It applied to people born in other countries who were lawful permanent US residents with valid visas. And it did not include a national security process, even though it was billed as a national security measure.

Many Democrats and members of the liberal legal establishment scoffed at the poorly drafted executive order and predicted that it would not survive review in the courts. In hindsight, they underestimated both Trump and Trumpism.

POLITICALLY, THE ORDER was a Trumpian masterstroke. It demonstrated to far-right conservatives that Trump would aggressively pursue the hard-line policies that they had sought for decades, and it energized voters who supported Trump's campaign vow to defend Americans from Muslim "terrorists" and "Mexican criminals."

After Trump issued the travel ban, some career Justice Department employees, along with large parts of the country, were bewildered by his first seven days in office. Trump had lied about the size of the crowd at his inauguration and falsely claimed that voter fraud had robbed him of the popular vote, foreshadowing the chaos he would sow in 2020. He ordered the US government to begin building a wall along the border with Mexico and told the Justice Department to defund so-called "sanctuary cities" that welcomed migrants who were seeking asylum.

Trump's actions immediately exposed the core tension in the DOJ's mission that attorneys general had struggled with since the department's creation. Should the Justice Department use its legal expertise to empower presidents or to constrain them?

The attorney general was expected to advance the president's broad policy agenda and at the same time enforce the law without fear or favor. The two priorities sometimes clashed. After 9/11, the George W. Bush administration and national security agencies placed enormous pressure on the Justice Department to legally bless policies that seemed illegal on their face, such as the use of torture and mass surveillance in response to the attacks.

In an apparent attempt to go around the department, no one at the White House had discussed the travel ban in detail with career DOJ officials before announcing it. Presidents before Trump would have wanted their top legal minds to bulletproof a controversial policy order that had such vast implications for civil liberties and national security, if for no other reason than to stave off crippling legal challenges.

Instead, the Justice Department's topmost officials learned of the travel ban from the news media. That pattern would continue.

WITH TRUMP'S NOMINEE for attorney general, Jeff Sessions, the conservative Alabama Republican senator, awaiting confirmation from the Senate, the decision of how to defend Trump's ban fell to career department lawyers and holdover Obama administration appointees, including Sally Yates, the acting attorney general.

"I got a call from my principal deputy," Yates later recalled at the Aspen Ideas Festival. "[He] says, 'You're not going to believe this, but I was just on the *New York Times* website, and it looks like the president has instituted some sort of travel ban.'" Yates scrambled to find a copy of the order on the internet, and then got to work trying to figure out, "What the heck is this thing, and to whom does it apply?"

Jody Hunt, a career DOJ civil servant and one of the directors of the Federal Programs Branch, which defends the federal government in civil suits, also heard about the ban from the news. Hunt's office would need to defend the United States in the many lawsuits that would be filed against the ban.

While presidents nominate the attorney general and several dozen other top DOJ officials, most of the department's day-to-day work is conducted by roughly nine thousand career department attorneys like Hunt. An Alabama native, he had worked as career civil servant for decades, serving under Bill Clinton, George W. Bush, and Barack Obama.

Hunt believed his role as a civil servant was to advise presidents and their aides on the legal defensibility of their policies—even if he disagreed with them personally. Hunt believed presidents, their appointees, and members of Congress should determine government policy, not career civil servants like himself.

"The Justice lawyer's job is to ask, 'Do we have a valid, viable legal defense of what is being done?'" Hunt said in an interview. "There might be a stronger argument on the other side, but it is the job of the department to defend the executive branch." He added, "If there is a viable argument, we're going to put that forward."

Yates, meanwhile, worked to sort out whether the ban was constitutional. Could the DOJ's Civil Division beat back the lawsuits filed in the wake of the travel ban announcement? Should federal prosecutors criminally charge people from Muslim countries who were on flights into the United States when the ban was announced?

Yates would ultimately declare the travel ban unconstitutional and order Justice Department lawyers not to enforce it. Liberals immediately lionized her for resisting the ban. Trump immediately fired Yates, who, in hindsight, came to be seen by the new president and his allies as an early example of the "deep state"—government workers who refuse to implement the policies of a democratically elected president with a mandate from voters to carry out the policies they promised.

After firing Yates, the Trump White House had DOJ lawyers repeatedly revise the executive order. More than a year and three versions later, Trump's travel ban ultimately triumphed. The Supreme Court's conservative majority upheld it in a June 2018 5–4 ruling, eighteen months after Trump's signing ceremony at the Pentagon.

In those early days of the administration, Hunt, for his part, did not believe that Trump wanted to flagrantly violate the Constitution. Trump had been president for only a week. He had no idea what most federal agencies did or how they did it. The main problem, as Hunt saw it, was that the travel ban had not gone through the DOJ's rigorous legal vetting process before being rolled out.

Hunt held out hope that Trump would learn on the job and begin to respect the norms of the presidency. He assumed that the presidency would change Trump. Instead, Trump would change the presidency.

ACROSS THE JUSTICE DEPARTMENT, its 115,000 employees faced the same difficult choice. Should they remain and try to defend the department's norms from inside, or should they depart? If they did stay, would they be violating their oath to defend the Constitution, uphold the rule of law, and apply the law equally to all Americans?

Erica Newland, a twenty-nine-year-old lawyer who joined the DOJ three months before Trump was elected, wrestled with the ethics of facilitating policies by the new administration that she did not believe were lawful. Newland declined to describe the specific cases she worked on, citing ethics rules that require lawyers to maintain confidentiality.

Raised in Auburn, Alabama, the Yale Law School graduate worked in the Office of Legal Counsel (OLC), a powerful entity in the Justice Department which, among other duties, helps revise executive orders from the president to ensure that they are constitutional.

Known as the department's brain trust, the OLC provides legal advice to the White House and executive branch agencies, often in the president's favor. An OLC staff position was one of the most coveted legal jobs in Washington. A civil libertarian, Newland was a skeptic of presidential power. She believed the law could serve as a constraining force on a president.

Newland decided to remain in the DOJ, believing that by upholding the rule of law she could help act as a check on Trump's excesses. "I thought it was really important to stay," Newland recalled in an interview, adding that working for presidents from both parties is "part of the obligation" of a career civil servant. "To keep the wheels of government turning, enforcing the constraints. Because the rule of law matters no matter who is in the White House."

Before arriving at the OLC, Newland had worked as a law clerk for then Federal Judge Merrick Garland, whose 2016 nomination to the Supreme Court had been blocked by Senate Republicans in a then unprecedented act of partisanship. Newland, who declined to comment on Garland or her work for him, had also worked as an intern at the State Department, the Justice Department, and the Senate Judiciary Committee.

Trump's travel ban was disorienting for career DOJ lawyers, a staid, insular group so buttoned up that, according to Newland, there were "conversations in the OLC lunchroom about whether blue shirts are appropriate under suit jackets."

She found that Washington lawyers tended to be highly conscious of their status in the capitol's elite legal community and usually obeyed authority rather than challenging it. The type of lawyers who pursued jobs in the Justice Department, in general, seemed to be both high-achieving and highly risk-averse. For some lawyers, positions at the DOJ were launchpads to politics or lucrative positions at Washington law firms or large corporations. For others, they were the beginning of lifelong careers in nonpartisan public service. "Some really believed in a career in government," Newland recalled. "A sense of collective mission."

Caution was also common among career DOJ lawyers. A major error could derail a career in a law firm or in the federal government. Due to Washington's small size, open conflict with superiors or colleagues was also avoided. "DC is a small town," Newland said. "You pop in and out of each other's lives all the time. You never know when you are going to end up at the same law firm or working together in government."

On a positive note, the work culture at the DOJ and in DC law firms was seen as less abusive than at large New York law firms. "It's a little less toxic and abusive than in New York," she said. "Because the attorney you're mentoring may someday oversee you." That intimacy also produced a tendency to remain silent. "It's part of why so few people speak out," Newland said.

Over time, Newland came to see the travel ban as an example of an intentional Trump administration legal and political strategy. She called it "LOL nothing matters lawyering." The term, LOL—from the abbreviation for "laugh out loud"—and the idea that "nothing matters" summarized what she saw as a deeply cynical approach to practicing law, which placed a high value on managing Trump and trolling liberals. The goal was to somehow win cases in court while simultaneously energizing Trump's political base.

Newland said the term was a derivation of a phrase that Quinta Jurecic, a fellow at the Brookings Institution, used in an article in Lawfare. Citing the 2005 book *On Bullshitting* by the late Princeton philosophy professor Harry Frankfurt, Jurecic called Trump's administration the "LOL nothing matters presidency." She argued that, unlike lying, which involves acknowledging that facts exist and intentionally obscuring the truth, bullshitting is a nihilistic effort "undertaken without any relationship to truth whatsoever." Jurecic contended that "bullshit . . . is faithless, because it denies the existence of anything constant in which to have faith."

Over time, Newland would come to see "LOL nothing matters

lawyering" as deeply corrosive and dangerous. The approach erodes public trust in judges, the fairness of the legal system, and basic fact. "It corrupts not just the department but our courts," she said. "It contributes to a corruption of the rule of law and our society at large."

THE CIVIL SERVICE JOBS held by Hunt, Newland, and roughly two million other workers across the US government were created in the wake of an assassination. On July 2, 1881, President James A. Garfield arrived at Washington's Baltimore and Potomac Railroad Station to depart for summer vacation. An Ohio Republican, Garfield was considered one of his era's most promising presidents; at forty-nine, he was the third-youngest man ever elected to the office. As he walked across the station, a middle-aged lawyer turned bill collector turned preacher named Charles Guiteau pulled out a revolver and fired two shots into the president's back. One bullet missed, grazing Garfield's arm; the other struck dead center.

Before being taken away by the police, Guiteau shouted his loyalty to Chester A. Arthur, Garfield's vice president: "I am a Stalwart, and Arthur is president now," he shouted. News of the shooting spread quickly, via telegraph, across the country. For the next seventy-nine days, Garfield lingered, his health improving and declining, in part due to botched medical care. On September 19, 1881, he died.

The public raged at Guiteau, a delusional political wannabe who believed he deserved an appointment from Garfield to serve as a US official in Europe. While Guiteau considered himself an important Garfield supporter, he was one of thousands of hangers-on who hoped to obtain a job in the federal government under the "spoils system," where each new president appointed thousands of their supporters to federal jobs, prioritizing loyalty over merit. ("To the victor belong the spoils," as one senator famously put it.)

Under such a system, corruption was rampant in Washington,

DC, but a country still divided after the Civil War lacked the political unity and will to address it. Garfield's death proved a turning point. Sixteen months later, on January 16, 1883, Congress passed into law the Pendleton Act, a historic government reform mandating that nearly all federal employees be hired based on skills, training, and education, rather than political connection. The act gave the American public an independent, professional civil service— one which was answerable to elected officials without being beholden to them.

Over 130 years later, Donald Trump derided Washington, and its federal workers, as "the swamp." The city's most nefarious actors were its corrupt politicians, establishment Democrats and Republicans alike, who Trump claimed betrayed ordinary Americans. After he took office, he came to distrust and denigrate career civil servants, and adopt a term introduced to a broad conservative audience by Breitbart News and its former chairman, Steve Bannon: the "deep state."

First used by political scientists to describe the Turkish military, the term morphed after 9/11 into a reference to the American "military industrial complex," which critics on the Left and Right accused of perpetually fueling conflicts abroad to secure government funding and profit.

Trump, Bannon, and their allies made the "deep state" something vaster: a permanent, unelected shadow government which relentlessly gathered power to itself. The "deep state" included not just power-mad FBI and CIA agents but military leaders, journalists, tech executives, and FDA regulators. Over time, Trump's presidency would be predicated on the idea that the US government—including federal civil servants like Hunt and Newland—was itself an enemy of the people.

Skepticism about government can be a sign of health in a democracy. Concentrations of power and secrecy have always struck Americans as unjust. Since the country's founding, politicians have been elected on promises to tame and change Washington. Resulting waves of reform have eased political division and distrust in government.

Over the last half century, however, distrust in government has grown relentlessly. In 1958, 73 percent of respondents to a Pew Research Center analysis said that they trusted the federal government to do the right thing most of the time. By 1974—toward the end of the Vietnam War, and after Watergate—only 36 percent of Americans felt that way. Since then, no president has been able to restore trust for a sustained period. Through Barack Obama's second term and Trump and Joe Biden's first ones, the percentage of Americans who say that they trust the government has hovered around 18 percent.

At the same time, trust in the news media has declined precipitously as well, with the percentage of Americans who say they trust the media "a great deal" or "a fair amount" declining from 72 percent in 1976 to 36 percent in 2023. The proportion of Americans who say they have no trust at all in the media has grown from 4 percent in 1976 to 39 percent in 2023. Rapid technological change has helped create an online information crisis. Partisan cable television and social media platforms both tend to amplify provocative voices, conspiracy theories, and disinformation. Fearful that politicians and government workers were conspiring against them, large numbers of Americans were eager to see if Trump could drain the swamp.

LINING THE HALLWAYS of the Justice Department headquarters in Washington, DC, are more than fifty stirring art deco murals that are a reflection of a bygone era. In highly idealistic depictions, they show how public service and the rule of law can help improve the lives of all Americans. For many career workers in the building, they remain a core part of the department's identity.

One of the most famous is *Law Versus Mob Rule*, which John Steuart Curry, a Wisconsin artist, painted above the entrance of the department's main law library in 1937. It depicts a shirtless white man, terrified and cowering, on the steps of an unidentified courthouse surrounded by a lynch mob. The leader of the angry crowd is a man clutching a rope tied into a noose. Around him, men on horseback and on foot carry clubs and torches. The sole figure protecting the frightened man is a judge clad in a black robe. The judge implores the crowd to trust the American legal system to dispense justice, rather than the mob.

Such images gloss over decades of abuses of power by the DOJ and the FBI. After the department's creation by Congress in 1870, it briefly battled the Ku Klux Klan and its campaign to terrorize freed slaves, segregate races, and prevent Black Americans from voting. Then, for nearly a century, the department—and the presidents it served—ignored the Klan-backed imposition of Jim Crow laws across the South. When Curry initially proposed that the mural celebrate the end of slavery in the United States, department officials rejected the idea.

That was just one example of the DOJ and FBI leaders failing to live up to their organization's professed ideals. The staff of the Justice Department, from the attorney general and FBI director down, reflect the norms, mores, and political divisions of the society they inhabit. Longtime FBI director J. Edgar Hoover rose to power in the 1920s by embracing the virulently anti-immigrant and anti-communist politics of that era.

At the age of twenty-four, Hoover created a system to gather intelligence on socialists, anarchists, and "alien negro agitators," including Marcus Garvey, as head of the department's newly created "Radical Division." Hoover biographer Beverly Gage wrote that he "forever changed the nature of American politics, launching an unprecedented experiment in peacetime political surveillance." Hoover also played a critical role in the Palmer Raids that resulted in the mass deportation of immigrants. For his efforts, Hoover was promoted in 1924 to run what became the Federal Bureau of Investigation.

Forty-eight years later, Hoover died in office a month before the Watergate scandal, when Richard Nixon's former attorney general, John Mitchell, sent a group of former CIA and FBI officials to break into the Democratic National Committee headquarters located in the Watergate complex. The burglars planted listening devices and photographed documents, all in service of Nixon's reelection.

In the wake of Nixon's resignation and Mitchell's federal criminal conviction for his role in Watergate, Presidents Gerald Ford and Jimmy Carter set out to clean up the Justice Department and the FBI. Ford appointed Edward Levi, the widely respected president of the University of Chicago, as attorney general in 1975.

Levi made restoring public trust in the Justice Department the central focus of his tenure. He instituted sweeping reforms requiring department officials to enforce federal law apolitically and issued the first-ever "Attorney General's Guidelines" for how the FBI should conduct domestic national security investigations. The new rules required the bureau to produce evidence of a crime before conducting wiretaps or searching homes, a step that reduced the number of domestic national security probes by two-thirds.

Levi, a revered figure in the DOJ, created the model of the post-Watergate attorney general. Under Levi, the attorney general implemented the president's policy agenda but did not target the president's political enemies. In a series of nationwide speeches, Levi described the apolitical way the department should work so convincingly that confusion surrounded his political leanings. News accounts questioned whether he was a libertarian, liberal, or conservative.

To reverse Hoover's legacy at the FBI, President Carter appointed William Webster as FBI director. A fifty-three-year-old St. Louis federal appeals court judge, former federal prosecutor, and practicing Christian Scientist, Webster vowed to depoliticize the bureau. He introduced a new motto, telling agents that the bureau could "do the work that the American people expected of us in the way that the Constitution demanded of us." The reaction among rank-and-file agents was mixed. Some Hoover loyalists—known internally as

*After the abuses of Hoover
and Nixon, Attorney General
Edward Levi instituted sweeping
reforms requiring DOJ and FBI
officials to enforce federal law
apolitically.* (KEYSTONE PRESS /
ALAMY STOCK PHOTO)

"Hoover hard hats"—initially resisted Webster's efforts to rein in the
bureau's tactics and diversify its workforce.

Over the course of his nine-year tenure, Webster, aided by Congress, implemented new laws and policies to undo Hoover's imprint:
a ten-year term limit for the FBI director; policies that clearly sub-
ordinated the bureau to the attorney general; coordination with the
Justice Department before bureau officials could publicly speak
about any criminal case; and strict rules governing communications
between the White House and the Justice Department. As the memory of Hoover faded, however, the norms and policies seemed less
urgent, more conditional. But the Justice Department's ability to
affect America's political present and future had not gone away.

A WEEK AFTER THE FIRING of Yates, Jody Hunt received a call on
his office phone from an unknown number. Busy in a meeting at the
Justice Department, he ignored it. When he listened to the voicemail
message, he instantly recognized the lilting voice. "It was a very dis-
tinct accent, I'll never forget it," Hunt recalled, chuckling.

Attorney General Jeff Sessions and his chief of staff, Jody Hunt,
were embraced and then denigrated by Donald Trump. (AP Photo /
Susan Walsh)

"Jody," the caller said. "This is Jeff Sessions, would you please call
my cell phone?" The two Alabama natives, who had never met, had
breakfast the following morning, Saturday, February 4, 2017, at Bistro
Bis, a popular restaurant on Capitol Hill.

Sessions, who was days away from Senate confirmation, asked Hunt
whether he would serve as his chief of staff. Hunt was startled at the offer
but said that he would be willing to serve in the role as long as he was
needed. Sessions responded, "Wonderful, that's what I wanted to hear."

Sessions said in an interview that he intentionally chose a DOJ
career civil servant as his top aide. "He was a highly respected
twenty-year veteran known for his integrity," he said of Hunt. "That's
why I chose him as my chief of staff."

The dizzying turn of events elated Hunt. "I actually felt honored,"
he recalled. "I thought this would be an interesting and fun challenge." Some attorneys general had filled the chief of staff position
with outsiders who alienated the department's career staff. "I thought
it was really great that he wanted someone who had familiarity with
the department."

A lifelong Republican, Hunt is the son of missionaries who had proselytized in Taiwan for ten years when he was a young boy. In 1971, at the age of nine, he wrote a letter to President Richard Nixon protesting US recognition of the Communist government in Beijing.

After attending high school in Alabama, he earned a degree in public administration from Samford University, a Christian college in Homewood, Alabama, and a master's degree in international affairs from Florida State University. Unsure whether to become a diplomat or professor, he decided to get a law degree and graduated from Columbia Law School in New York in 1989, after which he clerked for a federal judge in Birmingham.

An avid Auburn football fan, Hunt wears his hair slicked back, radiates Southern charm, and has a boyish face that makes him look younger than his years. For much of his career, Hunt had been seen as apolitical. But his role in a dispute over gay rights caused some Obama appointees to see him as politically biased. Hunt objected when Attorney General Eric Holder indicated that the department would no longer defend the legality of "Don't Ask, Don't Tell," a 1993 executive order issued by Bill Clinton that allowed gays to serve in the military if they did not publicly reveal their sexual orientation. Gay rights groups criticized the policy for institutionalizing and legitimizing homophobia.

Hunt personally thought that "Don't Ask, Don't Tell" was a "silly" policy, and that the Obama administration and the Democrat-controlled Congress should simply enact a law banning discrimination against gays in the military.

Declining to enforce certain laws for political reasons, Hunt believed, sent the message that officials could enforce laws only when they comported with their personal political beliefs. Hunt did not go public with his disagreements with the Obama administration because he believed that part of his job was to keep such disputes private.

Yates's decision to publicly order DOJ lawyers to not defend the travel ban in court astonished and infuriated Hunt. He believed it was the job of career department attorneys in his office to defend high-profile and complex constitutional challenges if a viable argument could be made that they were constitutional. While he personally opposed Trump's travel ban, he felt that a revised version of it could be deemed constitutional.

For the next twelve months, the question that would haunt Hunt, Newland, and other department employees was whether they—and the ideals and norms they had sworn to uphold—would constrain the new president. Hunt could not yet imagine that legality would have no bearing on what Trump would push the department to carry out. He could not imagine that Trump would attack the DOJ and FBI officials who opposed him, destroying their careers and their reputations.

FOUR DAYS AFTER RECEIVING the surprise call from Sessions, Jody Hunt moved into his spacious new office adjacent to the attorney general's suite on the fifth floor of the Justice Department. The speed of his appointment left Hunt's head spinning. "I sat down at the chief of staff's desk, and I thought, 'What am I supposed to do?'" Hunt joked.

In fact, his phone rang incessantly. Sessions was due to take office in two days and Hunt needed to immediately schedule a series of briefings. There was also confusion about where Sessions would be sworn in as attorney general. "I was fielding calls, and everyone had an issue," Hunt recalled. "You have this feeling that everyone wants a piece of the AG."

Democrats, meanwhile, dreaded the arrival of Attorney General Sessions, a man whose far-right positions on immigration and violent crime they perceived as disqualifying him from serving as the country's chief law enforcement official. But Sessions and Trump bonded over a shared sense of being outsiders disdained—and underestimated—by the political establishment. Eight days after winning the 2016 election, Trump chose Sessions as his nominee for attorney general.

In an interview in his home in Mobile, Alabama, Sessions called his tenure as attorney general one of the highlights of his life. Sessions, who worked as a US attorney and federal prosecutor in southern Alabama before entering politics, saw his return to the DOJ as a homecoming. "I spent fourteen years in the department. I was raised in the department. I loved the Department of Justice and I respected it," Sessions said. "And I did my best to serve it honorably, even though we had a hostile media."

Born Jefferson Beauregard Sessions III, the new attorney general, like his father and grandfather, was named after two infamous Confederate leaders: President Jefferson Davis and General Pierre Beauregard. Called "Buddy" as a boy, Sessions grew up in a one-story house about an hour's drive south of Selma.

Sessions's father, who did not have a college degree, ran a local country store and then an International Harvester dealership. "We certainly did not have much money," Sessions recalled. "I learned the importance, as a youth, of financial discipline. Both my parents were very frugal because of the great depression." But, he added, his facing lighting up, "Those were good times."

As a youth, Sessions attended segregated schools in one of the state's poorest counties. After graduating from Huntingdon College, a private Methodist school in Montgomery, he earned his law degree from the University of Alabama in 1973 and became a federal prosecutor.

Throughout the 1980s, Sessions served as the US attorney for the Southern District of Alabama under Ronald Reagan and George H. W. Bush. He said the experience instilled a belief in him that the law must be aggressively enforced. "It was a great group of prosecutors," Sessions recalled. "Crime can be reduced through effective law enforcement."

Sessions also supported mandatory minimum prison sentences in drug cases, which politicians across the political spectrum later called excessive.

After Bill Clinton won the presidency, Sessions was elected state attorney general, ousting a Democrat. During his two-year tenure, Sessions backed the revival of prisoner chain gangs, supported a county judge who posted the Ten Commandments in his courtroom, and defended a state law that banned funding for gay student groups at state colleges, contending that such groups encouraged violation of state sodomy laws. (A federal appeals court later struck down the law, declaring it blatant discrimination.) In 1996, he was narrowly elected to the US Senate.

During his two decades as a US senator, Sessions advocated for lengthy prison sentences and harsh measures to halt the flow of immigrants to the United States. He derailed attempts by George W. Bush and Barack Obama to pass bipartisan immigration reform. As Alabama and other red states grew more conservative, he grew so popular that he ran unopposed for Senate in 2014.

When the Reagan administration nominated Sessions to serve as a federal judge, a Black federal prosecutor testified that Sessions had once called him "boy" and said that the Ku Klux Klan was "OK until I found out they smoked pot." (Sessions adamantly denied calling the man "boy," and said his comment about the Klan had been a joke.

After Coretta Scott King and other Black civil rights leaders publicly opposed Sessions's nomination, support for him on the Senate Judiciary Committee dropped and Sessions withdrew.

During his political career, though, Sessions created a political base for himself in Alabama that included suburban, working-class, rural, and evangelical voters. "Sessions had a Trump movement before there was a Trump," Wayne Flynt, a history professor at Auburn University, told the *New York Times*.

When Trump launched his campaign in 2015, Sessions found a candidate who shared his political vision. While other Republicans expressed reservations about Trump's bombast and attacks against migrants, Sessions embraced them. Sessions supported some of the Trump campaign's most provocative tactics, such as having the victims of crimes committed by undocumented immigrants speak at the Republican National Convention. Steve Bannon, who once urged

Sessions to run for president, praised the senator for his role on the campaign, musing, "He has been the leader of this populist revolt against the political elite."

ON FEBRUARY 9, 2017, Sessions was sworn in by Vice President Mike Pence in the Oval Office as Trump looked on. Trump, Pence, and Sessions beamed. "It is with great pride, very great pride, that I say these words to you right now," Trump said: "Attorney General Jeff Sessions, welcome to the White House." Attendees clapped. Trump announced that he was signing three Sessions-like executive orders designed to reduce violent crime and "break the back of the criminal cartels that have spread across our Nation."

In his own remarks, Sessions echoed Trump's tough-on-crime messaging, but also struck a different note. "Mr. President, thank you for this great honor," Sessions said. "I look forward to making sure that every ounce of strength I have and that the people of the Department of Justice have is going to be focused on preserving and protecting the Constitution and the safety of this country."

Hunt attended as well. He found Trump warm and personable in private. "He's very likable one-on-one," Hunt recalled. "He wants you to like him and thinks that if he's nice to you, you'll always be loyal to him."

After the ceremony, Hunt decided to show Trump a photo that he thought might interest the new president. As Trump sat behind the *Resolute* desk, which Presidents Kennedy, Carter, Reagan, Clinton, George W. Bush, and Obama had all used, Hunt pulled a photo up on the screen of his phone.

"I leaned my arm across the desk and put my phone in front of him," Hunt recalled. The photo was a picture of Trump, when he was in his forties, dressed in a light-blue blazer and a white golf shirt, with his arm around a young woman standing beside him. Both of them smiled.

Trump, visibly surprised, asked "Wow, when was that taken?" Hunt recalled. He explained that the photo was shot on Trump's yacht during the 1989 Miss America pageant in Atlantic City. The young woman was Miss Maryland 1988, Lori Windsor, a contestant in the pageant. Several years later, Windsor and Hunt had met in Washington, DC, and married. Hunt had asked his wife to send him a copy of the photo that morning.

"She is beautiful," Trump declared. "Is she still that beautiful?" Hunt answered, "Yes, sir." The president joked, "I guess I messed up." Trump again zeroed in on the beauty of Hunt's wife. "She's really that beautiful, huh?" Trump said. "Well, I guess I really did screw up."

"That was my introduction to the Donald," Hunt said.

CHAPTER 2

DEMOLISH NORMS

O NE OF THE FIRST MEETINGS THAT JODY HUNT SCHED-
uled for Jeff Sessions was with three senior Justice Department
officials who said they had an important matter to discuss with the
new attorney general. Hunt, Sessions, and the three officials gathered in the secure command center on the department's sixth floor,
a "SCIF," or sensitive compartmented information facility, built to
thwart eavesdropping.

Scott Schools, the department's chief ethics officer and senior-
most career lawyer, led the meeting. A former federal prosecutor from South Carolina, Schools had been hired by Sally Yates to
replace David Margolis, a revered career civil servant who had served
for decades as the department's ethics chief before passing away
in the summer of 2016. Schools was under pressure to handle the
department's most fraught cases as ethically as Margolis had. Two
other officials joined them: James Crowell, who worked in the Deputy Attorney General's Office, and Tashina Gauhar, a career lawyer
in the Deputy Attorney General's Office who focused on national
security issues.

After a brief exchange of pleasantries, Crowell informed Sessions
and Hunt of a secret FBI investigation that would ultimately doom
Sessions's tenure as attorney general. It would also reveal Trump's
power to demolish the post-Watergate norms that presidents, attorneys general, and DOJ and FBI employees had followed for a
half century.

Crowell told Sessions that the FBI had opened a criminal investigation into whether individuals associated with Trump's campaign had coordinated with the Russian government's efforts to interfere in the 2016 election. The disclosure stunned Sessions and Hunt. "We were both surprised," Hunt recalled.

Sessions said that he knew that he had to recuse himself from a criminal investigation of an organization that he had helped lead. Sessions had served as a senior advisor to Trump's 2016 campaign and as a co-chair of its National Security Advisory committee. "It was obvious since I had a role in the campaign," Sessions recalled. "If you read these facts to a thousand lawyers, a thousand would say you have to recuse yourself. This is basic recusal. It happens all the time."

Sessions was right. Under department conflict-of-interest regulations mandated by the Ethics in Government Act of 1978, one of many post-Watergate reforms, DOJ employees were barred from participating in investigations if they have a "personal or political relationship" with the organization under scrutiny.

Schools had printed out a copy of the regulation, which stated, "No employee shall participate in a criminal investigation or prosecution if he has a personal or political relationship with any person or organization substantially involved in the conduct that is the subject of the investigation or prosecution." The regulation defined a "political relationship" as "a close identification with an elected official, a candidate . . . a political party, or a campaign organization, arising from service as a principal adviser thereto or a principal official thereof."

Sessions felt that he had no choice. As attorney general, he had to set an example and scrupulously follow the department's ethics rules. And Sessions, like Hunt, felt that politics had influenced some DOJ decisions during the Obama administration. "If you want the Department of Justice to follow the rules, you need the attorney general to follow them too," Sessions recalled.

When the meeting ended, Hunt made a note to schedule a follow-up meeting where Sessions would formally recuse himself.

The process entailed writing a recusal message that would be shared with various DOJ officials. In hindsight, Hunt said that he wished he had drafted and sent the recusal notice that day. He wrongly assumed that top DOJ and FBI officials would take Sessions at his word.

SOON AFTER THE RECUSAL MEETING, Hunt attended his first Oval Office meeting with Trump. It focused on a legal matter, the specifics of which Hunt declined to discuss. During the meeting, Hunt noticed something that later would emerge as a pattern for Trump concerning legal matters. Trump appeared skeptical of the legal system and had little faith that it would reach a fair outcome insofar as his own interests were concerned. He frequently suspected that those involved in a case, particularly a judge or lawyer, were biased against him. Trump would ask his legal team to try to get these perceived enemies removed from the case.

"These people don't really like me," Hunt recalled Trump saying at times.

Trump's legal advisors would warn him that trying to attack the parties in a case, or a judge or lawyer, could backfire. The move would likely fail in court and ultimately be detrimental to the president. After some back-and-forth, and while still declaring that he was right, the new president would usually relent and tell his legal team to do what they thought was right. Trump's advisors would then quickly leave the meeting and take the victory.

Hunt initially thought that Trump, who appeared to know little about the law, could be persuaded by his attorneys. Hunt assumed his own candor and frank advice would enable a good working relationship with the new president. That, too, ultimately would prove wrong.

Trump's interest in attacking his opponents reflected a core legal strategy that he had employed for decades in business and that he would employ during and after his time in the Oval Office. Based, in part, on the tactics of his infamous former lawyer, Roy Cohn, it also resembled Newland's concept of "LOL nothing matters lawyering." Legal cases and lawsuits were tools for achieving political or public relations victories, discrediting or smearing political opponents, business rivals, or silencing journalists and former employees. In 2023, a federal judge would summarize Trump's legal strategy in a ruling throwing out a false claim by Trump and ordering him and his attorney to pay nearly a million dollars in penalties for filing frivolous claims against three dozen of his political rivals, including Hillary Clinton.

"This case should never have been brought. Its inadequacy as a legal claim was evident from the start," Judge Donald Middlebrooks wrote in a scathing forty-six-page opinion. "No reasonable lawyer would have filed it. Intended for a political purpose, none of the counts of the amended complaint stated a cognizable legal claim." He called Trump's claims "implausible," "categorically absurd," and "a hodgepodge of disconnected, often immaterial events, followed by an implausible conclusion."

"A continuing pattern of misuse of the courts by Mr. Trump and his lawyers undermines the rule of law, portrays judges as partisans, and diverts resources from those who have suffered actual legal harm," Middlebrooks wrote. "Trump is a prolific and sophisticated litigant who is repeatedly using the courts to seek revenge on political adversaries. He is the mastermind of strategic abuse of the judicial process."

OVER THE COURSE of February, Sessions and Hunt put off the recusal meeting because of other demands. "His schedule was incredibly packed," Hunt recalled. In the last week of February, Hunt scheduled a meeting for March 2 to draft and finalize the recusal notice.

On March 1, the day before the scheduled recusal, the *Washington Post* broke the story that Sessions had met with Russian ambassador Sergey Kislyak during the 2016 campaign and not disclosed it during his Senate confirmation hearings. Asked by then-Democratic senator Al Franken if he had any contacts with Russian officials, Sessions had replied, under oath, "I did not have communications with the Russians."

Hunt suspected that the story had been leaked as a way to tarnish the new attorney general. Special Counsel Robert Mueller later found that Sessions's communications with Kislyak only included "a passing mention of the presidential campaign." Hunt believed that a colleague in the DOJ or FBI, who knew of Hunt's plan to have Sessions formally recuse himself from the Trump-Russia investigation on March 2, had leaked the story to the paper anyway. "I still am strongly suspicious that someone who knew about this [recusal] meeting leaked the Kislyak story so that it would look like Sessions had done something improper," Hunt recalled.

Top FBI officials did not trust Sessions. They had noted the discrepancy between Sessions's confirmation testimony and his meeting with Kislyak, and they were concerned about the fact that nearly a month had passed with no recusal.

And James Comey, the director of the FBI, was on edge about all things Trump and Russia-related. In late January, during a private dinner at the White House, Trump had asked Comey to shutter the bureau's ongoing investigation into Michael Flynn, the White House national security advisor who was later forced out for his contacts with Russia, particularly Kislyak. "I need loyalty, I expect loyalty," Comey would later testify that Trump had told him.

While Comey did not tell Sessions all that had happened, he implored Sessions to intervene and stop Trump from orchestrating such one-on-one conversations. Sessions said he told Comey to follow DOJ rules.

In short, the FBI did not trust the attorney general of the United States. After the leak, Sessions did not trust his top officials at the FBI and the DOJ. In a dynamic that would occur over and over, pressure from Trump fueled suspicion and division within and between Justice Department and FBI officials.

TO DEMOCRATS, AS WELL as journalists investigating potential coordination between the Trump campaign and Russia, Sessions's alleged contact with Kislyak was further evidence that the Trump campaign had, in fact, worked with Russia. But Trump remained defiant, and another early pattern emerged: he seemed impervious to being publicly shamed. He also appeared to have no faith that an independent DOJ investigation, from which Sessions was recused, would clear him of wrongdoing.

The morning after the *Washington Post* story broke, Trump flouted DOJ rules, and told McGahn that Sessions could not recuse himself from the Russia investigation. It was more important that Sessions have the power to protect Trump from his perch as attorney general.

Sessions ignored the pressure from Trump and formally recused himself on March 2, 2017, as planned. Minutes before the scheduled press conference to announce the recusal, Hunt sent out a three-paragraph email to top officials and highlighted the fact that the decision had been under discussion for several weeks. To clarify that the recusal was nonpartisan, Hunt wrote that Sessions would not oversee any investigation related to either the Trump or Clinton campaigns.

Two days later, Sessions and Hunt traveled with other top administration officials to meet with Trump in Mar-a-Lago. Before the group meeting, Trump pulled Sessions into a side room, told him to "unrecuse" himself, and said Bobby Kennedy and Eric Holder had protected the president while Sessions had not. Sessions left the meeting with the sense that Trump feared that the investigation could spin out of control and hamper his ability to govern.

Sessions and Hunt failed to grasp the new political reality of the Trump era. Trump cared little about ethics or preserving public trust in government. Hunt and Sessions, meanwhile, believed that abiding by the Department of Justice's norms would serve the department, the president, and the country well in the long term. They believed that the public retained faith in the department precisely because officials followed the rules. Trump, it would soon emerge, disdained them.

TRUMP ISSUED A STATEMENT publicly supporting Sessions, but privately the recusal infuriated the new president, who would incessantly pressure his attorney general to change his mind. Investigators would later scrutinize those efforts as possible attempts to obstruct the Trump-Russia investigation.

Reflecting on the pressure that Trump placed on Sessions to retract the recusal, Hunt said that he saw it as another example of the president's own ignorance of the office. "I really thought he just didn't get it, and at the time I thought, 'Maybe he'll understand this and get to it and move on,'" Hunt recalled. "In fact, I think a lot of people didn't, and still don't, actually understand what the recusal was about."

"I later came to realize that Trump did not care whether or not it was the proper thing to do as a matter of legal ethics," Hunt added. "The only thing that mattered to him was whether, in his mind, it hurt him in some way."

Trump spent the next twenty months publicly shaming Sessions and threatening to fire him—heretofore unthinkable behavior by a post-Watergate president. He wanted his supporters to distrust and despise Sessions and, by extension, the Justice Department and the principles that the recusal represented.

By the summer of 2017, Trump began to publicly call Sessions weak and "disgraceful." He avoided direct communications with Sessions, routinely communicating instead through his chief of staff, Reince Priebus, and Hunt. On social media and in public remarks, Trump said that Sessions failed to hold Democrats accountable for crimes of their own. He demanded that Sessions end the Russia investigation, all but saying that the president was above the law. And he said that he should have chosen a different attorney general.

"The Russian Witch Hunt Hoax continues, all because Jeff Sessions didn't tell me he was going to recuse himself," Trump said on social media. "I would have quickly picked someone else. So much time and money wasted, so many lives ruined."

Hunt noted that Trump's message was deliberately misleading. "Sessions could not have told the president he was going to recuse himself at the time," Hunt said. "Because Sessions did not know until after he became attorney general that there was such an investigation into the campaign that would require his recusal."

Hunt also later acknowledged the bigger picture. Trump could make statements out of ignorance, that, at the same time, deliberately undermined the department. "In hindsight," Hunt said. "I know that Trump was trying to make sure that his personal interests were protected, and that he was bullying the Department of Justice."

IN THE FACE OF TRUMP'S IRE, Sessions focused on his job. Many of the policies that Trump favored, Sessions favored, too, and the embattled attorney general leaned into them. Sessions vowed to be tough on crime, to go after MS-13 (a gang that Trump had demonized), and to have zero tolerance for illegal border crossings.

Sarah Isgur, who served as Sessions's DOJ spokesperson, said in an interview that the attorney general's enthusiasm reflected both his own long-held views on illegal immigration and the understanding that he may not be in his job for long. "It's Jeff Sessions. The goal is Sessions's goal," she said. At the same time, "He knew he could get fired any day."

Two months after Trump became president, border patrol agents in El Paso, Texas, quietly launched a pilot program called the "El Paso initiative," where agents referred all migrants caught crossing the border illegally for the first time for federal criminal prosecution. As a result of the new policy, migrant parents would be separated from their children.

During the George W. Bush and Barack Obama administrations, the Justice Department had used its discretion to not aggressively

Sarah Isgur, Sessions's spokesperson, saw the Trump and Biden years at the Justice Department as a Greek tragedy. (ZUMA PRESS, INC. / ALAMY STOCK PHOTO)

prosecute parents caught crossing the border illegally with their children who were first-time offenders. The department allowed families that applied for asylum to be released together and remain in the US until their cases were resolved in backlogged immigration courts. Other parents were charged with a misdemeanor that typically resulted in several days in jail before the entire family was deported.

Sessions, however, believed in enforcing immigration laws to their fullest. Like Trump, he supported the use of harsh tactics, such as family separation, to discourage illegal immigrants, and pressured federal prosecutors along the southern border to crack down on them.

Trump administration immigration officials spoke publicly of a planned crackdown but kept the pilot program secret. Asked in a March 2017 interview with CNN if migrant children were being separated from their parents, Homeland Security Secretary John Kelly said he was considering separating migrant families as a deterrent. The children, Kelly promised, "will be well cared for as we deal with their parents."

In April, Sessions traveled to Nogales, Arizona, to make an announcement. "This is the Trump era," he said. "The lawlessness, the abdication of the duty to enforce our immigration laws, and the catch-and-release practices of old are over."

In May, a second pilot program was quietly launched in Arizona. Over the course of 2017, at least 234 families were separated in Yuma, according to the Department of Homeland Security. All told, under the "El Paso initiative," roughly 280 families were separated between July and November 2017.

And that was just the beginning. Encouraged by Miller and the White House, Sessions would implement the plan at every US Attorney's Office that touched the southern border. Trump was a vehicle for immigration hard-liners to achieve policies they had long sought. But they were naïve to think that Trump cared about policy as much as they did. Being aligned with Trump's politics would not protect Sessions from Trump.

Instead of bringing order, the family separation program caused chaos. Prosecutors would later tell the DOJ inspector general that there were instances of infants being forcibly separated from their breastfeeding defendant mothers. No comprehensive system existed for tracking family members after they had been split apart, they said, and children had gone missing.

Despite the problems that plagued the pilot programs, on May 7, 2018, Sessions publicly announced the family separation policy: "If you cross this border unlawfully, then we will prosecute you. It's that simple. If you are smuggling a child, then we will prosecute you and that child will be separated from you as required by law."

Over the next three months, more than four thousand children were separated from their families. Images of children in crowded cages went viral and sparked a public uproar. Instead of being held near their parents, children were flown to shelters hundreds of miles away. When the prosecution of parents was completed, government officials could not find their children in hundreds of cases.

Sessions blamed other government departments. "Homeland

Security has the responsibility to house the children initially, and then Health and Human Services takes the children to ensure that they're in a healthy environment for longer periods," he said in an interview. "The Department of Justice had nothing to do with that but they blame me."

Accounts of his personally calling for the separation of children were taken out of context by the press, he claimed. "When we went to zero tolerance, as I recall, I was on a conference call with US attorneys and somebody asked about separating the children," he said. "I said they will have to be separated because you couldn't take them to court. We felt there would be a short separation and did not imagine that they wouldn't be reunited."

Worldwide, though, Trump, Sessions, and the chaos and cruelty of the policy were condemned. On June 20, 2018, Trump issued an executive order that largely ended family separation. Five years after the program ended, as many as one thousand children still had not been reunited with their families.

CHAPTER 3

TERMINATE AND
REMOVE

ON THE MORNING OF MONDAY, MARCH 20, JODY HUNT was at home sick with pneumonia, worn down by long hours on the job. Lying on the couch, he turned on his television to watch FBI Director James Comey testify before the House Intelligence Committee. What he heard caused Hunt to sit up and yell at the screen.

Comey said that he had been authorized by the Department of Justice to publicly disclose that the FBI had launched a criminal investigation into any links or coordination between the Trump campaign and the Russian government during the 2016 presidential election. "As with any counterintelligence investigation, this will also include an assessment of whether any crimes were committed," Comey said.

With his announcement, Comey had put Trump on notice: You will not interfere with an FBI investigation. Comey would fight back.

Hunt was astonished that Comey had disclosed an ongoing criminal investigation. He did not know who, if anyone, at the DOJ had authorized Comey to do so. The disclosure was a flagrant violation of a decades-old Justice Department rule that criminal investigations be kept secret. If an individual is indicted by a grand jury, the charges are made public. If no charges are brought, the investigation remains secret to protect citizens from being unfairly smeared by prosecutors.

"The prosecutor has more control over life, liberty, and reputation than any other person in America. His discretion is tremendous,"

Attorney General Robert H. Jackson implored prosecutors to not use their vast powers for political gain. "The citizen's safety lies in the prosecutor who serves the law and not factional purposes," he warned. (LIBRARY OF CONGRESS PRINTS & PHOTOGRAPHS DIVISION, WASHINGTON, DC)

Attorney General Robert H. Jackson had famously warned in a 1940 speech. "He can have citizens investigated and, if he is that kind of person, he can have this done to the tune of public statements and veiled or unveiled intimations."

Comey's announcement set off a frenzy in the press and immediately gave Democrats a new line of attack against Trump. It also reinforced Comey's carefully cultivated image as a dedicated public servant who was willing to stand for what he thought was right.

Comey had intervened in 2014 when George W. Bush's White House counsel and chief of staff had tried to pressure Attorney General John Ashcroft, then seriously ill in the hospital, to reauthorize a domestic surveillance program. When the program was reauthorized without changes recommended by the Justice Department, Comey and several other senior officials threatened to resign. Ultimately, President Bush bowed to their wishes.

But in Hunt's view, Comey's surprise disclosure of the Trump-Russia investigation was showboating. "He's trying to put himself on a platform equal to the president," Hunt said.

This was not the first time that Comey had made a bold public declaration that dismayed Hunt and other career DOJ civil servants. When department staff returned to work after the Fourth of July holiday weekend in 2016, many were stunned to see Comey on their television screens, wearing a dark blue suit and gold checkered tie, his six-foot, eight-inch frame dwarfing a lectern at FBI headquarters. On the sweltering morning of July 5, Comey began a now infamous press conference. "Good morning. I'm here to give you an update on the FBI's investigation of Secretary Clinton's use of a personal e-mail system during her time as Secretary of State." Comey then stated, "I have not coordinated this statement or reviewed it in any way with the Department of Justice."

To DOJ veterans, Comey's statement was reminiscent of when FBI Director J. Edgar Hoover had leaked damaging information about people he unilaterally deemed subversive. Comey would later blame the Obama appointees running the Justice Department at the time and say he was facing a "five-hundred-year flood."

Attorney General Loretta Lynch had declined to recuse herself from the Hillary Clinton email investigation after news broke that she had privately met with Bill Clinton on her plane during a stopover in Phoenix. FBI officials thought that Lynch and her senior advisors—Sally Yates and Matthew Axelrod—struggled to act as neutral law enforcement officials when it came to politically sensitive matters.

"Our assessment was that this crowd—Loretta, Sally, and Matt—over-emphasized the political element of things," said a retired senior FBI official close to Comey who asked not to be named.

In his surprise press conference, Comey announced, without the permission of the attorney general, that the FBI had not found "clear evidence" that Clinton had intentionally broken laws. "No reasonable" prosecutor would charge her, but he added that she had been "extremely careless" in her handling of classified information. Comey's comments violated Jackson's admonition against prosecutors denigrating defendants not charged with a crime.

Three months later, eleven days before the 2016 election, Comey again acted without the approval of the attorney general. FBI agents had discovered work-related Clinton emails on the computer of Anthony Weiner, the estranged husband of longtime Clinton aide Huma Abedin, while investigating illicit texts that Weiner had sent to a fifteen-year-old girl. For decades, Justice Department guidelines have said that officials should not take any actions before an election that could impact the outcome. Comey, ignoring pleas from the attorney general's aides to wait until the emails had been examined, sent confidential letters to the leaders of the congressional committees that had investigated Clinton's email use saying that the investigation of Clinton had been reopened.

Comey believed that the FBI could face a nightmare scenario: What if Clinton was elected and then evidence from the laptop showed that she had committed a crime? The FBI could find itself indicting the president-elect. Two days before the election, Comey announced that agents had found no evidence of wrongdoing in the emails but it was too late.

After Republicans leaked that the investigation of Clinton had been reopened by the FBI, Clinton's lead in national polls had dropped by roughly 50 percent. In swing states it dropped by roughly 60 percent, from 4.5 to 1.7 percent. The pollster Nate Silver later concluded that Comey's letter to Congress, and the intense media coverage of it, more than any other factor, likely swung the 2016 race to Trump. "The Comey letter had a fairly large and measurable impact, probably enough to cost Clinton the election," Silver wrote.

Sixteen months later, as Hunt watched Comey testify before the House Intelligence Committee, he believed Comey was again meddling in presidential politics. His disclosure of the Trump-Russia investigation set off a media firestorm that would engulf the White House for the next two years. Democrats, once furious with Comey over his handling of the Clinton investigation, now hailed him as a hero of the anti-Trump resistance.

JAMES COMEY AND HIS top deputies—including Andrew McCabe, the deputy director of the FBI; and Peter Strzok, the bureau's top counterintelligence official—were deeply alarmed when Trump upset Clinton in 2016. Comey, like most observers, had expected Clinton to win, according to a former senior FBI official. With Trump now in the White House, the bureau faced a new nightmare scenario.

Trump's win had set off "alarm bells" throughout the counterintelligence world, Strzok later wrote. As president, Trump was positioned both to learn about the Russia investigation and to stop it.

One hundred days before the election, Strzok and his agents had opened the bureau's Trump-Russia investigation after an Australian government official had told Strzok that a Trump campaign advisor knew about a Russian attempt to interfere in the election before it happened. The information was so alarming that Strzok and his agents decided that they needed to get to the bottom of the Trump campaign's ties to Moscow.

Trump himself was not under investigation, but FBI officials found his behavior concerning. In one instance, Trump publicly called on Russia to uncover more of Clinton's emails, weeks after the Russians had hacked other Democratic email accounts and leaked them to the press. Seemingly in response, FBI agents found that Russia tried to hack a server that Clinton's personal office used. And unlike past candidates, Trump seemed to admire Vladimir Putin, the Russian president.

Comey and his aides thought that they could figure out the relationship between Trump's campaign and Russia after Clinton won. Having badly miscalculated the election outcome, FBI officials were now in the unenviable position of investigating the soon-to-be president.

Comey, though, was not daunted. Two weeks before Trump's inauguration, he privately told Trump about a dossier of salacious, humiliating, and unproven allegations from what would eventually be dubbed "the Steele dossier," after Christopher Steele, the former British spy who compiled the information. Comey and James Clapper, the director of national intelligence, had thought that Trump should know about the claims.

Four days after Trump was briefed, BuzzFeed News published the unvetted document, which fueled suspicion by Trump and his supporters that the FBI had leaked the document to the press. Multiple US news organizations, in fact, had been in possession of the dossier for months but had not publicly reported on it because they were unable to confirm its contents. BuzzFeed's publication of the dossier, just before Trump took office, gave Democrats a way to cast Trump as an illegitimate victor and a threat to national security.

About a week after Trump took office, he asked Comey at a private dinner at the White House for a pledge of loyalty. Comey, awkwardly, did not reply. A month later, Trump held Comey back after an Oval Office meeting and asked the FBI director to drop the investigation of Michael Flynn, the White House national security advisor. While Comey was noncommittal, he briefed FBI officials about this worrisome private encounter. The team investigating the Trump campaign grew more alarmed.

After Trump falsely claimed that President Obama had wiretapped Trump Tower, Comey and his top aides did not know whether to trust Attorney General Jeff Sessions, who did not publicly refute Trump's claim. After the Senate sent the FBI a criminal referral on Sessions, based on his failure to disclose his contact with Sergey Kislyak during his confirmation hearing, the FBI considered opening a perjury case against the new attorney general.

The situation was unprecedented. For the first time in American history, the campaign of a sitting US president was being investigated for conspiring with a foreign power to win an election. And the FBI was considering investigating Sessions, their superior, for lying about his role in the potential plot. Instead of Comey and the FBI emerging as saviors, they would underestimate Trump and be sullied themselves.

———

AS THE SPRING OF 2017 progressed, Hunt believed that Sessions's relationship with Trump could survive the Russia investigation. The attorney general and Hunt attended meetings with the president after Comey had publicly revealed the probe where Trump didn't raise Sessions's recusal. "I thought we could get past it," Hunt recalled.

But Hunt began to think otherwise in early May, after he received a bewildering request from the White House counsel's office to attend an Oval Office meeting on Wednesday, May 3, 2017. Trump was meeting with Ed McNally, a potential nominee for US attorney for the Southern District of New York. Some Justice Department officials privately questioned McNally's close ties to former Illinois governor George Ryan, who had been convicted by federal prosecutors of participating in vast corruption in the state for more than a decade. During Ryan's trial, McNally had testified as a defense witness for the former governor, a step that surprised and angered federal prosecutors.

Trump's Oval Office meeting with McNally was yet another departure from Justice Department norms designed to keep the department independent of the president. Nominees for US attorney were usually vetted by the Justice Department and the White House counsel's office and rarely met with the president. Hunt believed the meeting would leak and fuel speculation that the president was trying to control federal investigations of his business in New York.

Hunt believed that if McNally was nominated, Democrats would ask McNally what Trump had said to him during their Oval Office meeting. Hunt was so alarmed that he phoned a lawyer in the White House counsel's office to find out what was going on. "We don't do this for other US attorneys," Hunt recalled saying of the meeting between McNally and Trump. Hunt was rebuffed. "I advised the White House not to do it. They insisted on it."

After Hunt arrived at the White House, it quickly became clear to him that Trump was using the McNally meeting as a pretext to again pressure Sessions. Before the meeting with McNally began, Trump asked Sessions, Hunt, and McGahn to meet alone with him in the Oval Office. Hunt recalled Trump asking McGahn, "How did Comey do today?"—a reference to the FBI director's testimony that morning before the Senate Judiciary Committee. "Not well," McGahn told the president. "He had several opportunities to say that you were not under investigation, but he did not."

McGahn's answer infuriated Trump, according to Hunt. "The president said, 'I don't know why he wouldn't say it,'" Hunt recalled. "'He has told me three times that I am not under investigation.'" Trump began berating Sessions. "This is terrible Jeff. It's all because you recused," the president said.

For several minutes, Trump castigated Sessions, in Hunt's view, saying his recusal was unfair, interfered with Trump's ability to govern, and undermined Trump's authority with foreign leaders. Sessions replied that the recusal was required under DOJ regulations. He also reminded Trump that he had advised him during the transition to immediately replace Comey after he took office—advice Trump had ignored.

After the meeting, Hunt returned home deeply frustrated. "In hindsight, I realized we were duped," Hunt said. "We were there so that the president could berate Sessions." He felt it was both unfair and unseemly for Trump to demean Sessions. "I was very upset," he recalled. "I was upset at how he treated Sessions."

The president's behavior fit a pattern that Hunt had grown to notice: Trump befriended people in the hope they would be loyal to him, then, at the slightest sign of perceived disloyalty, brutally attacked them. "He tries to be charming and likable and then he turns on you if he thinks you're doing something against him, even if it's the right thing, like recusal," Hunt said. "To him, it's only the right thing if it helps him and helps his image."

Before going to sleep, Hunt grabbed a legal pad and handwrote detailed notes about what had happened in the Oval Office that day, as he had on previous days. "These were my own personal notes,

I was doing it because I knew I was witness to some really historic events," Hunt recalled. "I wanted to remember these things for myself. At the time I took the notes, I never intended for them to see the light of day."

Democrats saw the Russia investigation as an opportunity to cast Trump as illegitimate or traitorous. Still reeling from Clinton's loss, they doubled down on the importance of the FBI's Trump-Russia investigation and vowed to protect it. Past presidents would not dare to retaliate under such circumstances, but Trump, as the FBI would learn, was different. Comey, for all his establishment credentials, could not outmaneuver the president and would not outlast him. Comey's demise, and that of the Russia investigation, sent a clear message: The FBI would pay dearly for defying Donald Trump.

A FEW DAYS AFTER Comey's May 3 testimony in the Senate, Sessions, Hunt, and Rod Rosenstein, the newly confirmed deputy attorney general, attended two White House meetings to discuss Comey's fate. During the meetings—one in the White House counsel's office and one in the Oval Office—Trump made fun of Comey for telling senators that he felt "mildly nauseous" to think that he might have had some impact on the outcome of the 2016 election. Rosenstein recalled Trump excitedly offering, "Do you want to watch it? I have it on TiVo."

Rosenstein, a hypercautious career DOJ lawyer and registered Republican who had a reputation for being apolitical, was the only US attorney to serve both the George W. Bush and Barack Obama administrations. Widely viewed as a model federal prosecutor, he had worked in the Justice Department, essentially, for his entire adult life. He graduated from Harvard Law School, clerked for a conservative federal judge in Washington, and then, at twenty-five, landed a job in the DOJ's Public Integrity Section, tackling public corruption cases. During his confirmation hearing to be the DOJ's number-two official, Rosenstein had told senators that "political affiliation is irrelevant to my work" and vowed to "support any properly predicated investigation related to interference by the Russians or by anybody else in American elections."

"The sooner the Senate confirms him, the sooner the administration will have another adult in its top ranks," the *Washington Post* said of Rosenstein. He was confirmed in a 94–6 vote.

But nothing in his long Justice Department career had prepared Rosenstein for his first days in the Trump administration. Days after Rosenstein was confirmed, Comey had sought his opinion on whether the FBI should criminally investigate Sessions, his boss, and Rosenstein did not express an opinion either way. (Rosenstein, in an interview, said that Comey never asked for his opinion.)

Rosenstein had been on the job barely two weeks, and now he was at the White House being asked to help determine whether Trump should fire his FBI director. When Trump asked Sessions and Rosenstein for their views, Sessions said that Comey should be fired. Rosenstein, ever cautious, recalled not calling for his removal. He did remark that Comey would never resign under pressure and would have to be fired if the president wanted him out. Ultimately, Rosenstein believed that if the president and the attorney general did not like the FBI director, he probably should go.

Rosenstein claimed in a series of interviews that it never occurred to him that Trump wanted to fire Comey to end the Russia investigation. He knew from his career as a federal prosecutor that the FBI would continue the investigation, even if Comey was dismissed. "Now that might be naïve," Rosenstein said, "but if it had occurred to me that Trump believed that this will stop the investigation, I would have spoken up."

Rosenstein's suspicions that he was being set up were not even piqued when Trump distributed copies of a draft termination letter, written with Stephen Miller, that Rosenstein recalled as a "screed of all these right-wing talking points" complete with a reference to

Andrew McCabe, the deputy FBI director, and his wife, who had run for state senate in Virginia as a Democrat and received campaign funding from a Clinton ally. Rosenstein, in hindsight, was one of a long line of DOJ officials who were manipulated by Trump.

The meeting concluded with Sessions and Rosenstein agreeing to each write memos that described Comey's failures. Trump told Rosenstein to include Comey's failure to tell Congress that the president was not under investigation. Rosenstein pushed back on that request.

That night, Rosenstein penned a thousand-word memo, titled "Restoring public confidence in the FBI," that said Comey should be fired for his Hillary Clinton email investigation press conference, citing former Justice Department officials in both Democratic and Republican administrations. Rosenstein, in a false statement or a sign of his guilelessness, said in an interview that he assumed that his memo would remain private.

Sessions wrote a 150-word cover letter that echoed Rosenstein's points. "I have concluded that a fresh start is needed at the leadership of the FBI," Sessions wrote.

When Hunt delivered the letters to the White House the following day, he watched Trump eat Hershey bars and drink Diet Coke while orchestrating Comey's ouster. Throughout the two-hour meeting, Trump gave no indication that he understood that Democrats, as well as numerous current and former law enforcement and intelligence officials, genuinely feared that he had colluded with Russia. He even asked a White House photographer to come to the Oval Office to capture what he saw as a historic moment.

In the end, the White House released a statement that read: "Today, President Donald J. Trump informed FBI director James Comey that he has been terminated and removed from office. President Trump acted based on the clear recommendations of both Deputy Attorney General Rod Rosenstein and Attorney General Jeff Sessions."

The White House also publicly released Rosenstein's memo, making it appear that the DOJ's new number two official was helping the new president scuttle the FBI investigation. Rosenstein acknowledged that he might have been naïve, but insisted that it did not occur to him that Trump was firing Comey to try to halt the Russia investigation.

"If they had said we want to fire Comey so we can end the Russia investigation, I would have said it's not going to stop the Russia investigation," Rosenstein asserted. "I would have set them straight."

TRUMP'S FIRING OF COMEY WAS the gravest political error of his first year in office. Democrats declared Trump a new Nixon. The move instantly turbocharged conspiracy theories that he was a Russian agent and an illegitimate president. And it reinforced fears among top FBI officials the Trump had cooperated with Russia.

Inside the FBI, Comey's firing stunned agents. Many of them had joined the bureau under Louis Freeh, who was director for eight years, and Robert Mueller, who was director for twelve years. Comey, like all FBI directors, was appointed to a ten-year term to give him independence from the four-year presidential election cycle.

The senior FBI official who later became involved in the search of Mar-a-Lago said Comey's firing created a sense of vulnerability among agents. "I remember where I was when the space shuttle exploded and when Comey was fired," recalled the official. "It had a massive impact inside the FBI," he added. "We all felt exposed."

Nate Huber, a supervisory intelligence analyst and instructor at the FBI Academy at Quantico, said he learned of Comey's firing from the press. "I was stunned, surprised, and angry," he recalled in an interview. "I was just about to attend or I was already attending my daughter's softball practice. I wanted to resign from the FBI and told my wife so. I believed Comey was stuck in a no-win situation with the way Trump and the Republicans were attempting to politicize the Justice Department and FBI."

The son of a used car salesman and a hospital registrar, Huber grew up in Jamestown, New York, a small rust-belt city in western New York that is the birthplace of both Hollywood star Lucille Ball and Attorney General Robert H. Jackson. When Huber was a 17-year-old high-school senior, the 9/11 attack cemented his decision to work in law enforcement. "That was it," he recalled.

After attending community college, SUNY Albany, and receiving a master's degree in applied intelligence from Mercyhurst University, he joined the FBI in 2008. Huber's starting annual salary was roughly $48,000. Huber taught a class on the history of intelligence gathering that described the findings of the Church Committee and the reforms put in place to guard against the FBI abusing its powers. He felt Trump's claims that the bureau was politically biased against him were false. "I had never seen any systematic politicization," Huber said. "Never saw anything like that. I know those are lies."

Contradicting claims from the White House that Comey was unpopular, Huber said Comey was generally popular: "He was a great leader who believed in the mission of the bureau and believed in and supported his employees."

At the highest levels of the bureau, Comey's firing fueled fears that Trump, indeed, was working with the Russians. The dismissal "gave new urgency to the FBI's investigation of Russian interference in the 2016 elections," McCabe would later write in his memoir. The intelligence community considered Russia's efforts to interfere in the 2016 election an established fact. The FBI wanted to know whether Trump's team played a role in it. Trump's firing of Comey allowed FBI officials to cross a threshold they had been avoiding—whether to investigate the president himself.

The day after Comey was fired, McCabe met with his senior staff to discuss where the Trump-Russia investigation stood, and what steps should be taken next. The team was still reeling from the firing, and Rosenstein's seemingly key role in the dismissal. Many team members privately worried that they could no longer trust Sessions and Rosenstein, who technically oversaw the bureau.

Trump interrupted the meeting by calling McCabe, the bureau's acting director, and pressuring him to say that rank-and-file FBI agents had disliked Comey. Trump said that he wanted to visit the bureau to "show all my FBI people how much I love them." And he then railed at McCabe for allowing Comey to fly home from Los Angeles to Washington on an FBI plane after he was fired. Trump raised his voice. "I don't want him in the building. I'm banning him from the building. He should not be allowed, I don't want him in FBI buildings," McCabe later recalled.

McCabe shared the alarming call with the team. Now their primary concern was that Trump would shutter the Russia probe. McCabe wanted it on the surest footing possible, he later wrote, so that if he were also fired, the investigation would continue. He began to discuss the idea of appointing a special counsel with Rosenstein, who seemed to McCabe to be obsessed with the fact that the White House had used him, wiping away his sterling reputation in a single day.

SINCE TRUMP'S INAUGURATION, members of the FBI team investigating Russian interference in the 2016 election had wondered whether they would ever focus their probe on Trump himself. Some argued that they were investigating him in all but name. Technically, there was no case open against Trump, but agents were examining whether his campaign coordinated with the Russians in a way that broke the law; and as the leader of the campaign, it seemed inevitable that some of the activity in question would implicate Trump. When Trump had asked Comey if he was under investigation, Comey chose to stick with the technical truth, and he reassured Trump that he was not personally under investigation.

Peter Strzok, a lead investigator on the Russia teams, seemed to reiterate that point two days after Comey's firing when he briefed Rosenstein on details of the Russia investigation on May 11. As Strzok went through the list of open cases against individual Trump campaign associates, he included the now-open perjury case against Sessions, he later recalled in his book.

The topic came up again several days later. On May 15, top officials, including McCabe, Strzok, and James Baker, the FBI general counsel, discussed the facts that could lead them to open a case against Trump, particularly any evidence that might point to obstruction of justice. They discussed Comey's firing, which no longer seemed to be the sole reason to suspect him of wrongdoing.

In addition to firing the FBI director, Trump had publicly denigrated the Russia investigation. He had privately asked Comey to drop the Flynn case, and he had sought a pledge of loyalty. He had even told the media that he fired Comey because of "the Russia thing," undermining his painstaking efforts to set Rosenstein up as an alibi.

Most surprisingly, Trump had also invited Russian foreign minister Sergey Lavrov and Russian ambassador Sergey Kislyak to the Oval Office the day after Comey's firing and bragged about it. "I just fired the head of the FBI. He was crazy, a real nut job," Trump had told the Russians. "I faced great pressure because of Russia. That's taken off. . . . I'm not under investigation."

Even though it was within Trump's purview to fire the FBI director and even though it was not illegal for the president to criticize a criminal investigation, those actions seemed, to senior FBI officials, deeply suspect. Senior FBI officials decided that, taken together, Trump's behavior formed an "articulable factual basis" that obstruction had occurred. A week after Comey was fired, McCabe and his officials made one of the boldest and most consequential moves in FBI history—and one that would also mark the high point of the FBI's bravado.

The FBI opened both criminal and counterintelligence investigations against the president of the United States. The question was what Rosenstein, who oversaw the FBI investigation, would do to protect it.

CHAPTER 4

INVESTIGATE THE INVESTIGATORS

DEMOCRATS PRESSURED ROD ROSENSTEIN TO APPOINT a special counsel, a step he was already considering due to Trump's conduct after he fired James Comey. Twice, the president had made public statements suggesting that he had fired Comey to halt the Russia investigation. The day after Trump told Sergey Kislyak, "I faced great pressure because of Russia. That's taken off. . . . I'm not under investigation," the new president told Lester Holt of NBC News that he had decided to fire Comey on his own, before Sessions and Rosenstein gave their recommendation. "I was going to fire Comey. My decision," he said. "I was going to fire regardless of recommendation." Both statements could be used in court as evidence that Trump had obstructed the Russia investigation.

Trump's boasts further alienated Rosenstein. "He tells Kislyak, I removed the problem, which was completely inconsistent with how you handle a federal criminal investigation," Rosenstein said in an interview. "That's another example of Trump making his problems worse."

For years, though, Rosenstein had questioned the appointment of independent counsels and been dubious of their utility. His skepticism was based on his own experience working for one. During Rosenstein's first years at the Justice Department, he had worked for Kenneth Starr, the independent counsel whose four-year investigation of President Clinton was widely criticized. Starr's initial assignment was to look into allegations that the Clintons' former business partners had committed fraud. Rosenstein was part of that early effort, working as prosecutor for Starr from 1995 to 1997. "It was an interesting opportunity," he recalled. "I was young and single and at liberty to move to Arkansas."

Rosenstein and a team of prosecutors convicted Clinton's business partners, Arkansas governor Jim Guy Tucker and James and Susan McDougal, of fraud. Bill and Hillary Clinton were not accused of wrongdoing in the case, but Starr learned that Clinton had pressured an intern named Monica Lewinsky to lie to investigators about her affair with the president.

Starr eventually proposed eleven grounds for impeaching Clinton, including perjury and obstruction of justice. Clinton was impeached by the House but easily avoided removal from office after five Republican senators voted to acquit him. Public opinion polls showed that most Americans disapproved of Clinton's actions but felt they did not merit removing a president from office. Democrats accused Starr of being a partisan attack dog.

The experience left Rosenstein skeptical. "It fueled my view that independent counsels were overly zealous," he recalled.

Republicans, too, had come to distrust special counsels. During the Reagan administration, a group of conservatives led by Attorney General Edwin Meese argued that the creation of independent counsels after Watergate had dangerously weakened the presidency. In 1988, the Supreme Court delivered a sweeping rebuke to that argument in the case of *Morrison v. Olson*, ruling 7–1 that independent counsels were constitutional. The dissenting justice was Antonin Scalia. He argued that the Constitution granted executive powers of prosecution solely to the president. Scalia warned that a politically biased independent prosecutor could endlessly carry out "debilitating criminal investigations" for minor crimes.

Republicans despised Lawrence Walsh, a lifelong Republican and former judge, for doing just that in their view. Walsh spent six years investigating the Reagan administration's covert sale of arms to Iran and its use of the proceeds to fund a group of right-wing "Contra" rebels in Nicaragua. George H. W. Bush blamed Walsh for his defeat in the 1992 presidential election, citing Walsh's filing of criminal charges and revealing of secret documents four days before the vote.

Bush pardoned four former officials whom Walsh had convicted and said that their cases represented "a profoundly troubling development in the political and legal climate of our country: the criminalization of policy differences." The proper forum for such disputes, he wrote, "is the voting booth, not the courtroom."

By the time the independent counsel law expired in 1997, both parties happily bid good riddance to it. The attorney general retained the power to appoint less powerful investigators known as "special counsels" due to a "conflict of interest," an "extraordinary circumstance" or if it would be "in the public interest." The attorney general could remove special counsels or ignore their recommendations, as long as they informed Congress.

Twenty years later, Rosenstein wrestled with whether to name a special counsel in the spring of 2017. His decision was critical for the department and the country. Democrats feared that Trump was a Russian agent. Republicans feared that the FBI was smearing a democratically elected president.

Rosenstein eventually decided that naming a special counsel was the best way to protect public trust in the Justice Department, the institution he revered. "I wanted the special counsel," he recalled. "I thought it was the best way to promote public confidence in the ultimate results."

His top choice, Robert Mueller, was Rosenstein's model FBI director. "Personally tough but impervious to criticism," Rosenstein said. Mueller had become FBI director one week before the 9/11 terror attacks and resisted calls afterward to break up the bureau into multiple agencies. Instead, he expanded the FBI's counterterrorism division. Rank-and-file agents revered his leadership. After serving both Democratic and Republican presidents, he retired from the FBI in 2013 with a sterling reputation. He was replaced by James Comey.

Rosenstein began secretly interviewing potential special counsel candidates on Friday, May 12—three days after Comey's firing. He did not inform Sessions of his plans because the attorney general had recused himself from the Russia investigation.

Comey also pressured Rosenstein to name a special counsel by leaking information to the press. On May 16, 2017, the *New York Times* reported that Comey had memorialized each of his private encounters with Trump, including the loyalty pledge incident and the pressure to drop the Flynn investigation. Those notes made their way to the press via Comey's friend Daniel Richman, a professor at Columbia Law School. Immediately, Democrats, and even a handful of Republicans, began to clamor for a special counsel. The day after the *Times* story ran, Rosenstein formally appointed Mueller. "I didn't decide until the day before I appointed him," Rosenstein recalled.

When Rosenstein spoke with Mueller, Rosenstein outlined what he believed would be an appropriate special counsel investigation. "My message to Mueller was to look at a very discrete set of issues," Rosenstein recalled.

He tasked Mueller with three things: "to ensure a full and thorough investigation of the Russian government's efforts to interfere in the 2016 presidential election"; to examine any "links and coordination" between the Russian government and the Trump campaign; and to investigate all prior and future obstruction of the Russia investigation, including the president's firing of Comey and his direction to drop Flynn's case.

Rosenstein intentionally chose a narrow remit that was the opposite of the sprawling mandate given to Ken Starr. "I thought we had an obligation to resolve it quickly," Rosenstein said. "People worried about it. Congress worried about it."

Rosenstein's confidence in the former FBI director and Mueller's willingness to accept the position facilitated the decision. "I knew it had to be someone who was respected," Rosenstein recalled. "I didn't want just a good lawyer. I wanted someone who knew national security. To me it was critical." Rosenstein added, "If Mueller hadn't taken it, I probably would have delayed. From my perspective, if you appoint the wrong person it's going to be worse."

TRUMP, SESSIONS, AND HUNT learned about the decision to appoint Mueller less than an hour before the Justice Department press secretary alerted the media. The men were at the White House, interviewing candidates to replace Comey, when McGahn asked Sessions to leave the room. Sessions, he said, needed to take an urgent phone call from Rosenstein. When the men returned, they waited for the officials to end an interview with a candidate, and then Sessions told Trump that Rosenstein had appointed a special counsel. The news would be public in half an hour.

Trump slumped back in his chair. After a moment of stunned silence, he said, "Oh my God, this is terrible. This is the end of my presidency. I'm fucked. It's horrible," according to notes taken by Hunt.

Trump then began berating Sessions in a way that Hunt had never seen before. "How could you let this happen, Jeff? How could you let it happen? I appointed you attorney general. You recused yourself. You left me on an island by myself. This guy, you don't even know," Trump said, referring to Rosenstein. "How could you hire someone you don't even know? Elijah Cummings called me and likes him for God's sake."

Sessions tried to explain. "Well, he went to Harvard," he said. "He is a member of the Federalist Society. He has a lot of Department of Justice experience."

Trump interrupted him and continued browbeating the attorney general. "But you don't even know him, Jeff. How do you hire someone you don't even know? You let me down Jeff. Kennedy named his brother attorney general. Obama named Holder. It's the most important appointment. And I appointed you. And you have let me down."

Sessions, growing angry himself, offered to resign. "I said it was an honor to serve in your administration," Sessions said, according to Hunt's notes. "I will promptly submit my resignation." Trump ignored him. "Everyone tells me that if you get one of these independent counsels it ruins your presidency. It takes years and years, and I won't be able to do anything. This is the worst thing that ever happened to me."

Pence spoke up and tried to play down the threat to Trump. "This may not be so bad," he said. "Nobody here thinks it's the end of your presidency. It could be a good thing in the end." The comment surprised Hunt, who assumed that the vice president was trying to make Trump feel better.

"It's not," Trump retorted. "It's terrible." He again lambasted Sessions. "Jeff, you really let me down. I think you should resign. I think you should submit your resignation."

Sessions, who was already standing, picked up some papers that he had left on the *Resolute* desk, shoved them into a legal folder he was holding, and said, "Okay, you'll have it." Sessions started to turn and walk out of the Oval Office and then stopped. He turned to Trump and said, "Let me just tell you this. You are doing some good things. Stay on your agenda. I support you." Sessions then extended his hand to Trump. As the two men shook hands, Sessions said, "It's been an honor to serve as attorney general."

Sessions offered his resignation the next morning, as requested, but the president did not accept it. Sessions would stay on as attorney general until Trump fired him a year and a half later. But the entire Oval Office episode would be described in vivid detail in Mueller's final report. When that report was released in March 2022, the public learned that, like Comey, Hunt had written detailed notes about his meetings with Trump. Hunt's notes, to his surprise, proved to be a valuable resource for Mueller's team as they examined whether the president had obstructed justice.

THE MUELLER APPOINTMENT was initially hailed by politicians from both parties. Rosenstein had made a decision that would help

restore "the credibility of the DOJ and FBI in this most serious matter," said Maryland's Democratic senator Ben Cardin. Mueller's
"record, character, and trustworthiness have been lauded for decades
by Republicans and Democrats alike," noted Nebraska's Republican senator Ben Sasse. Republican Chuck Grassley of Iowa said that
Mueller had "a strong reputation for independence." He added, "At
the end of the day, we need a public accounting of what went on to
restore faith in government."

Republican senator Lindsey Graham even introduced a bill,
co-sponsored by Democrat Cory Booker, that would block the president from unilaterally firing Mueller or any other special counsel.
Graham's calculated embrace of the measure, which never became
law, showed the broad political support for having Mueller conduct
an independent investigation.

It seemed for a moment that Mueller's sterling reputation and
impartiality might unite a country that was bitterly divided over
whether Trump should be the president. Eighty-two percent of Democrats believed that Trump campaign officials had definitely or probably had improper contacts with Russia in 2016, a Pew survey found.
Among Republicans, 26 percent—a third of that number—did.
Trump's detractors, especially, hoped that the Mueller inquiry would
reaffirm that the Justice Department should investigate evidence of
wrongdoing, even if it led to the president. Mueller initially embodied the rule of law itself—a view that would splinter along party lines
over the course of his investigation.

It is hard to overstate how obsessed with Mueller both Trump's
supporters and detractors would become. Throughout the special
counsel's twenty-two-month investigation, Trump allies dismissed
the probe as pointless and the idea that Trump coordinated with
Russia as absurd. Trump's opponents spoke of Mueller in reverential
tones, the last honest man who would bring Trump to justice. They
bought T-shirts that said MUELLER TIME, prayer candles depicting a Saint Mueller, and heroic Mueller action figures.

INITIALLY, THE STATURE of the former FBI director and his vast network of supportive former colleagues appeared to even restrain Trump himself. When Trump hired Ty Cobb, a veteran Washington lawyer and former federal prosecutor, to be his representative to the Mueller team, Cobb made the president promise, as a condition of his employment, that he would not publicly attack Mueller. Cobb later said that he made the request because he respected Mueller and knew him personally.

But after reports emerged in June 2017 that the special counsel's team was investigating Trump himself for obstruction of justice, tensions began to rise. Trump attacked Rod Rosenstein for appointing Mueller. "I am being investigated for firing the FBI Director by the man who told me to fire the FBI Director!" Trump tweeted. "Witch Hunt."

Pro-Trump House Republicans began attacking Mueller and discussing ways to undermine his probe. Representative Matt Gaetz, of Florida, called Representative Jim Jordan, the pro-Trump congressman from Ohio, and agreed on a joint strategy. Both men felt that Mueller should not have been appointed and felt that establishment Republicans were not doing enough to defend Trump. They decided to "play offense."

First, in June, the two men sent Sessions and Rosenstein a letter requesting that a special counsel be appointed to reinvestigate Hillary Clinton's handling of emails. Then, in October, House Republicans opened congressional inquiries of the Clinton email investigation as well as a review of the Clinton administration's approval of a 2010 agreement that left a Russian-backed company in control of much of the United States' uranium.

The inquiries would produce no significant new evidence of wrongdoing, but they were the first steps in what would become a concerted—and successful—effort by Trump and his allies to investigate the investigators and discredit Mueller in the eyes of Republicans.

Some Democrats, Republicans, and former colleagues thought that Wray was well-intentioned but weak, unable to lead the FBI through a period of unprecedented tumult. (ABACA PRESS / ALAMY STOCK PHOTO)

WITH THE CHAOS of the Russia investigation squarely in Mueller's hands, Justice Department officials were poised to return to something resembling normal order. Sessions and Rosenstein would carry out the president's policy agenda, including plans to crack down on immigration and violent crime. And a new FBI director would hopefully repair the damaged relationship between the White House and the bureau.

Both Sessions and Rosenstein were strong supporters of Christopher Wray, a fifty-year-old, Yale-educated, former Justice Department official and corporate lawyer who Trump had nominated to replace Comey. But some Democrats, Republicans, and former colleagues thought that Wray was well-intentioned but weak, unable to lead the bureau through a period of shocking tumult.

A wealthy introvert with an estimated worth of $23 million, Wray had little experience running large organizations. Conservatives feared that Wray would undermine Trump. Liberals questioned why Wray, as a young lawyer in the Justice Department, never spoke out against the Bush administration's use of torture after 9/11. Friends worried, most of all, whether Wray could hold his own in the most deeply partisan Washington in decades. They feared that Trump would try to badger him into becoming a new J. Edgar Hoover, albeit patrician and genteel.

But the Senate confirmed Wray on August 1, 2017, to lead the FBI, in a 92–5 vote. Rosenstein, who saw Wray as a younger version of Mueller, was delighted. He expected Wray to embrace Mueller's style of staying out of the spotlight, respecting norms, and allowing the bureau's work to speak for itself.

Inside the FBI, Mueller's appointment soothed nerves. Mueller, some hoped, would steady and help reinvent the bureau as he had after it failed to stop the 9/11 attacks. Scandals occurred, including the surveillance and profiling of Muslim Americans, but by the end of Mueller's twelve-year tenure the FBI again enjoyed broad support from the American public.

"I was relieved when Rosenstein appointed Mueller," recalled Nate Huber, the supervisory intelligence analyst and instructor at the FBI Academy in Quantico. "I knew Mueller was a no-nonsense, by-the-book investigator. I knew he and his team would follow the evidence no matter where it took them within the confines of their authority."

MUELLER'S TEAM TOOK UP residence in a beige office space in a nondescript complex of buildings called Patriots Plaza. Their most high-stakes job was to examine any links or coordination between Russia and Trump campaign associates—essentially the remit of the Crossfire Hurricane investigation—as well as any leads that arose from that inquiry. Rosenstein said they were to investigate anything "within the scope of 28 CFR § 600.4(a)," meaning crimes committed to interfere with the special counsel's investigation itself. Those crimes included perjury, obstruction of justice, destruction of evidence, and witness intimidation.

The special counsel's office divided itself into three teams:

"Team R" examined Russia's efforts to interfere in the 2016 election; "Team M" scrutinized links between Russia and a key Trump campaign advisor, Paul Manafort; and "Team 600" gathered evidence that Trump had attempted to obstruct the Russia investigation.

Team R oversaw the cases that Mueller came to see as the heart of the investigation, culminating in two indictments that charged 265 Russians and Russian national intelligence officials with various crimes intended to interfere in the 2016 election. They hacked email accounts belonging to members of the Hillary Clinton campaign, the Democratic National Committee, and the Democratic Congressional Campaign Committee, and then used sites like WikiLeaks to disseminate the most embarrassing and politically damaging messages online. The Russians traveled the US to better understand its deepening social divisions, stole the identities of hundreds of thousands of Americans, and then posed as political activists to foment unrest in swing states like Florida. And they deepened America's social divisions by spreading inflammatory propaganda on social media. The goal was not only to sow discord, but also to damage Clinton's campaign.

The team, led by Jeannie Rhee, a federal prosecutor who had tried public corruption and national security cases, also found that the Kremlin itself directed a host of Russian officials and intermediaries to contact Trump campaign officials, advisors, and associates during the election. For its part, the Trump campaign not only welcomed the contact; some campaign officials tried, but failed, to arrange a meeting between Trump and Putin. The Mueller team concluded that the Trump campaign expected to benefit from information that Russia stole and released to the public, but that it did not work with the Russian government to conduct these activities. And although the contact was unorthodox and troubling, Mueller's team said that it did not rise to the level of criminal conduct.

"While the investigation identified numerous links between individuals with ties to the Russian government and individuals associated with the Trump campaign, the evidence was not sufficient to support criminal charges," the team concluded.

For Team M, the Trump advisor who drew the most suspicion of actual collusion was Paul Manafort, Trump's campaign manager. The son of a former mayor of New Britain, Connecticut, who was indicted but not convicted of corruption, Manafort began his career as a campaign advisor to Gerald Ford, Ronald Reagan, and George H. W. Bush. He then became a Washington lobbyist known for representing a rogue's gallery of corrupt autocrats, from Ferdinand Marcos of the Philippines to Mobutu Sese Seko of the Congo, In the process, Manafort grew extraordinarily rich.

Manafort's work for pro-Russian Ukrainian president Viktor Yanukovych, who was backed by a raft of pro-Putin Russian oligarchs, interested prosecutors most. Even before Mueller was appointed, federal investigators were scrutinizing Manafort's finances and lobbying activities. Manafort had lived lavishly, spending $45,000 on cosmetic dentistry and buying three homes in a single year. After Yanukovich's fall in 2014, Manafort went into heavy debt and appeared desperate for money.

Team M, led by Andrew Weissmann, a federal prosecutor well-known for his work on the Enron fraud prosecution, scrutinized Manafort's byzantine business dealings. Manafort's man on the ground in Kyiv, Konstantin Kilimnik, a Russian citizen with ties to Russian intelligence, was a primary focus. Prosecutors found that Manafort was paid, in all, more than $60 million between 2010 and 2014 by various Ukrainian backers and used at least fifteen shell companies to hide much of the money in foreign bank accounts.

Declining to cooperate with prosecutors, Manafort was convicted of eight of eighteen counts of bank and tax fraud in federal court in Virginia in 2018. Sentenced to forty-two months in prison and facing a separate trial in Washington, DC, Manafort agreed to finally cooperate with Mueller's team. But Trump, through intermediaries, told Manafort that he might receive a presidential pardon. After Manafort repeatedly lied to prosecutors, they ended their cooperation agreement. Manafort was sentenced to seven years in prison.

Despite securing the full cooperation of Rick Gates, Manafort's deputy, prosecutors were unable to collect sufficient evidence to charge Manafort with conspiring with representatives of the Russian government to influence the outcome of the 2016 election. Trump, in one of his last acts as president, would pardon Manafort on December 23, 2020.

TEAM R RETURNED significant indictments that shed light on Russia's vast conspiracy to interfere in American democracy. Team M revealed Manafort's multiple crimes, lavish lifestyle, and rapacious greed. But it was the work of Team 600—to investigate all prior and future obstruction of the Russia investigation—that captured the public's attention, because it focused squarely on the president himself. Would he be held criminally accountable for public acts that seemed on their face designed to undermine the rule of law, and for the private acts that would be revealed when Mueller's final report was made public?

Team 600 was led by James Quarles, a veteran Washington lawyer and former Watergate prosecutor who worked with Mueller at the white-shoe law firm WilmerHale. Among the first pieces of evidence that his team examined was the original draft letter that Trump had written about firing Comey. The statement, written after Comey had told Congress about the Russia investigation and before Rosenstein knew that Trump intended to fire Comey, was laser-focused on Russia. It noted that Comey had assured Trump three times that he was not under investigation and it dismissed the idea that Russia had meddled in the election. Read alongside Comey's memos, it seemed to give investigators evidence that Trump wanted to fire Comey because he was investigating Russia, and that he had used Rosenstein's memo as a smokescreen.

Team 600 would interview nearly every top White House staffer, whose combined testimonies painted a picture of a president who wanted them to curb and even shut down the Russia investigation, before and after the inquiry fell under the purview of the special counsel. Ultimately, Quarles and his team identified ten possible examples of attempted obstruction of justice, such as firing Comey, pressuring McGahn to fire Mueller, lying about Donald Trump Jr.'s meeting with Russian government representatives, and trying to force Sessions to seize control of the Mueller inquiry.

But the team's inquiry eventually raised a question that they and Mueller could not answer: Could Trump have committed obstruction if he took actions that he was allowed to take under the Constitution, such as firing executive branch officials?

And Mueller also forced all of his teams to work within a set of norms that carried with it assumptions about the presidency and the kind of person who could become the president of the United States. Perhaps, in deference to the office of the presidency, some of the investigators "gave the benefit of every possible doubt to the president," Andrew Weissmann, the leader of Team M, would later write in his memoir. Others "thought that some of those doubts were fanciful and unrealistic," Weissmann wrote.

But in key moments, Weissmann concluded, the special counsel's office acted to appease the president and keep him from shutting down their investigation. Even as the president made blatantly false claims about the inquiry and the investigators, Mueller would not allow the office to respond, assuming that the public would duly consider the special counsel's court filings and weigh them against Trump's lies.

Throughout 2017 and 2018, blanket press coverage chronicled every move and potential move by Mueller's team of several dozen lawyers, FBI agents, intelligence analysts, forensic accountants, and support staff. Many journalists felt they were covering a story that was bigger than Watergate—a former reality television star had colluded with Russia and won the presidency. A witting or unwitting agent of Moscow now occupied the Oval Office. And Trump's erratic behavior, lies, and embrace of conspiracy theories increased suspicions of collusion rather than easing it.

As Mueller's team indicted multiple Trump advisors—Michael Flynn, Paul Manafort, Roger Stone, Michael Cohen, and others—anchors and analysts on MSNBC and CNN predicted that Trump himself would be forced from office. Anchors and analysts on Fox News noted that the charges against the Trump advisors centered on lying to investigators or tax fraud—not secretly conspiring with Russia.

IN JANUARY 2018, Erica Newland and other career lawyers in the Justice Department were stunned when one of their colleagues, Bruce Ohr, became the center of a media firestorm of his own. Ohr was accused of secretly funneling information from Christopher Steele, a former British intelligence officer who authored the unverified dossier of salacious allegations against Trump, to the FBI without telling his DOJ superiors. Steele, House Republicans later discovered, had told Ohr that he was "desperate that Donald Trump not get elected and was passionate about him not being president." Career DOJ staff were shocked that Ohr had worked with Steele.

Ohr's wife, Nellie, had worked for Fusion GPS, the firm hired by Hillary Clinton's campaign and the Democratic National Committee to conduct opposition research on Trump. And Fusion GPS had hired Steele. When Fusion GPS shared the dossier with major US news organizations, they declined to print the allegations during the 2016 campaign, citing their inability to verify its claims.

Rosenstein, the deputy attorney general, was bewildered by Ohr's behavior. "The idea that he had actually had some role in this Russia investigation was shocking to me," Rosenstein told investigators. "I had no idea that somebody on my staff had actually been involved in . . . an operational way in the investigation."

Ohr and his wife, who had also worked as a contractor for the CIA, became the focus of myriad far-right conspiracy theories. Over time, it emerged that Ohr had only played a peripheral role in the FBI's Trump-Russia investigation. To many career civil servants in the DOJ, Ohr had made a massive mistake by not telling his supervisors about the meetings and deserved to be reprimanded. But the portrayal of Ohr—and the DOJ—as part of a nefarious cabal out to discredit Trump was overblown.

Again, attacks by Trump and his allies on Ohr struck fear in the DOJ and FBI workforce, as the firings of McCabe, Strzok, and Page had. The public airing of personnel decisions that would normally be handled in private unnerved staffers. Career public servants were again being used as political punching bags. "We did not want a target on our back," Erica Newland recalled in an interview. "It speaks to how easy it is to chill lawyers. To the sense of vulnerability, especially for people who have security clearances. The standard for revoking is very low. They need it."

A full-time career job at DOJ was secure, with reasonable hours. A supervisor's refusal to provide a reference could derail a career and a family's life in Washington. "People were scared of that," she said. "And those who had kids were especially, and understandably, scared of losing a stable job."

In the Trump era, Republicans experienced a different fear. Young lawyers were expected to display the outspoken legal conservatism and boundary-pushing of Supreme Court justices Samuel Alito and Clarence Thomas. "There was a sense among the lower-level conservative lawyers you had to prove your bona fides," Newland recalled. "You have to push the contours of the law and be willing to make extreme arguments."

There was also "a real fear of being seen as at all critical of Trump," Newland said. "And that getting back to the White House."

Over time, relations between career civil servants and some Trump political appointees in the Justice Department grew strained. A culture clash of sorts emerged. "You have these deeply held views about punctuation and white shirts coexisting with this LOL nothing matters method of lawyering," Newland said. "During the Obama administration, people would try to impress by being precise and legally rigorous. Under Trump, to impress each other you had to get the punctuation right and to push the real extremes of the law. Punctilious punctuation became cover for extreme lawyering."

Newland found that her Trump-appointed supervisors were kind to her, but she vehemently disagreed with some of their policies, which she saw as not authorized by existing law. An audio recording of migrant children weeping as they were separated from their families published by ProPublica in June 2018 deeply angered her. "One of the hardest things was that these people were very nice," she recalled. "They were very kind to me when they were doing things in the world that I found despicable." She added, "Under those circumstances, it's easy to lose your grounding."

Newland also found that she disagreed with Trump appointees on basic facts. This surfaced not only in the legal work but also when people made jokes in the office. "People would say things and you wouldn't know if they were joking," she recalled, referring to political appointees. "And then I would make jokes and they wouldn't land because of the absence of some kind of shared values or facts."

Newland tried to rely on legal ethics as a guide. "For litigators, they defend something if there is a good faith plausible basis for it," she said. "My view is that those are terms that have substance and meaning." But when she and her supervisors disagreed on basic facts she found it difficult to agree on basic legal assessments. "That's one part of the devolution of the rule of law: the disintegration of shared reality."

Some fellow career lawyers believed that the best way to uphold the rule of law was to keep their heads down and rigorously apply the law to the facts. Trump, to Newland, challenged this because he was not constrained by facts and employed "alternative facts" for political gain. If career civil servants ignore that behavior, she thought, they facilitate the erosion of the rule of law.

Over time, Newland, who is Jewish, struggled with her conscience. She later told George Packer of *The Atlantic* that she often asked herself: If she and her colleagues had been German government lawyers in the 1930s, what would they have done?

She felt that DOJ lawyers fit into four categories: There were true believers and ideologues, like one lawyer who was a Clarence Thomas protégé. There were ambitious opportunists who got ahead by going along. And there were a small number of silent dissenters.

Most people, though, simply tried to keep their heads down, provide for their families, and hang on. "I guess I know what kind I would have been," Newland told Packer. "I would have stayed in the Nazi administration initially and then fled."

She imagined that she would have sought compromise as a government lawyer in 1930s Germany, such as pushing for carve-outs in the Nazi race laws that would preserve citizenship rights for Germans with only partial Jewish ancestry. Newland suspected that she would have told herself that this was better than nothing—that it justified working on policies that she personally opposed.

Trump's executive orders and other requests, some of which were legally dubious, appeared to trouble her supervisors as well. Newland told Packer that one of her supervisors began telling her, "We're just following orders." It was without irony, according to Newland, as a way of reminding DOJ career lawyers that "we work for the president."

One day, when he again told Newland, "We're just following orders," and she gave him a quizzical look, he added, "I know that's what the Nazis said, but we're not Nazis." Newland told Packer that she responded, "The president has said that some of them are very fine people." Her supervisor replied, "Attorney General Sessions never said that. . . . And I've never said that. We're not Nazis." The fact that she could still have such a blunt exchange with her boss seemed, on one level, like a reason to soldier on at the DOJ.

TRUMP, MEANWHILE, began calling Rosenstein, who oversaw Mueller and his investigation. Their conversations, usually at night, varied in frequency, but the president was always cordial. "There were periods when he called me frequently," Rosenstein recalled. "He's one of these people who likes to talk by phone." The deputy attorney general, like many other observers, noticed that Trump managed his White House like he managed his company. "He ran the Trump Organization like a small business. He treated the government the same way."

The Russia investigation hung over their conversations. Rosenstein declined to discuss it with Trump. "In retrospect, all that he wanted was someone to say that Donald Trump has nothing to do with Russia," Rosenstein said. Rosenstein expected to be called to testify before Congress and feared being accused of trying to aid Trump. "The last thing I was going to do was discuss Russia with Trump," Rosenstein recalled. "From my point of view, I need to be the guy who marches into Congress and says we did a proper investigation."

Topics ranged from the historic to the mundane. Trump, an avid cable television watcher, sometimes commended Rosenstein for how he handled himself during congressional testimony and press conferences. Rosenstein understood Trump's focus on television. "His view was that's the way he got to be president," he said. "He said if you look bad on TV, I look bad on TV."

Other times, television reports on Fox News prompted calls from the president for the Justice Department to prosecute his rivals. Trump reacted to what he saw on Fox News, Rosenstein recalled, citing, for example, a claim by Fox commentator Gregg Jarrett that former FBI deputy director Andy McCabe had "committed felonies."

Rosenstein said that he would change the subject or speak in generalities, telling Trump "We should do the right thing for the right reasons." Trump would listen and then push again. "He's the kind of guy who is always testing limits."

CHAPTER 5

DISPARAGE AND DISCREDIT

I N DECEMBER 2017, PRO-TRUMP HOUSE REPUBLICANS received an extraordinary political boost from the Sessions Justice Department. In a move that unnerved FBI officials, the department gave congressional investigators the private text messages of two FBI officials involved in the Trump-Russia investigation—Peter Strzok and Lisa Page. The texts leaked to the media and detonated like a political bomb in Washington. They immediately damaged Republican views of the FBI and the Mueller investigation.

Strzok and Page, who were having an extramarital affair at the time, had disparaged Trump throughout the 2016 campaign in text messages. Page had called Trump a "loathsome human" and said that Hillary Clinton "just has to win." Strzok wrote "this man cannot be president" and called Trump an "idiot" and a "douche."

When the texts leaked, Strzok was working as a senior investigator on the special counsel's team. As soon as Mueller learned of the texts, he fired Strzok, but it was too late. Republicans declared the texts evidence of anti-Trump political bias in the Mueller investigation and FBI. Page, who did not work for Mueller, later resigned from the bureau.

Asked why his Justice Department had turned over the private text messages, Sessions said he did not recall playing any role in the decision, which was made by the DOJ's Office of Legislative Affairs. "Technically, it had to be Leg Affairs," he said, without offering further details.

At a House Judiciary committee meeting the day after the messages leaked, Jordan and other Republicans assailed the bureau. Rosenstein, who was previously scheduled to testify, tried to defend the FBI, the DOJ, and Mueller. He argued that an official holding a personal political view was different from an official letting their own partisan bias impact their official decisions. "We recognize we have employees with political opinions," Rosenstein testified. "And it's our responsibility to make sure those opinions do not influence their actions."

Jordan flatly dismissed Rosenstein's argument. He demanded that Rosenstein appoint a special counsel to investigate the FBI and end the Mueller investigation. "The public trust in this whole thing is gone," he said, suggesting a secret cabal was at work.

In another blow to Mueller. Steve Chabot, a Republican representative from Ohio, then read out the names of several members of Mueller's team and the political contributions that they had made to Democratic causes. Mueller, a registered Republican, who had been appointed by Rosenstein, a registered Republican, oversaw a team of seventeen people, thirteen of whom had previously registered as Democrats. The four others were not registered with any party, or their affiliation could not be found by journalists.

Nine of the seventeen had made donations to Democrats, which totaled roughly $57,000. The majority came from one person, Quarles, Mueller's partner at WilmerHale, the Washington law firm. Quarles contributed roughly $54,000 to Democrats, and also gave $2,750 to moderate Republicans. Quarles and five other members of the team had also all donated to Hillary Clinton when she ran against Trump in 2016.

Jeannie Rhee, who also left WilmerHale to work on Mueller's team, had given $5,400 to Clinton for her 2016 race and $7,300 to Obama's two runs for the presidency. Rhee had also twice served as Clinton's private lawyer, representing the former secretary of state when conservative advocacy groups had sued for access to her private

emails and filed a lawsuit accusing the Clinton foundation of racke-
teering. Both cases were dismissed by judges.

The GOP attacks intensified the caution inside Mueller's team.
Weissmann was alarmed by what he saw as Aaron Zebley's tendency
to narrow the investigation. Zebley, for example, said that the team
should not investigate Trump's financial ties to Russia. "There's an
old FBI saying," Weissmann, who served as the bureau's general
counsel, said in an interview. "Big cases big problems, little cases
little problems, no cases no problems."

Fearing they would be fired by Trump, Mueller's team also created
a centralized system for storing its work, from witness interviews to
subpoenas, on FBI computers so that it would be preserved. They
also used the court system to maintain a backup record of their investigation, packing search warrants with information.

In all, Mueller's team filed more than five hundred search warrants, filling them with details to ensure that a separate branch of
government had access to the information if Trump fired them.
Finally, they referred multiple investigations—such as the investigation of Trump's private lawyer, Michael Cohen, to the US attorney
in Manhattan—to make it harder for the Trump DOJ or the White
House to destroy or seal off the investigation's records.

ON MARCH 16, 2018, Trump, with Jeff Sessions's help, achieved a
goal that he had pursued for over a year that sent a clear message to
investigators. Just over twenty-four hours before Andrew McCabe—
a Comey ally and former FBI deputy director—was set to retire, Sessions fired him. The move meant that McCabe, who had served in
the FBI for two decades, would lose most of his pension. McCabe
immediately released a lengthy statement saying his removal was
politically motivated.

"This attack on my credibility is one part of a larger effort not
just to slander me personally, but to taint the FBI, law enforcement,
and intelligence professionals more generally," McCabe said. "Their

persistence in this campaign only highlights the importance of the special counsel's work."

Sessions, in a statement at the time, said he was simply following the recommendation of the DOJ inspector general and the DOJ's Office of Professional Responsibility. Attorney General Levi established the office in 1975, following revelations of ethical abuses and serious misconduct by senior department officials during Watergate. The office concluded that McCabe had made "an unauthorized disclosure to the news media and lacked candor—including under oath—on multiple occasions." Sessions noted that the department's top civil servant had recommended McCabe's firing as well. "I'm confident I made the right decision," Sessions said.

At the same time, Trump had tweeted or retweeted messages that attacked McCabe as a corrupt Comey ally. Trump's evidence of wrongdoing, which he cited over and over, was that when McCabe's wife, a pediatrician, had run as a Democrat for the Virginia state legislature in 2015 she had received several thousand dollars from a political action committee controlled by Terry McAuliffe, a longtime Clinton ally and then the state's Democratic governor.

McCabe's wife had lost the election, part of a failed push by McAuliffe and other Democrats to win control of the state senate. Trump, seemingly emboldened by McCabe's firing, began publicly attacking Mueller. "The Mueller probe should never have been started in that there was no collusion and there was no crime," he tweeted. "It was based on fraudulent activities and a Fake Dossier paid for by Crooked Hillary and the DNC. . . . WITCH HUNT!"

The following day, he echoed the attack line of House Republicans tarring Mueller's team as "angry Democrats." "Why does the Mueller team have 13 hardened Democrats, some big Crooked Hillary supporters, and Zero Republicans?" he tweeted, ignoring the fact that Mueller, the team's leader, was a longtime Republican. Days later, he tweeted, "Special Council is told to find crimes, whether a crime exists or not."

The Washington establishment, from politicians to pundits, dismissed Trump's Twitter tirades, which at one point included 181 tweets that used the term "witch hunt." "Many of the President's detractors snorted at the broadsides, dismissing them as the ravings of a cornered man," Brian Bennett later noted in *Time* magazine. "But there was power in the mayhem. The President's campaign to discredit the decorated former Marine and lifelong Republican as a rogue prosecutor seems to have had a real effect. Over time, Trump was able to convince supporters that a meticulous inquiry was politically motivated, and the public's views became more and more entrenched along party lines."

INSIDE THE MUELLER INVESTIGATION, some prosecutors began to feel that the team was too deferential to Trump, in part to avoid playing into his narrative of victimization.

Prosecutors began interviewing witnesses about a June 9, 2016, meeting in Trump Tower that had fueled widespread suspicion that Trump was colluding with Russia. Donald Trump Jr., Paul Manafort, and Jared Kushner had met with Natalia Veselnitskaya, a Russian lawyer with ties to the Putin government.

Several weeks later, at a press conference on July 27, 2016, Trump publicly called for Russia to hack Hillary Clinton's email. "Russia, if you're listening, I hope you're able to find the 30,000 emails that are missing," Trump said. "I think you will probably be rewarded mightily by our press." Investigators from Mueller's team found that, on or around that same day, Russian hackers sent phishing emails to accounts at a domain used by Clinton's personal office. They also targeted seventy-six email addresses on the domain used by the Clinton campaign.

Ivanka Trump did not attend the Trump Tower meeting, but she talked with those who did afterward. She was also later involved in conversations with her father about how the administration could hide the details of the meeting from reporters. Mueller's team did not request an interview with Ivanka due to concerns that it would reinforce Trump's narrative that he and his family were being persecuted by the DOJ and FBI. Mueller's team feared that the request would enrage Trump and cause him to fire Mueller and shut down his investigation. Weissmann again blamed Zebley, the team's second ranking official, for being too cautious.

"The specter of our being shut down exerted a kind of destabilizing pull on our decision-making process," Weissmann wrote in his memoir. "Repeatedly during our twenty-two months in operation, we would reach some critical juncture in our investigation only to have Aaron say that we could not take a particular action because it risked aggravating the president beyond some undefined breaking point; that it might either upset our endless negotiations with the Justice Department and the White House as to whether and under what condition the president would sit for an interview with our office, or anger him to such an extent that he'd lash out and fire us."

BY THE TIME HE FIRED SESSIONS, Trump's attacks on the Justice Department—on top officials and career civil servants, and on the very idea that no one was above the law—had taken a toll on the department and the FBI. Sessions's public statements in defense of the department had done nothing to quiet Trump. Worse still, Wray adopted a strategy of not publicly responding to Trump's attacks.

What had seemed like paranoia in 2017 was now abundantly clear: Trump had wiped away the norms designed to protect the department, and the cost of holding him to account was now devastatingly high. With Sessions out, the department was temporarily under the control of Matthew Whitaker, a Trump devotee who the rank and file feared would undercut the DOJ's ability to investigate the president and his allies. Whitaker's ascension to power was so alarming that some Democrats were privately eager to confirm Trump's nominee, William P. Barr, who they perceived as a moderate Republican. Barr, in fact, was a staunch supporter of presidential power.

Barr had served as George H. W. Bush's attorney general in the 1990s, and he believed that the administration had been hamstrung by Lawrence Walsh, the independent counsel whose investigation of Reagan-era misdeeds had helped Bush lose the 1992 election. "[Walsh] was certainly a headhunter and had completely lost perspective and was out there flailing about on Iran-Contra with a lot of headhunters working for him," Barr recalled in a 2001 interview for an oral history on the Bush presidency. "The whole tenor of the administration was affected by that."

Barr enthusiastically supported Bush's decision to pardon the four former officials whom Walsh had prosecuted for lying to Congress. And he later said that such independent counsel probes reinforced his belief that the post-Watergate reforms had gone too far in weakening the presidency and shifting prosecutorial power away from presidents and other elected officials.

"The other big problem is this notion that has gained currency that there's something wrong about political officials reviewing cases," Barr recalled in the 2001 interview. "This has largely been precipitated by the liberal critics of the Department of Justice and by the Democrats on the Hill. It's very destructive to personal liberty because what they're trying to do is to say that political-level people shouldn't be reviewing cases."

Barr argued that if elected leaders abused prosecutorial powers, they could be voted out of office. "The second-guessing is not for political reasons," Barr said. "It's really because someone is exercising some maturity of judgment, and putting things in perspective and saying, 'Why would you indict this person over this?'"

Barr was espousing a view that was the polar opposite of the apolitical approach established by Edward Levi after Watergate. Skeptics of presidential power argued that political leaders do not always show maturity of judgment. Intense pressure to win the next election can distort an elected official's thinking. Prosecuting one's political rivals to gain an electoral edge could prove tempting.

When Barr promised during his confirmation hearing to let the Mueller inquiry run its course, most Democrats on the Senate Judiciary Committee were deeply skeptical. Minnesota senator Amy Klobuchar said that the Trump era was "not the time to install an attorney general who has repeatedly espoused a view of unfettered executive power." California senator Dianne Feinstein argued that a twenty-page memo, written by Barr while a private citizen, disqualified him from serving as attorney general. In the memo, Barr argued that it was within Trump's authority as the president to fire Comey after asking him to drop the Flynn matter. Treating those acts as obstruction of justice would be "fatally misconceived," Barr wrote, and doing so would ultimately damage the power of the presidency.

But the Republicans had the votes necessary to confirm Barr. In a largely party-line 54–45 vote, they ensured that he would be the attorney general when Mueller submitted his final report.

THREE WEEKS LATER, on March 5, 2019, a Justice Department security detail drove four visitors into the building's basement. They hustled the group, all men, into a back elevator to prevent employees from spotting them. Arriving on the building's fifth floor, the visitors were escorted into the attorney general's wood-paneled conference room.

Waiting for the visitors were Barr; Rosenstein; Ed O'Callaghan, one of Rosenstein's top advisors; and Brian Rabbitt, Barr's chief of staff. The four men greeted the three visitors warmly. After two years of work, Special Counsel Robert Mueller and his three top aides, James Quarles, Aaron Zebley, and Andrew Goldston, had arrived to share the final results of their two-year investigation into whether the Trump campaign had colluded with Russia during the 2016 election.

After Barr, Mueller, and their aides took their seats in the conference room, Mueller began the meeting by pulling out a piece of paper with notes on it. After a few perfunctory remarks, the special counsel handed the meeting over to Zebley, who summarized their findings regarding Russian interference. Russia had mounted a sophisticated hacking and disinformation campaign to aid Trump during the 2016 election and sow division among Americans. But Mueller's investigation did not establish that the Trump campaign had conspired or coordinated with the Russian government in its effort.

Zebley said that Mueller's team had identified numerous links between individuals with ties to the Russian government and associates of the Trump campaign. But they had not found sufficient evidence to charge any member of the campaign with conspiring with Russia. Zebley said that investigators still had questions about Trump campaign manager Paul Manafort but that they were comfortable saying there was no conspiracy.

Mueller's team had regularly updated Rosenstein and O'Callaghan on the status of their investigation, but the formal confirmation came as a relief to Justice Department officials. "We all at a very basic level felt good that we didn't have a Russian plant in the Oval Office," said a former DOJ official. "We felt very good that we didn't have to deal with that scenario."

Quarles then presented the team's long-awaited findings regarding whether Trump had obstructed justice. Quarles first said that Mueller's team agreed with a 1973 DOJ memo, issued during the Watergate scandal, that concluded that Congress was the only body with the power to investigate, impeach, and remove a sitting president. That finding would disappoint liberal legal commentators who had predicted for months that Trump's public attacks on Mueller's investigation could result in him being charged with obstruction.

But Quarles's next statement surprised and puzzled Barr, Rosenstein, and their aides. Mueller's team, he said, had decided to make no recommendation regarding whether enough evidence existed for Trump to be prosecuted for obstruction of justice. Quarles said that the prosecutors had not reached a conclusion whether Trump's conduct was criminal. He said that Mueller's report would present the facts, evidence, and analysis dispassionately.

In the view of Barr, Rosenstein, and O'Callaghan, one of Mueller's core tasks as a special counsel had been to determine whether anyone, including Trump, should be prosecuted for committing a crime. "It was a little confounding on the obstruction piece," O'Callaghan recalled in an interview. The former DOJ official called it "the most confusing thing ever." Barr, according to his memoir, asked Mueller and Quarles to clarify their position. "So, you're saying that, because you couldn't indict at this stage," Barr recalled asking, "you aren't even embarking on the analysis to determine whether the evidence is strong enough to show an obstruction?"

Mueller and Quarles replied that Barr was correct. Barr asked Mueller if the report provided a record on which someone else could decide whether a crime had been committed. Mueller replied yes.

Inside the special counsel's office, staffers had been flummoxed by Mueller's position as well. They felt it was well-intentioned and fueled by respect for a defendant's rights and the DOJ norm that it was wrong to publicly accuse someone of a crime if they were not given a chance to defend themselves in court. And the 1973 OLC opinion said that the only way to prosecute a president for a crime was for Congress to do so through impeachment. As a result, Mueller had concluded he was barred from indicting Trump.

Weissmann feared that Mueller had made a nuanced decision that could confuse the public and appear mealymouthed. He felt it would have been better for Mueller to say that Trump had committed or not committed obstruction of justice—even though prosecuting the president while in office was not possible. "Far better to have just made the difficult factual and legal calls we were supposed to make and let the attorney general deal with their inconvenient consequences," Weissmann later wrote.

At the same time, Trump's attacks had continued to successfully undermine public confidence in the investigation. At roughly the same time as Mueller prepared to deliver his final report, *Time* magazine was given access to a series of focus-group sessions convened in Des Moines, Iowa, by a Democratic polling firm. One panel was made up of college-educated Republicans. The other was made up of college-educated independents, and one of Democrats without college degrees.

The groups shared a sense that the investigation was merited, the matters were serious, and it was important that justice be done, *Time* found. They were troubled by the idea that politicians and the privileged might get away with things regular people wouldn't. But many of the allegations against Trump didn't strike the participants as a big deal. The prevailing view was that there was a lot of funny business going on around Trump—but that the president had likely found a way to keep his hands clean.

"I do think he probably did some stuff, but I'm pretty sure he did a good job insulating himself," a thirty-five-year-old Republican man told the magazine.

Surprisingly, none of the focus-group participants expected the Mueller report to be a game changer. "There may be a lot of pistols, but there probably isn't going to be a smoking gun," a sixty-nine-year-old male independent said. Most important, few said the report was likely to alter their opinion of Trump. A Fox News poll showed the same result. Roughly 70 percent of respondents said there was only a small chance the report would change their views.

Adding to that morass of public opinion and growing indifference, Mueller's conclusion regarding obstruction was confusing. But the special counsel's office could not have imagined, in the end, how the attorney general himself would brazenly take advantage of Mueller's eagerness to be fair. Together, Barr's aggressiveness and Mueller's caution would put a stake in the special counsel investigation, its reputation, and its mission—supercharging Trump to see himself as having defied and defeated a special counsel, as no president had in fifty years.

FOR ROSENSTEIN, THE END of the special counsel's investigation was a relief. He had endured two years of incessant attacks from Trump, Republicans in Congress, and other critics. Mark Meadows, a member of the House Freedom Caucus who later became Trump's chief of staff, had filed articles of impeachment against Rosenstein. "He was a career prosecutor who was thrown in the middle of this political maelstrom in his capacity of acting attorney general," O'Callaghan recalled. "Rod defended the integrity of the Mueller investigation, and he was right to do it."

Rosenstein and O'Callaghan felt that history, overall, would look favorably on the special counsel's investigation. They viewed the former FBI director's conduct during the probe as a model for future special counsels. In all, Mueller had indicted thirty-four people, including two dozen Russians, and secured eight convictions and guilty pleas without losing a single case. "I think it went very well," Rosenstein said. "What they accomplished in under two years was remarkable."

But Barr had an entirely different view of Mueller and his investigation. The new attorney general dismissed the idea that Trump had conspired with the Russians as ludicrous, and saw investigating it as unnecessary, illegitimate, and engineered by Democrats. "Trump's victory sent Democrats on a treasure hunt to find an explanation for their loss," Barr wrote in his memoir. "And what they came up with, thanks in part to Jim Comey's conduct, was a preposterous theory about Russian collusion and an illegitimate election." He viewed Mueller, then seventy-four, as a once-commanding figure diminished by age. The former DOJ official said some of Mueller's aides were biased against Trump. "There were a couple of people who were in this 'get Trump' mode. I think the people in Mueller's office felt they were on to something big and then couldn't find it."

Rosenstein and O'Callaghan disagreed with Barr's view of Mueller's health. "I shared his view that Mueller was a little shaky but people at that age are often shaky and that doesn't correlate with being mentally impaired," Rosenstein said. O'Callaghan believed that Mueller was not diminished. "My impression at that meeting was that he didn't have diminished capacity," O'Callaghan recalled. "There is nothing that led me to think that."

TWO WEEKS AFTER the secret meeting at the Justice Department, on Friday, March 22, Mueller's 448-page final report was hand-delivered to O'Callaghan at his office. O'Callaghan, Barr, Rosenstein, Rabbit, and Steve Engel, the head of the Office of Legal Counsel, began to read it. O'Callaghan also asked the department's top civil servant, Bradley Weinsheimer, to review it. O'Callaghan included Weinsheimer, who held the position once occupied by the late David Margolis, to ensure that a career prosecutor, not only political appointees, were involved.

Barr, as required by special counsel regulations, sent a letter that afternoon to the House and Senate Judiciary committees informing them that he had received Mueller's final report. Unsurprisingly, the letter quickly leaked and a media feeding frenzy ensued. Television crews camped out in front of Barr's home and the Justice Department. Journalists reported in real time on Barr's movements around Washington. In liberal circles, suspense built that Mueller might have discovered evidence Trump had colluded with Russia, or evidence that the president had obstructed the special counsel's investigation.

As DOJ officials read through the final report, they were more focused on logistics. They quickly saw that confidential grand jury information had not been redacted from the report. Instead, Mueller's team had added footnotes indicating which information needed to be removed. Barr feared that it could take as long as three weeks to fully redact and release the report. He set an internal deadline of Sunday to notify Congress of Mueller's principal conclusions within 48 hours. Barr feared that delaying the release of the report any further would fuel speculation that the Justice Department was trying to hide Mueller's findings.

Returning to the department on Saturday morning, Barr, Rosenstein, and O'Callaghan reviewed Volume II of the report, which described fourteen instances when Trump potentially obstructed justice—ranging from the president firing Comey to the president ordering Don McGahn to fire Mueller.

Barr bluntly dismissed the legal arguments in Volume II as strained, tortuous, and based on fuzzy logic. His conclusion was no surprise. In Barr's unsolicited, nineteen-page memo to the White House counsel's office and to Rosenstein, he had argued that it was essentially impossible for Trump to obstruct justice, given his power as president.

The legal views of Rosenstein, who had long been lauded by Democrats for his nonpartisanship, carried more public weight. Mueller's team had found fourteen separate episodes where Trump tried to have Mueller fired or otherwise slowed his investigation. Rosenstein, though, agreed with Barr that there was not enough evidence to prosecute Trump of obstruction. "The facts are clear," Rosenstein said.

O'Callaghan agreed. He believed that Trump had followed the advice of his lawyers and stopped just short of obstruction. "He has advisors who told him where the line was," O'Callaghan said. "He didn't cross it. He got very close to the line and did not step over it."

Together, the four men compiled a four-page letter that described the report's principal conclusions that Barr could release to Congress and the public by his Sunday deadline. The letter stated that Mueller had not concluded whether Trump had obstructed justice but that Barr, as attorney general, had ruled that the president did not. They included language from the report that was damaging to Trump as well, including that it "does not exonerate him." By the time they finished, Rosenstein and O'Callaghan were comfortable with the four-page document. "I defend the letter," Rosenstein later said.

O'Callaghan called Zebley and informed him that Barr planned to release the letter publicly that afternoon. He asked if Mueller's team wanted to review it first. Zebley had expected Barr to publicly release Mueller's prewritten summaries of the report instead. After discussing it with Mueller and other members of the special counsel's office, Zebley called O'Callaghan and said that Mueller didn't want to see Barr's letter.

Their reasoning was simple: the special counsel didn't want to be seen as vouching for Barr's summary. Weissmann said it was the job of the attorney general to write such a letter, not the special counsel.

In hindsight, Mueller and his team had made a pivotal communications error. If they had reviewed Barr's letter beforehand and disagreed with it, they could have quickly issued a short statement saying so and blunted its impact. Instead, they remained silent and allowed Barr to frame the report's findings.

At roughly 3:30 p.m. on Sunday, Barr sent the four-page letter to the chairs of the House and Senate Judiciary committees, who immediately released it. Blanket coverage of Mueller's long-awaited findings exploded across television screens, websites, and social media. Trump, once again, quickly won the messaging war by shamelessly distorting Mueller's findings.

Standing on an airport tarmac dressed in a suit and signature red tie, he triumphantly declared the report a "complete and total exoneration." "It was just announced there was no collusion with Russia, the most ridiculous thing I ever heard," Trump said. "There was no collusion with Russia. There was no obstruction, none whatsoever." Trump then called Mueller's investigation "an illegal takedown that failed."

Adopting a familiar tactic, Trump called for an investigation of his investigators. "It began illegally, and hopefully somebody's going to look at the other side," he said, hinting at a probe of the FBI's Trump-Russia investigation.

Dismayed Democrats demanded that the full report be released. And Mueller's team privately expressed fury at Barr for releasing his own summary of Mueller's report. In hindsight, Mueller's embrace of traditional Justice Department reticence was no match for Trump's willingness to blatantly lie about Mueller's findings. Mueller had intentionally not used the word "collusion," which is not a legal term, in his report. Yet initial media coverage of the report featured Trump's "no collusion" language in headlines and stories. As occurred throughout his presidency, Trump's false and intentionally provocative tweets dominated the news cycle. Trump's performative messaging triumphed.

On Monday morning, Zebley called O'Callaghan and asked him to release the six-page summaries of the report that Mueller's team had prepared. O'Callaghan promised to look into it, but questioned why Mueller's team had not provided a version of the report with confidential grand jury material redacted. Later that day, Zebley sent O'Callaghan the executive summaries with all grand jury material redacted, so that they could be released immediately. O'Callaghan did not respond.

Many members of Mueller's staff were livid at Barr, who they felt had mischaracterized their work to help Trump. Two days later, Mueller sent a letter to Barr stating that the attorney general's summary letter "did not fully capture the context, nature and substance of this office's work and conclusions. There is now public confusion about critical aspects of the results of our investigation."

Mueller, though, followed traditional Justice Department reticence and did not release the letter to the public. If Mueller had, it would have caused a firestorm and potentially impacted public views of the report. Instead, the letter did not become public for a month.

Soon after receiving the letter, Barr called Mueller and asked why he hadn't simply called him and made the request. Mueller then suggested that Barr release the report summaries prepared by his staff. Barr said he would consider it and then failed to do so for weeks.

THREE WEEKS AFTER first receiving the report, Barr released a redacted version of the voluminous document at an April 18 press conference at the Justice Department. Weinsheimer, the career civil servant, had worked tirelessly with intelligence agency lawyers to rapidly redact classified information and prepare the report for public release. Barr asked Rosenstein and O'Callaghan to join him on stage for the press conference.

At 9:34 a.m. Barr walked up to the lectern. Rosenstein, dressed in a gray suit and blue striped tie, stood behind Barr's left shoulder. O'Callaghan, wearing a charcoal suit and red striped tie, stood behind Barr's right shoulder. The two men stared blankly ahead. They both appeared stone-faced, as Justice Department officials have been trained to do for years, to appear impartial.

In a twenty-two-minute presentation, Barr delivered a full-throated defense of Trump before releasing the report to the reporters in the room. He stated four times that Mueller's team found no evidence that Trump, or anyone in his campaign, had "colluded" with Russia. Barr painted the president sympathetically, saying, "There is substantial evidence to show that the president was frustrated and angered by a sincere belief that the investigation was undermining his presidency, propelled by his political opponents, and fueled by illegal leaks."

As Barr spoke, Rosenstein and O'Callaghan continued to stare ahead blankly. Rosenstein appeared to focus his gaze on the cameras in the back of the room. O'Callaghan glanced down at times or from side to side. When Barr took questions from reporters, he grew testy when asked why his statements appeared sympathetic toward Trump, noting that he seemed to take into account Trump's feelings and emotions. Rosenstein and O'Callaghan, by standing behind Barr, appeared to support what the attorney general said. Liberal critics later accused both men, longtime career prosecutors, of helping Barr whitewash the Mueller report.

William Barr, Rod Rosenstein, and Ed O'Callaghan releasing the
Mueller report. O'Callaghan privately considered Barr's public
defense of Trump that day a mistake. (BILL O'LEARY / WASHINGTON
POST VIA GETTY IMAGES)

Rosenstein declined to comment on his thoughts during Barr's
press conference. O'Callaghan said that, as he listened to Barr speak
that day, he felt Barr went too far in defending Trump. "I do think it
was an attempt by him to get behind the report as released. And he
wanted to have the two people in his inner circle who lived the longest with the investigation there with him." O'Callaghan recalled. "I
think it's a fair criticism that the remarks, as they came out, seemed
to bend too heavily toward defending the president. But I believe that
Barr sincerely meant everything he said."

The twenty-two-minute presentation and Barr's handling of the
Mueller report proved pivotal in Barr's second tenure as attorney general. In the short term, it won Barr cachet with Trump. For the next
year, according to a former DOJ official, Barr was the "golden boy"
of the cabinet.

To Democrats, Barr's press conference was the first of myriad
acts of norm-shredding by the new attorney general. Barr, to them,
appeared to be a partisan who was using his position as attorney gen-

eral to aid Trump politically. A combination of overconfidence, ideology, and isolation resulted in Barr and his team operating in a bubble.

To Republicans, Comey and the Democrats had improperly used the FBI, the Office of the Attorney General, and now the special counsel law to delegitimize Trump's presidency. They believed that Comey, Hunt, and Mueller were trying to force a democratically elected president from office. In their view, the "Russia hoax," as Trump called it, was the most egregious FBI abuse since the tenure of J. Edgar Hoover.

Two lessons emerged. Mueller's decision to pass judgment on whether Trump had obstructed justice was an example of how the norms of the 1970s were ill-suited for the Trump era. Mueller said nothing and Trump said everything. Mueller worked in secret, allowing Trump to fill the void with baseless accusations of a witch hunt. Mueller's conclusions were muddied by legal jargon, which Barr and Trump distorted into a vindication.

Anyone who remained silent and failed to fight back against Trump would be defined by Trump.

CHAPTER 6

SHIELD AND PROTECT

I N THE MONTHS AFTER WILLIAM BARR'S CONTENTIOUS
release of the Mueller report, Trump and his new attorney general enjoyed a honeymoon. "The president loved Bill at that point,"
recalled the former DOJ official. Like Jody Hunt, the former official
was struck by Trump's ability to charm people. "He's an engaging,
gregarious, funny guy," the former official said. "He remembers you."

Barr also steadfastly supported Trump's policies. He directed
judges to deny migrants the opportunity to post bail and restricted
their ability to claim asylum. He tried to reverse a court decision that
helped protect people from fast-track deportations and sued "sanctuary cities" in California and other states.

In early July, Barr deftly handled an embarrassing legal setback.
The Supreme Court ruled, 5–4, against the administration's attempt
to add a citizenship question to the Census, a measure that liberals said disadvantaged Hispanics. Chief Justice John Roberts concluded that the "sole stated reason" for the change "seems to have
been contrived."

Barr and other officials convinced Trump to issue an executive
order that gave him the ability to collect the citizenship data by other
means. Legal experts widely dismissed the order as a pointless fig
leaf. But in a Rose Garden ceremony, Barr declared it a triumph.
"Congratulations again, Mr. President," Barr said, "on taking this
effective action."

Privately, Barr and his aides saw the Census question as a quixotic distraction proposed by Jeff Sessions and Stephen Miller. They were grateful to Barr for finding a solution that would allow the administration to focus on other policy priorities. "That is a classic example of Bill Barr taking a bullet for the administration," the former official recalled. "And lying on the ground and letting his personal credibility bleed out."

While Barr remained in Trump's good graces, other cabinet members did not. In an Oval Office meeting with multiple other officials, the president berated Wilbur Ross for mishandling the Census question issue. Like Hunt, the former DOJ official was struck by how Trump could quickly pivot from charismatic to cruel. Trump humiliated Ross, a billionaire, as he had Sessions. The former DOJ official said that Trump spoke to Ross as if he were scolding a pet. "He turned to Wilbur Ross, he said 'Wilbur, you're a very bad, bad secretary.' It was like he was a dog," the former DOJ official recalled. "I've never seen one man degrade another man like that and have the other man not respond."

TWO WEEKS LATER, Barr enjoyed another triumph. Democrats held two three-hour congressional hearings with Robert Mueller as the star witness on July 24. The former FBI director made no bombshell revelations regarding Trump and Russia. He also largely declined to attack Barr.

Mueller, true to form, comported himself as a model, nonpartisan public servant. He was meticulously fair to Trump and tried to hew strictly to the department's rules against revealing negative information about an individual who has not been charged with a crime. A decorated Vietnam War veteran and lifelong prosecutor and law enforcement official, Mueller struggled cognitively. His answers were halting and labored at times. He asked repeatedly for questions to be clarified or repeated. According to a count compiled by MSNBC, Mueller "deflected or declined to answer questions" at least 198 times.

The report itself revealed multiple unseemly, unethical, and arguably criminal acts by Trump that enraged Democrats. But the revelations appeared to have little impact on Trump's core supporters. More than a year of false attacks on Mueller and his team by Trump and his Republican allies had left them convinced that Trump was the victim of a Democratic smear campaign. The hearing also showed, yet again, how the norms of the 1970s were no match for the online smears, partisan cable TV coverage, and hyper-partisanship of the Trump era.

BILL BARR, MEANWHILE, quickly emerged as one of the most partisan attorneys general in decades. In a series of public appearances, he argued that Hillary Clinton advisors, Obama administration officials, and members of the media had spread a conspiracy theory that Trump was a Russian agent.

He dismissed the possibility that FBI officials genuinely feared that Trump had colluded with Russia due to Trump's own actions. To FBI officials, Manafort's long-running ties to Russia; Manafort, Kushner, and Donald Trump Jr.'s Trump Tower meeting with the Russian lawyer Natalia Veselnitskaya; Trump's call for Russia to find Hillary Clinton's emails; and the subsequent hacking of Clinton's emails by Russians were alarming.

Barr publicly argued that Democrats had used the "Russiagate nonsense" to try to discredit and destroy Trump's presidency. Throughout his tenure, Barr repeatedly argued that Trump was being politically persecuted and echoed conspiracy theories spread by the president.

During congressional testimony in the spring of 2019, the new attorney general publicly argued that the FBI had improperly spied on Trump. The statement gave credence to the president's false claim that the FBI had illegally wiretapped Trump Tower during the 2016 campaign, a claim flatly denied by FBI officials. "I think spying did occur," Barr said. "The question is whether it was adequately predicated."

Giving more credence to pro-Trump conspiracy theories, Barr asked the US attorney for the District of Connecticut, John Durham, to conduct a sweeping criminal investigation of the origins of the FBI's Trump-Russia investigation. Barr's actions sent a message to law enforcement and intelligence officials: if you investigate Trump, we will investigate you.

A former senior Justice Department official said that Barr's suspicions of career civil servants, the liberal elite, and the news media were sincere and longstanding. "He was someone who came to the job with the view that conservatives are persecuted by the media, by the elite," this former official said, adding that Barr's suspicion extended to career DOJ lawyers, like Hunt. "He really has a deep belief that there is a liberal bias among the career people." Whatever Barr's thinking, his key role in helping Trump survive the Mueller investigation failed to humble Trump. Instead, it emboldened him.

A DAY AFTER MUELLER'S testimony gave Trump an opportunity to shift the focus away from his conduct, the president created a new scandal that sullied Barr and energized Democrats. In a phone call with Ukrainian president Volodymyr Zelensky, Trump appeared to withhold US military aid to Kyiv as a way to pressure Ukraine into opening an investigation of Hunter Biden's business activities there.

Twice during the call, Trump told Zelensky that Barr would be in touch with him regarding the Ukrainian government's criminal probe of Hunter Biden's business practices in their country. Trump's statement suggested that Barr was actively participating in the president's effort to pressure Ukraine. Barr, in fact, had never spoken with Trump about asking Ukrainian officials to investigate Hunter Biden. When the new attorney general learned of the call, and that Rudy Giuliani was the driving force behind the scheme, he was livid.

In a single, reckless phone call, Trump had created the grounds for a new Democratic investigation of a potential presidential abuse of power and ensnared Barr in the scandal. As Democrats investigated and then impeached Trump over the call, Barr faced a decision. Would he uphold his own reputation, or that of the president, who was impugning him?

Privately, Barr felt that the Ukraine call was idiotic and harebrained, but not criminal. He predicted that Giuliani would go down as the man who helped Trump get himself impeached. But he continued publicly defending Trump and argued that impeaching the president for his Ukraine call was another example of Democrats' willingness to use any tactic to destroy his administration.

Barr and White House Counsel Pat Cipollone both urged Trump to declassify and release the transcript of his call as soon as possible, believing it would help the president politically. Trump initially refused to do so, claiming the call was "perfect." The delay allowed Nancy Pelosi and other Democrats to build political support for impeaching Trump on abuse of power charges.

ON JANUARY 9, 2020, as the Senate prepared to hold Trump's impeachment trial, Barr had a private meeting with Jessie Liu, the US attorney for the District of Columbia. Several weeks earlier, Liu had received a seemingly generous offer from the Trump administration. She would be nominated for the number-three job in the Treasury Department if she agreed to resign from her position as US attorney in D.C. Liu accepted the offer.

Normally, as a courtesy, US attorneys are allowed to remain in their position while waiting for Senate confirmation of their new position. Instead, Barr and his aides told Liu to depart immediately, saying that they needed new, stable leadership in the office and felt that her confirmation could drag on due to Trump's impeachment.

Soon after, Barr announced that he was appointing Timothy Shea, a longtime aide and loyalist, to become the acting US attorney for Washington, D.C. Shea, who was working as Barr's counselor, had also worked for Barr when he was attorney general under George H. W. Bush.

To DOJ staffers, the timing was suspicious. Shea, a member of Barr's inner circle, would now oversee the pending criminal cases against three Trump allies—Roger Stone, Rick Gates, and Michael Flynn—as well as two former FBI officials that Trump had said should be jailed, Andrew McCabe and James Comey. Within days, prosecutors planned to send a recommendation for how long a judge should sentence Roger Stone to prison for his conviction the previous month on charges of lying to Congress and witness tampering.

The prosecutors, after seeing Barr's handling of the Mueller report and his ousting of Liu, were suspicious that Barr was again trying to aid Trump politically. Like many other prosecutors, they revered the department's apolitical norms and feared that Barr was destroying public trust in it. On February 5, the four prosecutors told their superiors that they planned to recommend that Stone be sentenced to seven to nine years in prison.

Over the course of the investigation and trial, prosecutors had concluded that Stone was a hustler who had exaggerated his ties to WikiLeaks to stay in Trump's good graces. "We think he was bullshitting," one of the prosecutors said, referring to Stone. "All of the evidence we had was that he was bullshitting." Prosecutors said they uncovered no evidence that Trump or Stone had actually coordinated with Russia during the 2016 campaign, calling them "the gang that couldn't shoot straight."

Five days later, on February 10, Shea, the new US attorney for DC, told Barr that he believed the Stone seven-to-nine-year sentencing recommendation was excessive and that the prosecutors were trying to create a political spectacle. The standard sentence for obstruction of Congress, according to Shea, was three years. But the four prosecutors, citing the fact that Stone had threatened to use violence to stop a witness from testifying, had more than doubled the potential time Stone could spend in prison. In the end, though, the judge would determine Stone's sentence.

Barr felt that Stone was being treated unfairly by left-leaning career prosecutors. One of them, Aaron Zelinsky, had worked on Mueller's investigation of Trump. Another, Jonathan Kravis, had worked for two years as an associate White House counsel in the Obama administration. The other two prosecutors, Adam Jed and Michael Marando, were career civil servants.

After talking with Barr, Shea suggested to the prosecutors that they submit a sentencing memo that would not recommend a specific sentence. All four flatly dismissed the idea. "We would never, as prosecutors, not recommend a sentence," recalled one of the prosecutors, who asked not to be named. "We couldn't stand back and say we didn't have a recommendation."

The deep divisions of the Trump era had again fueled mistrust inside the department. Barr's management style complicated the process as well. He micromanaged, making most major decisions himself and often ignoring the head of the department's largest divisions.

Aggressive and confident, Barr's manner discouraged low-level prosecutors from raising problems or challenging him, former DOJ officials said. He disdained pro forma government meetings and grew bored with presentations that he felt did not quickly get to the point. "He comes to conclusions and makes decisions very quickly," said a former Justice Department official. "He doesn't like to change his mind and he takes it a little personally if people disagree with him."

Barr's willingness to take risks and his disdain for procedure earned him a nickname: "the Buffalo," a reference both to his aggressiveness and his thick skin. A former DOJ official said that when Barr learned of the moniker, he embraced it. "He heard it and he liked it," the official recalled. "He had a tendency to be imperial," the official added. "The Buffalo thing was great because he would charge through minefields."

Barr surrounded himself with a small circle of young aides and often made decisions on his own. Barr "was very impatient with process" and, as a result, his style sometimes alienated people. "I would say that there is a way to rush through something," another former DOJ official said, "and there's a way where you follow the process, and the DOJ likes that." Barr, though, simply plowed ahead.

Most important, Barr, unlike Levi and Mueller, was openly political. "He is a partisan," said the former DOJ official. "He likes to fight, and he wants Republicans to win. So, I think he had a hard time restraining himself."

AT HOME ON THE EVENING of Monday, February 10, Barr saw news reports that DOJ prosecutors had recommended that Stone be sentenced to seven to nine years in prison. Barr called Shea and told him that he would not accept what he saw as a disproportionate sentence.

The following morning, Barr, his aides, and Rabbitt were discussing whether to file a supplemental sentencing memo to the judge in the Stone case when other DOJ officials arrived for a daily staff meeting. Jeff Rosen, whom Barr had chosen to be his deputy attorney general, asked Barr if he had seen Trump's latest late-night tweet. At 1:48 a.m., Trump had publicly assailed the Stone sentencing recommendation. "This is a horrible and very unfair situation," Trump tweeted. "The real crimes were on the other side, as nothing happens to them. Cannot allow this miscarriage of justice!"

After reading Trump's tweet, Barr cursed. Now that Trump had publicly criticized the Stone sentencing recommendation, Barr was trapped. If he filed a new sentencing memo that recommended a shorter prison term for Stone, he'd be accused of doing Trump's bidding. Barr insisted that he had never discussed the Stone case, or his sentencing, with Trump, and vowed to file a new sentencing memo anyway, no matter the political cost.

Some of Barr's advisors described to the attorney general the downsides of filing the new memo. Barr overriding the four prosecutors' sentencing recommendation would be perceived as the attorney general protecting the president's ally. Barr went ahead anyway. Without

SHIELD AND PROTECT 95

informing the four prosecutors on the case, Barr's office submitted a sentencing memo that rescinded their call for Stone to serve seven to nine years.

The four prosecutors were astonished. In their careers at the Justice Department, no elected official—let alone a president—had publicly criticized one of their sentencing recommendations. And no attorney general had reversed one. Later that day, anonymous senior DOJ officials bad-mouthed the four prosecutors to reporters from Fox News and CBS, calling their seven-to-nine-year sentence recommendation "extreme, excessive, grossly disproportionate."

That afternoon and evening, two of the prosecutors resigned from the DOJ and two others withdrew from the case, one of the largest group resignations in the department since Watergate. Zelinsky, who had worked on Mueller's team, later said he withdrew from the case because a bedrock American principle was being flouted—equal justice under law.

"In the United States of America, we don't prosecute people based on politics and we don't cut them a break based on politics," Zelinsky said in subsequent testimony to the House Judiciary Committee. "But that wasn't what happened here. Roger Stone was treated differently because of politics."

Adam Jed resigned from the case as well. Michael Marando resigned from the case and Jonathan Kravis resigned from the DOJ altogether. Kravis believed that Barr was carrying out Trump's orders. "The president made his wishes known in a tweet and the attorney general acts on it," Kravis said. "This has never happened before in the history of the Justice Department." Kravis added, "I just felt like this was wrong. I felt that a bedrock principle had been violated."

Trump had interfered in other cases being investigated by the DOJ. In 2018, Trump suggested during a press conference in Helsinki with Russian president Vladimir Putin that a "Pakistani gentleman," not Russian hackers, had stolen the DNC emails that damaged Hillary Clinton's 2016 campaign.

The "Pakistani gentleman" was Imran Awan, a Pakistani American IT technician who had provided tech support to the offices of more than thirty House Democrats. DOJ prosecutors had investigated allegations reported by a right-wing news outlet, and then Congressman Ron DeSantis, that Awan had violated accounting rules and skirted employment rules. DOJ officials found that Awan was innocent of virtually all of the allegations.

After the four prosecutors quit the Stone case, Trump, yet again, called for the investigators to be investigated, tweeting, "Who are the four prosecutors (Mueller people?) who cut and ran after being exposed for recommending a ridiculous 9-year prison sentence to a man that got caught up in an investigation that was illegal, the Mueller Scam, and shouldn't ever even have started?"

A former DOJ official said Trump's threats caused prosecutors to fear for their safety and that of their families. "You will never feel more alive than when you are on the end of a presidential tweet and you know his seventy million followers know your name," said the former official. "You're a sitting duck. I don't have the guards. I don't have marshals. I have a briefcase. That is overwhelming pressure."

BARR COMPLAINED ABOUT Trump as well. In an interview with ABC's Pierre Thomas, Barr said Trump's tweets "make it impossible for me to do my job" and vowed he would not be "bullied or influenced" by the president regarding DOJ decisions. "I think it's time to stop the tweeting about Department of Justice criminal cases," Barr said.

After the interview aired, Trump called the attorney general and said that he had never told Barr what to do. The attorney general then told Trump to stop publicly commenting on cases, which made them both look bad. Trump said okay, and hung up.

Later that day, Trump withdrew the nomination of Jessie Liu to serve in the number-three position in the Treasury Department. Barbara Ledeen, a right-wing conservative activist, had sent him a memo

calling Liu a member of the "deep state" who was plotting to undermine his presidency. Ledeen's husband had co-written a book with
Michael Flynn, the former Trump National Security Advisor who
had been prosecuted by Liu's office for lying to FBI agents.

The memo criticized Liu for not carrying out a string of prosecutions favored by the Far Right. They included prosecuting Supreme
Court Justice Brett Kavanaugh's accusers, former FBI deputy director
Andrew McCabe, and what Ledeen said were "violent inauguration
protesters" who tried to disrupt Trump's 2017 inauguration. All the
allegations were false or exaggerated. Liu, like Sessions, was forced
out of her job and publicly humiliated.

TWO MONTHS AFTER Trump withdrew Liu's nomination, Barr
made a move that cemented Democrats' views that he was using his
power as attorney general to reward Trump allies. Barr dropped all
charges against Flynn.

Barr said that even if Flynn had lied to the FBI, he should not be
charged, because, in Barr's view, Flynn should not have been investigated in the first place. Flynn was allowed to withdraw a guilty plea
he had previously made twice, under oath, in federal court.

As the Stone prosecutors had done, Brandon Van Grack, the
senior prosecutor on the Flynn case, withdrew from it. Whatever
Barr's motivation, his decision signaled to members of Trump's inner
circle that they would be rewarded for their loyalty. The move also
immediately boosted the standing in Republican circles of Flynn's
then-obscure attorney, Sidney Powell. In a preview of the role that
she would play in Trump's attempts to remain in power after the
2020 election, Powell falsely said that the dropping of charges against
Flynn was "a restoration of the rule of law."

Trump hailed Barr's move and accused Obama administration officials of trying to "take down a president." "I hope a lot of people are
going to pay a big price because they're dishonest, crooked people,"

Trump said. "They're scum—and I say it a lot, they're scum, they're human scum. This should never have happened in this country."

In a television interview with CBS, Barr said that he was "doing the law's bidding," not President Trump's. Asked if Flynn had lied to FBI agents, the attorney general said that "people sometimes plead to things that turn out not to be crimes." In other interviews, Barr also attacked career prosecutors, saying the Stone prosecutors lost "perspective" and the Flynn prosecutors became "wedded to a particular outcome."

In the end, the judge in the Stone case, Amy Berman Jackson, an Obama appointee, gave Stone the sentence Barr had recommended: three years and four months in prison. Berman Jackson agreed that, while Stone had threatened violence, the four prosecutors' recommendation of a sentence of seven to nine years was excessive.

Trump later commuted Stone's sentence days before his longtime political ally was scheduled to report to federal prison. Mitt Romney tweeted, "Unprecedented, historic corruption: an American president commutes the sentence of a person convicted by a jury of lying to shield that very president."

IN AN ASTONISHING four-month-period between February and May 2020, myriad Justice Department and post-Watergate norms had been shredded by Trump and Barr with little political consequence. Barr had intervened in the Stone sentencing, Liu's promised nomination in the Treasury Department had been withdrawn, all charges against Flynn had been dropped, and Barr had appointed John Durham to investigate the origins of the FBI's Trump-Russia investigation. At the same time, Barr had asked a group of prosecutors he had handpicked to review other investigations, several of which were personally and politically important to Trump. Trump could not have asked for a better attorney general.

Trump, though, wanted more. Instead of Barr's support satisfying

the president, he seemed further emboldened. A former DOJ official said that after the Senate had acquitted Trump in his Ukraine
impeachment trial in February 2020, a desire for revenge consumed
Trump and his inner circle over the course of that spring. "The
turbocharged vindictiveness which permeated his inner circle was
alarming," the official warned.

CHAPTER 7

STOKE CONSPIRACY THEORIES

O N MAY 25, 2020, DONALD TRUMP CALLED WILLIAM Barr to vent his anger at an unlikely group: police officers. Trump had just seen the cell phone video showing a Minneapolis police officer choke George Floyd to death by kneeling on his neck for nine minutes and twenty-nine seconds. Trump said that he wanted to make sure that the DOJ was aggressively investigating the case and that the US attorney in Minneapolis would soon address the public.

Trump's sentiment quickly shifted over the next week, a period that badly damaged his presidency and solidified his relationship with Barr. As protests over Floyd's killing turned violent in multiple cities, Trump demanded that active-duty US Army soldiers be deployed in American cities to quell the unrest. The president, apparently fearing that he would appear weak, demanded a hard-line law-and-order response.

While Barr privately believed that deploying active-duty military forces was excessive, he publicly supported the president's get-tough stance. Barr's own political views dating back to Vietnam War protests—a deep-seated belief that leftist groups were stoking chaos—appear to have colored his response. Instead of acting as the country's nonpartisan chief law enforcement officer, Barr echoed, reinforced, and amplified the president's false claims and conspiracy theories.

FOUR DAYS AFTER Floyd's death, Barr read a prepared statement in the Justice Department press room on Saturday, May 30. Initially speaking in a calm, measured tone, Barr said that public anger regarding Floyd's death was "real and legitimate" and promised that "justice will be served." Barr then displayed his own decades-long belief that shadowy leftist groups were stoking violence in the hopes of implementing their revolutionary agenda. "The voices of peaceful protest are being hijacked by violent radical elements," Barr warned. "Groups of outside radicals and agitators are exploiting the situation to pursue their own separate and violent agenda."

Barr then said he would use the Anti-Riot Act, a federal law enacted in 1968 that allows prosecutors to indict individuals who cross state lines to incite violence. He blamed antifa, a loosely organized left-wing group of anti-fascists that were regularly vilified by Trump and many on the Far Right. "In many places it appears the violence is planned, organized and driven by anarchic and left extremist groups, far-left extremist groups using antifa-like tactics," Barr said.

Later that day, like clockwork, Trump echoed Barr's claims, tweeting, "Crossing State lines to incite violence is a FEDERAL CRIME! Liberal Governors and Mayors need to get tougher on protestors or the federal government will use the unlimited power of our Military and many arrests." A subsequent review of Minnesota court records by journalists from the *Star Tribune* found no evidence of shadowy outside groups coordinating the violence as Barr and Trump alleged. Barr and Trump, though, continued blaming antifa.

On Sunday, May 31, Trump tweeted, "The United States of America will be designating ANTIFA as a Terrorist Organization." Political analysts dismissed the tweet as an attempt by Trump to fire up his base by blaming the demonstrations on the shadowy left-leaning group. Barr, undeterred, issued a statement that afternoon parroting Trump. "The violence instigated and carried out by Antifa and other similar groups in connection with the rioting is domestic terrorism."

Since his days as a student at Columbia University during the Vietnam War, Barr had opposed the radical Left, which he accused of using bullying tactics to get their way. Decades later, he held similar views of Black Lives Matter, contending that the organization was Marxist, extremist, and based on a lie. Barr argued that BLM and the news media had falsely claimed that an epidemic of unjustified police killings was caused by institutional racism among police.

Shadowy leftist forces, in Barr's view, were at work in the protests following Floyd's murder. He argued that agitators, often white radicals, used the crowd to conceal their attacks on police and property.

A WEEK AFTER FLOYD'S DEATH, Barr arrived at the White House for a 10:30 a.m. meeting regarding how the administration would respond to intensifying protests nationwide. Barr arrived late and the Oval Office was so packed with officials that some stood against its walls. Trump, seated behind the *Resolute* desk, was denouncing violent demonstrations in multiple cities, including clashes with police in Lafayette Park across the street from the White House. He motioned for Barr to sit down in a chair in front of his desk alongside Secretary of Defense Mark Esper, Chairman of the Joint Chiefs of Staff Mark Milley, and Acting Secretary of Homeland Security Chad Wolf.

Infuriated by news reports that he had been taken into the White House bunker on a recent night for his safety, Trump lost his composure. Glaring at the cabinet members in front of him, he pointed his index finger at them. "You're all losers!" he thundered, his face reddening. "You're all losers. Fucking losers." As Trump bellowed, Barr noticed that small flecks of spit landed on his historic desk. The outburst angered Barr, who considered it a tantrum. He noted that Joint Chiefs Chairman Milley appeared angry as well.

After taking a moment to regain his composure, Trump said the violence in the capital made the US look weak. "Can you imagine the impact these scenes have around the world? Fires and rioting directly across the street from the White House," Trump said. "This is an invitation for our enemies to take advantage of us. We can't have this continue."

White House staffers told Trump that a plan was under way to extend the police perimeter around Lafayette Park and that roughly 1,200 military police from the DC National Guard were being deployed to support the Metropolitan Police, US Park Police, and the Secret Service. Over the weekend, the Park Police operations commander and Secret Service officials had decided to push back demonstrators and install a large fence around Lafayette Park.

Forty-nine Park Police, as well as several Secret Service agents and members of the DC National Guard, had been injured after protesters hurled bricks, rocks, caustic liquids, frozen water bottles, and fireworks at them. On Sunday night, a fire had been set in the basement of St. John's Church, the "Church of Presidents," where every chief executive since its construction in 1816 had attended ceremonies.

Trump asked Barr what he thought of the plan. Barr praised it and said that the DOJ and DHS would have another 2,000 officers as backup if needed. Trump said that he had the power as president to take control of the DC Metropolitan Police and added that he would like to do so. Barr replied that he would look into it.

Trump then raised the role of the military. He asked Milley if he should invoke the Insurrection Act, an amalgamation of federal laws enacted between 1792 and 1871 that gives the president the power to deploy active-duty troops inside the United States to suppress a rebellion or civil disorder. The act had been employed thirty times by American presidents, including George Washington, who used it to respond to early rebellions, and Abraham Lincoln, who invoked it at the outset of the Civil War.

Eisenhower, Kennedy, and Johnson used it—over the objections of southern governors—to enforce federal laws mandating the desegregation of public schools. It had last been invoked in 1992, when George H. W. Bush, with Barr's support, sent federal military forces to Los Angeles when riots erupted after four white police officers were acquitted of beating Black motorist Rodney King.

Legal experts have long argued that the law is too broad, permitting the president to deploy active-duty troops whenever "unlawful obstructions, combinations, or assemblages, or rebellion" make it "impracticable" to enforce federal law by the "ordinary course of judicial proceedings." A wayward president could use the loosely worded act to unleash the American military on civilians.

Milley and Esper both told Trump that they opposed the invocation of the Insurrection Act. They both contended that the military should only be used as a last resort. Unless an actual rebellion emerged, they felt the military should act in support of civilian law enforcement. Esper, Milley, Barr, and Wolf all told Trump it would be prudent to have active-duty military police units on standby but to not actually deploy them. Barr promised Trump that he would not hesitate to recommend that the president invoke the Insurrection Act, if needed, but he did not feel it was necessary at that point.

Trump then pointed to Milley and told him to support the attorney general. Trump pointed at Barr, and told him to take the lead and tell Milley what he needed. The meeting ended and Trump and his senior aides began a conference call with mayors and governors.

In the rambling call, a recording of which quickly leaked to the press, Trump was bellicose. "You have to dominate. If you don't dominate, you're wasting your time," he said. "They're going to run all over you. You'll look like a bunch of jerks." Barr then spoke and blamed "extremist anarchist agitators" for the violence and said, "Law enforcement response is not going to work unless we dominate the streets." He urged law enforcement officials to "go after troublemakers" and then signed off.

The call was a six-minute stream-of-consciousness diatribe from the commander in chief. "These are terrorists, these are terrorists, they're looking to do bad things to our country," he said. "They're antifa and they're radical Left."

After the call, Barr was so worried about Trump deploying active-duty troops that he met privately with Esper and Milley in the White House Situation Room to confirm that they opposed the use of the active-duty military as well.

BARR SPENT THE NEXT several hours in meetings in command centers in the Justice Department, the FBI, and the FBI's Washington field office. A former senior FBI official said that Barr barked orders at local law enforcement officials he did not oversee, some of whom ignored him. Some law enforcement officials felt that Barr was parading around the capital and trying to impress Trump.

At the meeting in FBI headquarters, the Park Police briefed Barr on the plan to push demonstrators back from Lafayette Park and install the taller fence. Barr said he supported it.

After the meeting at the FBI field office, Milley and Barr returned to the White House to brief Trump. At roughly 6:10 p.m., news cameras captured images of Barr entering Lafayette Park with his security guards and White House staff members. Standing behind a line of police officers, dressed in a suit but not wearing a tie, Barr surveyed the area.

After protesters in the crowd recognized Barr, they began shouting at the attorney general. When the Park Police operations commander heard the commotion, he walked over to Barr, told him the area was unsafe, and suggested that he and the other officials move away. The attorney general asked, "Are these people still going to be here when POTUS comes out?" The commander, who had not known that Trump planned to come into Lafayette Park, said to Barr, "Are you freaking kidding me?"

TRUMP PLANNED TO SPEAK in the Rose Garden, walk through Lafayette Park, and visit St. John's Church. Barr, Esper, and Milley were told to accompany Trump when he entered the park. Barr later said that he, Esper, and Milley were not thrilled with the idea but agreed to do so.

Across the street in Lafayette Park, Park Police gave three warnings to the crowd to disperse but investigators later found that many protesters could not hear the announcements. At 6:30 p.m., police advanced on the mostly peaceful protesters. On live, national television, law enforcement officers in riot gear beat demonstrators and fired flash grenades, chemical spray, and smoke at others.

At 6:43 p.m., Trump delivered a Rose Garden address that was one of the darkest speeches of his presidency. Trump exaggerated the scale of the violence nationwide and blamed Democrats and antifa for fomenting it. "In recent days, our nation has been gripped by professional anarchists, violent mobs, arsonists, looters, criminals, rioters, antifa, and others," Trump falsely claimed. "A number of state and local governors have failed to take necessary action to safeguard their residents."

The president then issued a threat. "If the city or state refuses to take the actions that are necessary to defend the life and property of their residents," Trump vowed, "then I will deploy the United States military and quickly solve the problem for them."

Trump concluded his speech with what sounded like a military occupation of the nation's capital. "I am dispatching thousands and thousands of heavily armed soldiers, military personnel, and law enforcement officers to stop the rioting, looting, vandalism, assaults, and the wanton destruction of property," the president said. He then added, "I am going to pay my respects to a very, very special place."

Trump then walked through Lafayette Park with Barr, Milley, Esper, and other cabinet members trailing behind him. His daughter, Ivanka, carried a borrowed Bible in her Max Mara purse. Standing in front of St. John's Episcopal Church, Trump conducted an awkward photo op, clumsily brandishing the Bible.

Trump's goal had been to create an iconic moment that displayed strength. Instead, it spurred outrage and fear. Religious leaders, protesters, and Democrats immediately condemned Trump's use of force to stage a photo op. Within days, Milley and Esper both apologized for their participation in the event. "I should not have been there," Milley said. "My presence in that moment and in that environment created a perception of the military involved in domestic politics."

A former senior Justice Department official said that Barr had been used by Trump in Lafayette Park. The attorney general "got bamboozled," said the former official, who called the photo op "fantastically stupid."

Barr, unlike other cabinet members, publicly defended the photo op in front of the church. At a press conference at the Justice Department several days later, Barr said, "I don't necessarily view that as a political act. I think it was entirely appropriate."

Barr again blamed antifa for the violence. One federal law enforcement official contradicted Barr's claims and said that a small number of extremists from various left- and right-wing groups had tried to infiltrate the protests. "What we're seeing is a broad spectrum of motivations, various people who identify as part of various groups," this official said.

In an interview on *Face the Nation*, Barr downplayed Trump's threats. He denied that Trump had demanded that active-duty troops be deployed in US cities, stating, "That's completely false." Barr's power had reached its zenith. His public support for Trump, seemingly no matter what the president did, had allowed him to become arguably the most effective and feared member of Trump's cabinet.

THREE WEEKS AFTER Lafayette Square, Barr badly miscalculated, and his descent from power began. At 9:15 p.m. on Friday June 19, Barr issued a statement that the US attorney for the Southern District of New York, Geoffrey Berman, had agreed to step down from his position. "With tenacity and savvy, Geoff has done an excellent job leading one of our nation's most significant US Attorney's Offices,"

Barr said. "I appreciate his service to the Department of Justice and our nation, and I wish him well in the future." Barr then announced that Jay Clayton, the current head of the Securities and Exchange Commission, and a golf buddy of Trump's, would replace Berman in the powerful post.

Two hours later, in a startling act of defiance, Berman issued his own statement: "I have not resigned, and have no intention of resigning, my position," Berman wrote. "I will step down when a presidentially appointed nominee is confirmed by the Senate. Until then, our investigations will move forward without delay or interruption."

Behind the scenes, the stakes were clear. Barr was trying to install a Trump loyalist in the US Attorney's Office in Manhattan, which was carrying out a series of politically embarrassing investigations of Trump allies in New York, including Michael Cohen and Rudy Giuliani.

In a 2018 case that had consumed the headlines for months and infuriated Trump, federal prosecutors in Berman's office had brokered a plea deal with Cohen, Trump's former personal lawyer, in which he confessed to having violated campaign-finance laws by facilitating hush-money payments to the adult-film actress Stormy Daniels and the model Karen McDougal. Cohen stated under oath that Trump ordered him to make the payments.

Berman, who had donated to Trump's 2016 campaign, recused himself from the Cohen case. Trump, as he had been with Jeff Sessions, was irate with Berman for not acting as the president's personal lawyer and making politically embarrassing cases go away.

In 2019, prosecutors working in Berman's office had indicted two associates of Giuliani, Lev Parnas and Igor Fruman, and accused them of making illegal campaign contributions to a US congressman and other officials. Berman's office was also investigating Giuliani for violations of foreign-lobbying disclosure requirements.

Berman's defiance appeared to catch Barr off guard. So did the response from Congress. The morning after Barr attempted to fire Berman, one of Trump's strongest backers in the Senate, Lindsey Graham, indicated that he would not support the nomination of Clayton to replace Berman. Graham, who was locked in a tight reelection race with Democrat Jaime Harrison, tried to distance himself from Trump. Several other Senate Republicans also declined to support Clayton, who had never worked as a prosecutor.

Outmaneuvered by Berman, Barr agreed to appoint Berman's deputy, career prosecutor Audrey Strauss, as an interim US attorney in New York. Berman issued a statement that the Southern District of New York could be "in no better hands." "I stepped aside because I had full confidence that the work of the office—its ongoing investigations of anyone, whether they be friends or enemies of the White House—would continue unabated with Audrey in charge," Berman later wrote.

Barr, in interviews, continued to fervently defend Trump. In a Fox News appearance two days after his failed ouster of Berman, Barr warned of mob rule if protests over Floyd's killing continued. He also endorsed a Trump conspiracy theory that the president had been invoking on the campaign trail—that Democrats were planning to steal the 2020 election. Barr, without citing any evidence, said in the interview that mail-in voting "opens the floodgates to fraud."

The next morning, Trump tweeted a link to Barr's interview and wrote, "This will be the Election disaster of our time. Mail-In Ballots will lead to a RIGGED ELECTION!"

BEHIND THE SCENES, Barr also tried to suppress another politically embarrassing allegation against Trump as the 2020 presidential election approached. The Justice Department filed a lawsuit to stop the publication of a book by former national security advisor John Bolton that said that Trump had repeatedly interfered in criminal investigations of his friends, political allies, as well as of the president himself.

Bolton described several instances involving major companies in

Turkey and China where Trump expressed a willingness to halt criminal investigations "to, in effect, give personal favors to dictators he
liked," Bolton wrote. "The pattern looked like obstruction of justice
as a way of life, which we couldn't accept," Bolton said, adding that
he had reported his concerns to Barr.

Bolton also claimed that Trump had used tariff talks with China
to boost his chances of winning reelection by asking President Xi
Jinping to buy American agricultural products and bolster Trump's
standing in farm states. Bolton wrote that Trump was "pleading
with Xi to ensure he'd win" and "stressed the importance of farm-
ers, and increased Chinese purchases of soybeans and wheat, in the
electoral outcome."

Barr, yet again, defended Trump. He dismissed Bolton's claim
that the president intervened in criminal cases to aid autocrats and
allies. He also falsely claimed that no White House aide had ever
written a memoir. "This is unprecedented, really," Barr said during
an exchange with reporters at a White House event. "I don't know of
any book that's been published so quickly while, you know, the office-
holders are still in government." Barr also claimed that the release of
information in the book posed a national security risk, a claim that
law enforcement officials denied.

Finally, a veteran DOJ official felt that Barr's support of the White
House effort to halt publication of Bolton's book was a spurious violation of DOJ protocols. Jody Hunt, the Alabama native who had served
as Jeff Sessions's chief of staff for nine months, had been working as
the head of the DOJ's Civil Division, where he had served for almost
two decades. For two years, as assistant attorney general in charge of
the Civil Division, Hunt had defended the administration's policies
in civil suits, including ones that he disagreed with personally. Hunt
believed, as he had with the travel ban, that it was his responsibility
as a civil servant to defend the policies of a democratically elected
president—as long as they were constitutional and ethical.

Hunt and his colleagues had defended the administration's decision to no longer defend the Affordable Care Act in court, its adoption of harsh immigration policies, as well as Trump's fight to add a citizenship question to the census. The Civil Division also defended Trump against lawsuits accusing him of illegally profiting from his personal business while serving as president. Morale suffered at times. At one point, so many lawyers in the Civil Division resigned or asked to be temporarily reassigned to other parts of the department that Hunt had to freeze reassignment requests.

But Hunt, who had vast experience handling the government's prepublication review litigation over the course of many years, believed that the attempt to halt the publication of Bolton's book was a clear example of the president using the DOJ to aid himself politically, not to carry out a government policy.

Over time, Trump's public attacks on the DOJ and the FBI had worn on Hunt, who had worked as a civil servant in the department for two decades. When Hunt returned home to Alabama, he was alarmed by how many people believed Trump's claims that career government employees like him were part of a "deep state" cabal that was undermining Trump. "It really did damage to the institution and to the FBI to call them 'the deep state,'" Hunt said.

"Politicians of both parties have taken to this name-calling with respect to DOJ and the FBI," Hunt added, calling it "shameful." "If Americans have lost faith in our institutions of government, it is not founded in reality," Hunt added. "Instead, it is because legislators and politicians have jumped on the bandwagon for political gain and have made unfounded and outlandish allegations about career government officials."

Barr's insistence on tightly controlling decision-making himself frustrated Hunt as well. By comparison to other attorneys general, Barr rarely met with senior DOJ leaders on key issues. He had a small tight-knit group of associates with whom he consulted. One senior DOJ official referred to Barr as "The Lawgiver," Hunt recalled. "He would say 'This is the law, now go do this.'"

"Once Barr took a call from someone outside the department insisting that the Civil Division file a statement of interest in a case," Hunt recalled, "and he had an associate tell me to 'shake it loose' without even knowing the facts and without understanding the legal implications." Hunt responded by telling the associate to tell Barr "the civil division is not going to file it."

The way that Trump had treated Sessions in the Oval Office had convinced Hunt that the president could not be controlled. Barr, he believed, continued to think Trump would change. "I think Barr was a strong believer in executive prerogative, but I think he underestimated that an executive could be a loose cannon like Trump," Hunt said. "You want to believe that the chief executive is going to behave rationally and obey the regulations and the norms. But when you have someone sitting there who doesn't respect the institutions of government, and doesn't respect the civil servants, that's very different from Bush and Obama."

Hunt was not alone. Support for Barr among current and former DOJ officials was eroding. Two senior DOJ officials had recently announced their departures: Brian Benczkowski, the head of the Criminal Division; Noel Francisco, the solicitor general. More than a thousand former Justice Department officials had signed a letter demanding Barr's resignation, citing his repeated interventions in Trump-related probes in ways that appeared to aid the president politically.

The breaking point for Hunt was the failure of DOJ leadership to stand up to the demands of White House officials regarding Bolton's book. Although a prepublication review specialist had reviewed the manuscript and had succeeded in getting Bolton to remove the classified information, the White House demanded that the DOJ file a prior-restraint lawsuit to halt publication of the book on the ground that it contained classified information.

Bypassing normal process, DOJ leaders insisted on filing the prior-restraint lawsuit despite the fact that it had no chance of success. The deputy attorney general, Jeff Rosen, who appeared to be working closely with the White House, demanded that the Civil Division pursue the prior-restraint lawsuit. Barr personally authorized it as well.

At around 3:00 p.m. on Tuesday, June 16, 2020, Hunt was told that White House Chief of Staff Mark Meadows had demanded that the lawsuit be filed within one hour. "Heads will roll if it isn't filed by four o'clock," Hunt recalled being told. Justice Department lawyers missed the four o'clock deadline but filed the lawsuit that day.

Trump's White House aides had succeeded in pressuring the DOJ to pursue a case in court that was both factually wrong and legally untenable. Copies of Bolton's book had already arrived in bookstores. "As is often the case with the Trump administration, this motion is all hat and no cattle," Ben Wizner, a lawyer with the American Civil Liberties Union, said at the time. "The audience for this filing is not the court; it's the president."

Hunt, after nearly two years of trying to hold the line on political interference, resigned as head of the Civil Division that same day. "I won't do something if it's frivolous or making a misleading statement," Hunt recalled. "Civil was my home there for almost thirty years."

In the end, he felt that Trump, Meadows, Barr, and Rosen had rendered him powerless to support the division and department that he loved. "They did not care that they circumvented the process, prevented the Civil Division from doing its due diligence, and ultimately undermined the good will of the department," he said. "It was manipulation and political interference in a manner that ran contrary to the standards of the Department of Justice, and it should not have been permitted."

CHAPTER 8

MENACE

ONE WEEK AFTER THE CLEARING OF LAFAYETTE PARK the president tweeted a dire warning at 11:38 p.m. on a Wednesday night, "Domestic Terrorists have taken over Seattle, run by Radical Left Democrats, of course. LAW & ORDER!" The following day, Trump issued a threat: "Take back your city NOW. If you don't do it, I will. This is not a game. These ugly Anarchists must be stopped IMMEDIATELY. MOVE FAST!"

Trump was referring to a decision by Seattle's mayor Jenny Durkan, after days of violent clashes, to abandon a precinct house in Capitol Hill, the city's most densely populated neighborhood. After the officers withdrew, protesters established a police-free, self-governing, six-block area that they declared the "Capitol Hill Autonomous Zone." Durkan, a Democrat and the city's first lesbian mayor, saw it as a temporary way to reduce tensions in the area. Trump, trailing Joe Biden in 2020 presidential election polls, saw a political opportunity.

The next morning, Trump blamed Biden for the police-free zone in Seattle. "Sleepy Joe Biden refuses to leave his basement 'sanctuary' and tell his Radical Left BOSSES that they are heading in the wrong direction," Trump tweeted. "LAW & ORDER!"

To Trump, Barr, and other Republicans, Seattle represented the first-ever antifa takeover of a major American city. Fox News ran apocalyptic stories that exaggerated the level of lawlessness in Seattle. One story featured a photograph of a demonstrator sprinting past a car and building engulfed in flames. "CRAZY TOWN," the head-line said. "Seattle helpless as armed guards patrol anarchists 'autono-mous zones,' shake down businesses: cops."

The photo, in fact, had been taken the previous month in Saint Paul, not Seattle, during the height of the unrest near where George Floyd was killed, the *Seattle Times* later reported. When reporters from the newspaper asked Fox for comment, they said the "photo illustration" that had run with the story had been updated and issued an apology. (The new image, the *Seattle Times* pointed out, com-bined separate images of a gunman and a shattered storefront in Seat-tle that were taken ten days apart.)

With the election five months away, Trump may have been pos-turing, trying to rally his base, or genuinely outraged. Whatever the cause, former Justice Department officials said that the presi-dent put intense pressure on Barr to crack down in Seattle. "Trump went crazy," recalled the former senior DOJ official. "He wanted to send the military into Seattle." Barr and other DOJ officials advised Trump to allow local law enforcement officials to handle the demon-strations. The question became how long Trump would wait.

TRUMP PRESSURED Justice Department officials to take action in Portland, Oregon, as well. For weeks, demonstrators there had gath-ered outside the city's federal courthouse, clashed with local police, spray-painted graffiti on the building, and shattered its first-floor win-dows. "The president wanted a strong response in Portland, to send a message," recalled the same former DOJ official. "It was harder and harder to get the White House from doing something dramatic."

On June 26, Trump issued an executive order that gave him the power to send federal officers to cities around the country to protect federal property, including monuments and statues. Senior Justice Department officials again feared that Trump would invoke the Insur-rection Act and dispatch federal troops. "We were highly motivated in that period trying to figure out how to somehow fix the Seattle problem and the Portland problem, so that the president wouldn't insist on using the insurrection act or use the military against the protesters," recalled the same former DOJ official.

On July 1, the standoff in Seattle ended when local police took control of the autonomous zone after four shootings, two of them fatal, occurred inside the area. In Portland that night, clashes intensified, with federal law enforcement officers emerging from the boarded-up federal courthouse for the first time and firing pepper balls at demonstrators. Instead of ending the protests in Portland, a series of more aggressive federal law enforcement steps that were caught on video and went viral exacerbated tensions.

On July 11, federal officers blocked an off-duty EMT and a volunteer from treating an injured man lying on a sidewalk. The following day, a federal officer shot a twenty-six-year-old protester in the head with an impact munition, fracturing his skull and requiring facial reconstruction surgery. Oregon's two US senators, both Democrats, called for federal officers to immediately leave Portland. Trump ignored them.

Three days later, on July 15, a protester who was several blocks from the demonstrations was grabbed off the street by federal officers and thrown into an unmarked van. The officers, who had no insignias on their uniforms, drove him to the federal courthouse and read him his Miranda rights. After ninety minutes, he was released with no paperwork or record of his arrest. More accounts of abductions by federal officers emerged in news reports and on social media. Democrats were outraged by the federal tactics in Portland, but Barr appeared nonplussed.

Part of the problem, according to former DOJ officials, was that senior White House and DOJ officials, as well as many Republicans, simply did not believe the mainstream news media reporting from the two cities. They believed the lawlessness there was being hushed up by the media. Barr had come to disdain the mainstream media, which he felt had covered Trump unfairly since he took office.

Barr regarded progressives as "Maoist," "totalitarian," "Bolshevik" radicals bent on creating universal government dependence. He blamed the media for allowing a progressive "ideological Blitzkrieg." "In the latter years of the Obama presidency, formerly respectable news outlets simply stopped producing and instead churned out consensus left-liberal opinion cloaked in the garb of 'objective' news," Barr wrote in his memoir. "Well before the rise of Donald Trump, the media had become the progressive movement's propaganda arm."

Inside the Justice Department, Barr's top advisors felt that the mainstream media covered the department far more negatively and skeptically during Republican administrations than during Democratic ones. Another former senior DOJ official said the journalists assumed nefarious motives drove every action taken by Barr and presented his every move in the worst possible light.

As a result, Barr and his aides often minimized interactions with the media and largely ignored it. "If you're a public official and you feel like you're going to get hit no matter what you do, you don't really care," said the former senior DOJ official. "If you're conservative, you know that the mainstream reaction is going to be so hyperbolic that it's not worth worrying about it." The official added that the dynamic was destructive for both sides and "leads to a reduction in accountability."

Barr and his aides instead focused on the coverage they received from conservative news outlets, particularly Fox News, which Trump watched avidly. "The civil unrest and the crime surge was getting so extreme on Fox News world," the former DOJ official said. "This was the focus. It was driving the president crazy."

AS FOX NEWS and other conservative news outlets continued to portray chaos in Portland, Trump and other White House officials made repeated calls to Barr and his aides demanding action. The fifty-year-old post-Watergate norm that presidents should not direct law enforcement operations for political gain was weakening.

Throughout the summer of 2020, Trump, White House Counsel Pat Cipollone, and White House Chief of Staff Mark Meadows repeatedly called Barr and his aides and demanded more aggressive steps in Portland. "The White House put a lot of pressure on us in the summer of 2020. I would get harangued and Barr would get harangued about exact responses, how many prosecutions we had brought," said the second former senior DOJ official. For the White House to call for an increase in the number of federal prosecutions brought in Portland, as Trump publicly attacked the city's Democratic mayor during a presidential election, was yet another violation of 1970s reforms designed to keep the DOJ from being used as a political weapon.

WITH TRUMP STILL TRAILING Biden in public opinion polls, his behavior and demands, both in public and in private, grew more desperate and improper. On August 13, in a rambling forty-minute interview with Fox News' Maria Bartiromo, Trump made a declaration that no modern American president, not even Richard Nixon, had employed.

He publicly called for the attorney general he had appointed to criminally prosecute his election opponent, the previous vice president, and the previous president, for treason. "Obama knew everything," Trump said. "Vice President Biden, as dumb as he may be, knew everything, and everybody else knew."

Trump was referring to his years-old false claim that Obama and multiple other senior members of his administration secretly engineered the FBI's investigation of his campaign's ties with Russia. The plot, according to Trump, involved former FBI director James Comey, former CIA director John Brennan, and former director of national intelligence James Clapper.

"They spied on my campaign, which is treason," Trump said. "They spied, both before and after I won, using the intelligence apparatus of the United States to take down a president, a legally elected president, a duly elected president of the United States. It is the single biggest political crime in the history of our country."

Both Trump's claims were false. Two Republican-supervised investigations—one conducted by John Bash, the then US attorney for the Western District of Texas, at Barr's request, and an exhaustive inquiry by the Republican-controlled Senate intelligence Committee—had found that none of the individuals had committed treason or engaged in criminal conduct.

Trump then publicly pressured Barr and John Durham, the federal prosecutor conducting a separate review of the origins of the FBI's Trump-Russia probe, to prosecute his two greatest political rivals. If Barr and Durham failed to do so, Trump insinuated, they were either cowardly or corrupt. "Bill Barr can go down as the greatest attorney general in the history of our country, or he can go down as an average guy," Trump said. "We'll see what happens." Later in the interview, Trump pressured his attorney general again, "Bill Barr is great most of the time, but if he wants to be politically correct, he'll be just another guy." Trump also repeated the false claim that there was evidence that Obama and Biden had committed a crime. "They have all the answers," Trump said, referring to Barr and Durham. "It goes all to Obama, and it goes right to Biden."

The interview infuriated Barr. He felt that Trump had invented evidence of criminal behavior by Obama and Biden that didn't exist and, more important, flagrantly overstepped his role as president to meddle in individual investigations. "Even accounting for the president's habitual hyperbole and imprecision, these comments were grossly improper for a president," Barr later wrote. "There had been no determination of criminality as described by the president. His labeling of individuals, including President Obama and Vice President Biden, as criminals far outstripped the existing evidence and, as chief executive, the president had no business prejudging an investigation and calling for scalps."

After Trump's interview, Barr, as he had in the past, remained silent. Barr could have challenged Trump publicly, as he had during the Roger Stone sentencing controversy, but he said nothing.

Instead, Barr continued to back Trump's false claims that the election would be stolen from him. In an interview with the *Chicago Tribune* on September 11, 2020, Barr predicted that mail-in ballots would abet massive Democratic voter fraud. "So now we're back in the business of selling and buying votes," Barr told John Kass, a long-time conservative columnist for the newspaper. "Capricious distribution of ballots means harvesting, undue influence, outright coercion, paying off a postman, here's a few hundred dollars, give me some of your ballots."

Barr also predicted that Trump would accept the results of the election and, if he lost, leave office amicably. He contended that Democrats were projecting and blamed them, not Trump. "All this bulls— about how the president is going to stay in office and seize power? I've never heard of any of that crap," Barr said. "I mean, I'm the attorney general. I would think I would have heard about it. They are projecting."

AT THE END OF THE SUMMER OF 2020, Barr had a tense exchange with Trump in the Oval Office. After a long meeting Trump asked Barr why the Durham investigation was taking so long. Barr responded that he trusted Durham and that some leads, such as alleged criminal activity by the CIA, had not panned out. Trump erupted and asked, "You buy that bullshit, Bill?" according to Barr. "Everyone knows Brennan was right in the middle of this," Trump said, referring to former CIA director John Brennan. According to his memoir, Barr shot back, sarcastically, "Well if you know what happened, Mr. President, I'm all ears. Maybe we are wasting our time doing an investigation. Maybe all the armchair quarterbacks telling you they have all the evidence can come in and enlighten us."

While privately seething, Barr again defended Trump publicly. On September 3, Trump issued a memorandum ordering Barr and other federal officials to identify "anarchist jurisdictions," and consider cutting off federal grants to them. Several days later, Barr designated Portland, Seattle, and New York "anarchist jurisdictions" and recommended that they lose their federal funding. "We cannot allow federal tax dollars to be wasted when the safety of the citizenry hangs in the balance," Barr said.

The *New York Times* later reported that Barr and other Justice Department officials had ordered federal prosecutors and FBI agents to shift from investigations into violent white supremacists to cases involving rioters or anarchists, including those who might be associated with antifa. Experts considered white supremacists, who have killed far more Americans than antifa, a larger threat to public safety. But federal law enforcement resources had been directed at the president and the attorney general's obsession: antifa.

JOHN DURHAM'S INVESTIGATION into the origins of the FBI's Trump-Russa investigation, an inquiry driven by Barr's political views, was also unraveling. On September 10, 2020, Nora Dannehy, a longtime colleague of Durham's and a respected prosecutor, discovered that other members of Durham's team had written a draft report about their investigation into the FBI's launch of its Trump-Russia probe. Durham had not told Dannehy about the draft report and for months she had been growing increasingly frustrated with the investigation, the *Times* reported.

Dannehy erupted and told Durham that no report should be issued before the investigation was complete—and particularly not before an election. She also denounced the draft for taking disputed information at face value. After sending several colleagues a memo detailing her concerns, Dannehy resigned on September 11.

Dannehy, a widely respected prosecutor, had complained to Durham about how Barr kept hinting darkly in public about the direction of their investigation. In April 2020, for example, Barr had suggested during a Fox News interview that officials could be prosecuted, saying that "the evidence shows that we are not dealing with just mistakes or sloppiness. There is something far more troubling here."

Dannehy urged Durham to ask the attorney general to adhere to Justice Department policy and not discuss an ongoing investigation publicly. But Durham was unwilling to challenge Barr. Two people close to Barr said he had pressed for the draft to evaluate what a report on preliminary findings would look like and what evidence would need to be declassified. But they insisted that he intended any release to come during the summer or after the November 3 election—not in the weeks before Election Day, when it would have the most potential political impact.

THE OTHER MAIN AREA of Republican investigation was the business affairs of Hunter Biden, Joe Biden's son. For years, the younger Biden appeared to have played off his family name, securing a lucrative seat on the board of a Ukrainian energy company and lavish business deals with Chinese firms. Hunter Biden also abused drugs, consorted with prostitutes, and failed to pay his taxes. The central question, from a political perspective, was whether his father had improperly aided him or profited from his business dealings.

Various Republican-led congressional committees had been investigating Hunter Biden as the 2020 race approached. On September 19, a long-awaited investigation by the Republican-controlled Senate Homeland Security and Finance committees found no evidence of improper influence by Joe Biden regarding his son's business dealings in Ukraine, as Trump and Giuliani had claimed for months.

The GOP-led investigation found that the younger Biden had "cashed in" on his family name to make high-paying business deals around the globe. It also found that Hunter Biden's work for a corrupt Ukrainian energy firm while his father directed US policy toward the country created the appearance of a conflict of interest and alarmed American diplomats. But witnesses rebutted claims that Joe Biden had directed policy in ways that aided his son. Senator Ron Johnson, the head of the Homeland Security Committee, conceded that no "massive smoking guns" had been found.

On October 8, Trump—still behind in the polls—did a second interview with Maria Bartiromo of Fox News. This one lasted fifty-five minutes. The sitting president, in an extraordinary step, again demanded that his attorney general bring criminal charges against Obama, the former president, and Biden, his opponent in 2020. "Unless Bill Barr indicts these people for crimes—the greatest political crime in the history of our country—then we're going to get little satisfaction, unless I win," Trump warned. The president said that the crime "includes Obama, and that includes Biden."

Trump later said that "Bill has got to move" and that he would go down in history as a "very sad situation" if he didn't indict people, an apparent reference to Hunter and Joe Biden. Trump said the Justice Department kept asking for more information but that it already had all the information it needed for indictment. A week later, Trump again pressured Barr during an interview on Newsmax, saying he was "not happy" with Barr. Again, Barr remained silent.

On October 14, the New York Post published a story saying that incriminating emails had been found on a laptop that Hunter Biden had abandoned in a Delaware repair shop in 2019. The laptop contained tens of thousands of emails as well as videos of the younger Biden smoking crack and having sex with prostitutes.

A 2017 email described potential ownership stakes in a joint venture with a Chinese company known as CEFC. An email from James Gilliar, a business associate of the Bidens, said that each of the deal's four partners would receive a 20 percent stake in the firm (except for Hunter's uncle Jim, who would get 10 percent). Gilliar then posed a question: "10 held by H for the big guy?" One of the recipients of the email, Anthony Bobulinski, said at a press conference organized by Giuliani that the "H" was a reference to Hunter and that "big guy" was a reference to Joe Biden.

But Gilliar, the author of the email, told the *Wall Street Journal* that Joe Biden played no role in the venture and that the proposed business never generated any income. "I am unaware of any involvement at any time of the former vice president," he said. "The activity in question never delivered any project revenue."

Soon after Rudy Giuliani leaked the contents of the laptop, Trump called Barr and asked the attorney general about it. Barr cut him off twice, he later said, and told Trump that he would not discuss the department's criminal investigation of Hunter Biden with him.

During a presidential debate on September 29, Trump tried to raise the matter of Hunter Biden, accusing the former vice president and his son of corruption. "That's been totally discredited," Biden said, jabbing his pen at the camera. "Totally discredited."

At the same time, aides to Barr began reaching out to reporters and arguing that Barr was breaking with Trump. They insisted that Barr's comments over the summer—such as his statement that Obama and Biden were not under investigation in May—were intentional. One associate said that Barr deserved credit for refusing to engage in a tactic that has spread across American politics—accusing one's political opponents of criminal activity based on flimsy evidence. "The real October surprise is Bill Barr," that aide said. As the 2020 election approached, Barr said nothing publicly about Hunter Biden and privately declined to name a special counsel to investigate him.

TO BARR AND HIS AIDES, the clearest, and most egregious, attempts by Trump to pressure them were the ones that he conveyed in public. The former Justice Department official put it simply, "Trump says the quiet part out loud."

Throughout 2020, as the presidential election approached, it was obvious to Barr and his inner circle the two things that Trump wanted from the Justice Department. First, for John Durham to bring criminal charges against the Obama administration and FBI officials for launching the Trump-Russia investigations. And second, launching a federal criminal investigation of Hunter Biden, and, by extension, his father, and, hopefully, the indictment of both men.

But Barr and his aides managed to keep two things secret from the public, and, apparently, Trump himself. On October 19, three weeks before Election Day, Barr secretly made Durham a special counsel. The appointment ensured that, if Trump lost the election, Durham's investigation would continue after he left office. And if Trump won the election and fired Barr, which Barr and his aides expected, the ability of the president and his new attorney general to pressure Durham would also be limited. Keeping the special counsel announcement private also prevented Trump from using it politically in 2020.

More important, the Justice Department had managed to keep secret for two years news that Trump would have eagerly used to savage Joe Biden throughout the 2020 race. Since 2018, Hunter Biden had been under criminal investigation by federal prosecutors in Delaware. During the final months of Jeff Sessions's tenure as attorney general, David Weiss, the Trump-appointed US attorney in Delaware, had quietly launched a criminal investigation of Hunter Biden. Prosecutors and FBI agents had spent two years scouring the younger Biden's business dealings inside and outside the US, including China and Ukraine.

Investigators uncovered strong evidence that Hunter had committed tax fraud, solicited prostitutes, and made a false statement on a federal form when he purchased a gun. They found evidence that Hunter Biden did not declare all of the income related to his business ventures, both inside the US and around the world. And when the younger Biden bought a handgun in October 2018, a period when he was using crack cocaine, he had falsely answered "no" to a question that asked if he was "an unlawful user of, or addicted to, marijuana or any depressant, stimulant, narcotic drug, or any other controlled substance?"

While Barr had tolerated Trump's violations of other departmental norms, he had defended a sacrosanct one: leaking news of a DOJ criminal investigation in order to potentially sway an election. The priority was keeping the "DOJ out of a presidential election," said the second former senior DOJ official. "It's why the memo exists," he added.

The official was referring to a department memorandum, issued by both Republican and Democratic attorneys general, that bars prosecutors from announcing criminal investigations actions that might influence elections. "There's a recognition that the department's work can be misunderstood and have an outsized influence on people's thinking," the same official said.

Again, Justice Department officials had taken solace in the fact that they had held the line on an inviolable norm in an election year. Trump, though, would soon violate an even larger one.

CHAPTER 9

FRAUD

O N TUESDAY, NOVEMBER 3, 2020, BILL BARR AND HIS wife, Christine, arrived at the White House for what Trump and his supporters predicted would be a victory party. In the final days of the presidential campaign, massive crowds had attended Trump rallies. After months of Biden leading in the polls, Trump had narrowed the gap, just as he had done in 2016. Trump, to the delight of his core supporters, would defy expectations and the establishment again.

In the State Dining Room and the East Room, the attorney general mixed with senior Trump administration officials, members of Congress, and longtime Trump supporters. Rudy Giuliani and several of his colleagues sat at a table in the center of the Red Room studying the latest election returns on their laptops. Barr, who had grown to disdain Giuliani since the Ukraine scandal and impeachment, felt the former New York mayor was posturing.

Unlike in 2016, when Barr woke up convinced that Trump would pull off an upset win, he rose on Election Day in 2020 with a gut feeling that Biden would prevail in the election. Barr admired the stamina that Trump had displayed in the final weeks of the election—holding forty-eight rallies in twenty-one days, twice as many as Biden—but he felt that the president had ignored his advice to curb his crass behavior, which alienated college-educated suburban voters.

Barr hadn't spoken with Trump since mid-October, when he had cut short the president's call regarding Hunter Biden's laptop. Barr expected that any election night interaction with Trump would be awkward. As the evening wore on, though, Trump remained upstairs in the White House residence. Barr and his wife departed at 10:30 p.m. and headed home.

Just before 2:30 a.m., Trump emerged from the residence to speak to his supporters. News organizations had not declared a winner in the presidential race but Trump's lead in key battleground states was shrinking as mail-in ballots were counted. "This is a fraud on the American public," Trump declared. The president's words marked the beginning of the most serious constitutional crisis in American history since the Civil War.

For the next eleven weeks, an incumbent president, for the first time in US history, would mount a political, legal, and, ultimately, violent effort to remain in power.

Barr quickly concluded that Biden had, in fact, won the election by a wide margin. But for the next four weeks, as Trump spread false election theft conspiracy theories, Barr kept his conviction that Biden had won private.

Throughout the final months of the 2020 campaign, in fact, Barr himself, like Trump, had publicly predicted widespread voter fraud, reinforcing the belief of the president and his supporters that Democrats would steal the presidency.

BARR VIEWED UNIVERSAL mail-in voting, where election officials mail ballots to all eligible voters, as particularly vulnerable to fraud. In the years before the pandemic, four states—Oregon, Washington, Colorado, and Hawaii—had instituted universal mail-in balloting. After the pandemic began, four other states—California, Nevada, Utah, and Vermont—adopted the practice as well.

In the days and weeks after the election, though, Barr was repeatedly told by DOJ officials that there was no evidence of large-scale voter fraud, including via mail-in ballots. On Election Day, the US attorneys had been told to monitor voting for any signs of irregularities. Since then, the US Attorney's Offices received isolated allegations of fraud, but none were widespread enough to change the outcome in any single state.

Giuliani led Trump's effort to challenge the election results and a pattern quickly emerged. In cable television interviews and press conferences, Giuliani and other pro-Trump lawyers claimed that widespread fraud was occurring without citing specific examples. In their court filings—where they risked being disbarred for making false statements—they did not describe specific incidents of fraud. Instead, they cited examples of state election officials sometimes not following election rules.

Barr believed that Trump had lost to Biden. Barr noticed a drop in support for Trump in swing-state suburbs in 2020, where he received fewer votes than in 2016. Other Republicans, in fact, outperformed Trump in those same areas in 2020, suggesting that Trump's unpopularity with suburban voters, not voter fraud, explained his loss. There was also no surge of unexplained votes in Democrat-dominated cities. In many of those cities, Trump had performed better than he did in 2016.

Republican voters and television pundits, though, overwhelmingly embraced Trump's stolen-election claim. False stories about voter fraud attracted enormous audiences on Fox News and Facebook, energizing and enraging the president's supporters. A Politico/ Morning Consult survey released two days after Biden was declared the winner found that 70 percent of Republicans did not think the 2020 election was "free and fair."

BARR, UNDER GROWING PRESSURE to at least look into Trump's fraud claims, yet again backed one of Trump's false narratives, as he had done with the Mueller report, the Stone and Flynn cases, and the George Floyd protests. On Monday, November 9, Barr issued an unprecedented memorandum authorizing US attorneys to investigate claims of voter fraud.

Barr tried to strike a nonpartisan tone, instructing US attorneys to only investigate "if there are clear and apparently credible allegations of irregularities that, if true, could potentially impact the outcome of a federal election." He urged US attorneys to "maintain the Department's absolute commitment to fairness, neutrality and non-partisanship" and said that "specious, speculative, fanciful or far-fetched claims should not be a basis for initiating federal inquiries."

One of his aides said, off the record at the time, that Barr himself did not believe that the election was stolen. Yet, inside and outside the department, the memo was seen as an affirmation of Trump's false voter fraud claims.

Within hours of Barr issuing the memo, Richard Pilger, the head of the DOJ's Election Crimes Branch, which oversees investigations of voter fraud, resigned. "Having familiarized myself with the new policy and its ramifications," he wrote in an email to colleagues, "I must regretfully resign from my role as director of the Election Crimes Branch."

For years, the Justice Department had not investigated allegations of election fraud until after local officials finished certifying the vote. The practice was designed to prevent federal prosecutors from potentially pressuring local officials to change the results of an election that they did not like. Barr's memo, despite the caveats, had violated another long-running DOJ norm.

A former senior DOJ official said that the attorney general had again chosen the path of rapid, top-down action rather than waiting a few days and following departmental process. "Barr went in too quickly."

After releasing the memo, Barr met Senate Majority Leader Mitch McConnell, who, in a speech on the Senate floor, defended Trump, saying he was "one hundred percent within his rights to look into allegations of irregularities and weigh his legal options." Barr and McConnell publicly declined to condemn Trump's false election fraud claims and, to some observers, sounded somewhat sympathetic to them.

In private, they were both skeptical of Trump's claims. "My suspicion all the way along was that there was nothing there," Barr later told journalist Jonathan Karl. "It was all bullshit."

Whatever Barr's intent, his memo emboldened Trump. On the same day Barr released it, Trump fired Defense Secretary Mark Esper, who had opposed the president's threat to invoke the Insurrection Act and deploy active-duty troops. In a final letter to the president, Esper signaled his loyalty: "I serve the country in deference to the Constitution, so I accept your decision to replace me." In a final interview with the *Military Times*, Esper predicted that Trump would replace him with a "yes man," warning, darkly: "And then God help us."

In addition to firing Esper, Trump appointed Michael Ellis, a partisan loyalist, to be the general counsel of the National Security Agency. Rumors swirled that Trump also planned to fire FBI Director Christopher Wray, CIA Director Gina Haspel, and Barr as well.

In fact, Trump offered the job of attorney general to John Ratcliffe, a Texas congressman whom he appointed director of national intelligence after his aggressive questioning of Robert Mueller during Congressional hearings. Ratcliffe had briefed Trump that no foreign powers had tried to sway the election, a finding that contradicted Trump's claims of a secret international plot that changed vote totals in Biden's favor. Ratcliffe declined to become attorney general. Unlike Barr, he was apparently unwilling to entertain the president's voter fraud conspiracy theories.

OVER THE NEXT TWO WEEKS, Barr worked with the US Attorney's Offices and FBI agents examined the various fraud allegations made by Trump and his lawyers. Trump's team made six core claims: that voting machines made by Dominion Voting Systems were rigged to aid Biden; that a video from Georgia purportedly showed a box of fake ballots being added to the vote tally; that a large number of Biden votes had been added late on election night in Milwaukee and Detroit; that more absentee votes had been cast in Pennsylvania than the number of absentee ballots applications filed in the state; that a truckload of ballots had been driven from Bethpage, New York, and counted in Pennsylvania; and that several thousand votes in Nevada had been cast by people living outside the state. All of them proved to be false.

Barr was particularly disdainful of the claim about Dominion voting machines. The core flaw in the Dominion conspiracy theory was that election officials who used the machines also kept paper ballots. Hand recounts of the paper ballots showed that Biden had won. In Georgia, the US Attorney's Office found that the ballots shown in the video were legal votes and not double-counted.

In Michigan, Barr and his staff learned that it was normal for boxes of votes to arrive over the course of the night in Detroit, where for years ballots had been brought from Wayne county's 662 voting precincts to be counted in the city's convention center. Trump, in fact, won 5,000 more votes in the county than he did in 2016, while Biden received 1,000 fewer votes than Hillary Clinton had four years earlier. Trump had lost the state, as Barr suspected, because Biden had won far more support in the suburbs than the president, not because of secret fraud in Detroit.

In Pennsylvania, the claim regarding absentee ballots was based on a simple math error. Giuliani had cited the number of absentee ballots requested for the Pennsylvania primary, in June, and compared it to the number of ballots cast in the November general election. The claim that a truckload of ballots was driven in from Bethpage was disproven as well. And the Republican secretary of state and local US attorney found the claims of illegal out-of-state votes to be not consequential.

In Nevada, the Republican Party initially claimed that more than 9,000 out-of-state voters had improperly cast ballots. When the US attorney for Nevada looked into the matter, the Nevada secretary of state, a Republican, told him that he had already dismissed the claims. Sampling conducted by his office showed that the vast majority of the 9,000 voters cited were out of state for proper reasons, such as military service.

ON NOVEMBER 23, at the request of White House Counsel Pat Cipollone, Barr met with Trump in person to discuss the fraud allegations. Trump, to Barr's surprise, was initially cordial. As the conversation continued, though, Trump began to insist that he had won the election "by a long shot" and was the victim of "major fraud." Trump eventually confronted Barr and said that he'd heard that the Justice Department wasn't looking into the voter fraud allegations seriously.

Barr responded that the department had investigated the complaints. He said that Giuliani and his legal team were serving him poorly by presenting such poor examples. Trump gave Barr a chart depicting another claim of fraud, that it was "impossible" for mail-in ballots to break so strongly in Biden's favor. Barr believed that the pattern was normal but promised to look into it.

Barr then violated DOJ norms and spoke to the president as if he were a GOP political strategist, not the country's apolitical chief law enforcement officer. The attorney general raised something he believed was "critical" and advised Trump to campaign for the Republican candidates in two Georgia runoff elections that would decide control of the Senate. The attorney general's argument appeared to have little impact on Trump, who, according to Barr, stared at him sullenly.

Barr had also been speaking with Republican senators, including McConnell, and a few GOP members of Congress. All of them said they were worried about how far Trump would pursue the false election claims. None of them, though, publicly criticized Trump. McConnell, focused on preserving the Republican majority in the Senate, feared that acknowledging Biden's victory would prompt Trump to undermine Republican chances in the Georgia Senate runoffs.

Six days after Barr's Oval Office meeting with Trump, the president gave another rambling forty-five-minute interview to Fox News host Maria Bartiromo. Again, Trump repeated myriad false claims about the election. When Bartiromo asked Trump what the Justice

Department and FBI were doing to investigate, Trump said they were both "missing in action." Trump then complained about James Comey not being criminally investigated, asked why the Durham investigation had not been completed before the election, and repeated his false Dominion voting machines claim. "It all started with the mail-in. But it also goes to Dominion," Trump said.

After seeing the interview, Barr decided to finally speak out publicly against Trump's false fraud claims. On Tuesday, December 1, four weeks after the election, Barr invited Mike Balsamo, the DOJ reporter for the Associated Press, to lunch in the attorney general's private dining room. Soon after the lunch ended, Balsamo published a story that said the "Justice Department had uncovered no evidence of widespread voter fraud that could change the outcome of the 2020 election."

As Balsamo's piece dominated news coverage, Barr went to the White House for a previously scheduled meeting with Mark Meadows and Pat Cipollone. As they sat in Cipollone's office, an aide told Barr that Trump wanted to speak with him. Barr and Cipollone walked into the Oval Office and into the small, personal dining room where Trump often worked. Trump, sitting at the table, showed Barr Balsamo's AP story.

"Did you say this?" the president asked, according to Barr's memoir.

"Yes, I did, Mr. President," Barr responded.

"Why would you say that?" Trump asked, his voice rising. "How the fuck could you do this to me? Why did you say it?"

"Because it's true, Mr. President," Barr responded. "The reporter asked me what the department had found to date and I told him."

"But you didn't have to say that. You could've just said no comment. This is killing me—killing me. This is pulling the rug out from under me." The president, livid, responded by referring to himself in the third person: "You must hate Trump. You must hate Trump."

Barr told the president that he didn't hate him. The two men argued over Trump's fraud claims and Barr replied, "The department is not an extension of your legal team. Our mission is to investigate and prosecute actual facts. The fact is, we have looked at the major claims that your people are making and they are bullshit."

Barr added, "Your legal team continues to shovel this shit out to the American people. And it is wrong." After arguing over the Dominion voting machines, reports of fraud in Detroit, why the Durham investigation hadn't been completed yet, and why Comey had not been prosecuted, Barr offered to resign. "I understand that you are very frustrated with me, Mr. President, and I'm willing to submit my resignation. But I have . . ."

A loud banging noise surprised Barr, according to his memoir. "Accepted!" Trump shouted, as Barr began to realize that the president was smashing his hand against the table. "Accepted," the president yelled again. Trump, whose face was quivering, struck the table a third time and said, "Leave, and don't go back to your office. You are done right now. Go home!" Barr nodded, said "I understand," and began to walk out of the Oval Office.

As had happened with Sessions's firing, other White House aides implored Barr to stay. He listened carefully but then chose to leave, as Sessions had. Trump's habit—befriending people and then demonizing them after he viewed them as insufficiently loyal—prevailed.

ALMOST IMMEDIATELY, BARR was vilified online and on cable for his AP interview. Joe Hoft, at the Gateway Pundit, wrote that Barr had destroyed "his name for all eternity," and claimed that he had spent his time in office working surreptitiously to keep Hillary Clinton, James Comey, and Robert Mueller out of jail.

That night, Fox News host Lou Dobbs denounced Barr on his nightly show. "Today, a member of his own cabinet appeared to join in with the radical Dems, and the deep state, and the resistance," Dobbs said. "For the attorney general of the United States to make that statement, he is either a liar or a fool or both. He may be, um, perhaps, compromised. He may be simply unprincipled. Or he may be personally distraught or ill."

The week's events exemplified the self-destructive nature of the Barr Justice Department. Barr has clear legal and political convictions—many of which infuriate liberals—but he had pursued them consistently throughout his career. Like other Republicans, he had struck an alliance of convenience with Trump. As a long-time adherent to the view that the post-Watergate reforms had dangerously weakened the Presidency, Barr overcorrected and created a turbo-charged presidency that he, belatedly, realized posed a threat to democracy.

EIGHT DAYS AFTER Barr's AP interview, Hunter Biden released a statement on December 9, confirming that he was under criminal investigation by federal prosecutors in Delaware regarding "my tax affairs." The younger Biden said he was "confident that a professional and objective review of these matters will demonstrate that I handled my affairs legally and appropriately." He said no other Biden family members, including his father, were under investigation.

The following day, Trump attacked Barr. "Why didn't the Fake News Media, the FBI and the DOJ report the Biden matter BEFORE the Election," he wrote. Trump attacked again over the weekend, tweeting, "Why didn't Bill Barr reveal the truth to the public, before the Election, about Hunter Biden."

Forty-eight hours later, on Monday, December 14, Barr's nearly two-year tenure as Trump's attorney general came to an end. The president, true to form, announced the departure of another cabinet member via Twitter. "Just had a very nice meeting with Attorney General Bill Barr at the White House," Trump wrote. "Our relationship has been a very good one, he has done an outstanding job! As per letter, Bill will be leaving just before Christmas to spend the holidays with his family."

Barr, who had bitterly clashed with the president for months, submitted an effusive resignation letter to Trump. "I am proud to have played a role in the many successes and unprecedented achievements you have delivered for the American people," Barr wrote. "Your record is all the more historic because you accomplished it in the face of relentless, implacable resistance."

Barr then said that after winning the 2016 election Trump was "immediately met by a partisan onslaught . . . in which no tactic, no matter how abusive and deceitful, was out of bounds. The nadir of this campaign was the effort to cripple, if not oust, your Administration with frenzied and baseless accusations of collusion with Russia."

Barr hailed what he called Trump's many achievements. "Few could have weathered these attacks, much less forge ahead with a positive program for the country. You built the strongest and most resilient economy in American history—one that has brought unprecedented progress to those previously left out," he wrote. "You have curbed illegal immigration and enhanced the security of our nation's borders. You have advanced the rule of law by appointing a record number of judges committed to constitutional principles."

Legal scholars and former DOJ officials assailed Barr's tenure. "The few times Barr put the nation ahead of the president will not atone for the many times he chose the opposite. He leaves a wounded department," Stephen Gillers, an expert in legal ethics at New York University School of Law, said. "His tenure as attorney general will be akin to the plague years at the Justice Department," David Laufman, a former Justice Department official, added. In hindsight, Barr's resignation letter was telling. An attorney general who was a political actor praised the president for his political actions, and ignored the damage Trump did to the independence of the Justice Department.

To be fair, Barr sincerely viewed the 2016 Trump-Russia investigation, the subsequent appointment of Robert Mueller as special counsel, and the subsequent convictions of Paul Manafort, Michael Flynn, and Roger Stone as illegitimate. Barr had done his best to reverse each of those steps, undermining Mueller's report and lessening the punishment of the Trump allies who were successfully prosecuted by Mueller. Critics maintained that Barr's politicizing of the

Justice Department made him one of the most destructive attorneys general in modern American history.

OVER TIME, ERICA NEWLAND and some of her colleagues began to worry that they were saving Trump from his own lies. They used their legal skills to launder his false statements and jury-rig arguments so that presidential orders would pass constitutional muster. When she read that producers of *The Apprentice* had had to edit episodes in order to make Trump's decisions seem coherent, she realized that the attorneys in the Office of Legal Counsel were doing something similar.

"There was hardly any respect for the other departments of government—not for the lower courts, not for Congress, and certainly not for the bureaucracy, for professionalism, for facts or the truth," she told me. "Corruption is the right word for this. It doesn't have to be pay-to-play to be corrupt. It's a departure from the oath." Loyalty to the president was equated with legality.

In 2018, the Supreme Court, in a 5–4 decision, ruled that the third version of Trump's travel ban was legal. Career DOJ lawyers had repeatedly revised the executive order to make it constitutional. She and her Justice Department colleagues were acting as the executive branch's law firm, as they should. But the ruling and the office's role in achieving it deeply troubled Newland. She began to question whether her work was restraining or enabling Trump's abuse of the legal system.

On October 30, 2020, she gave her notice. On November 21, she worked her last day at the department. "I burst out in tears when I was talking with one career supervisor who I really respected," she recalled. "It was awkward and hard."

Newland felt, on one level, that she was giving up on American democracy. "It felt like giving up on the Department of Justice and of our country in a sense," she said. "It felt like I was abandoning my child in some way."

After watching Trump challenge the 2020 election results, Newland decided to write about her experience in the Trump DOJ and about her decision to leave. On December 20, 2020, the *New York Times* published an op-ed by her with the title, "I'm Haunted by What I Did as a Lawyer in the Trump Justice Department." She hoped the piece would inform the public and help other federal workers.

"I felt I was abandoning the ship," she wrote, referring to how she originally felt when she left. "I continued to believe that a critical mass of responsible attorneys staying in government might provide a last line of defense against the administration's worst instincts." As Trump's campaign lawyers took center stage and facilitated his open attacks on American democracy, she felt she had made an enormous error by remaining in the DOJ.

"Watching the Trump campaign's attacks on the election results, I now see what might have happened if, rather than nip and tuck the Trump agenda, responsible Justice Department attorneys had collectively—ethically, lawfully—refused to participate in President Trump's systematic attacks on our democracy from the beginning," she wrote. "The attacks would have failed."

"No matter our intentions, we were complicit," she added. "We collectively perpetuated an anti-democratic leader by conforming to his assault on reality."

THE DAY AFTER BILL BARR submitted his resignation as attorney general, Trump asked to speak with Deputy Attorney General Jeff Rosen, the man who would serve as the acting attorney general until Trump left office. During the George W. Bush administration, Rosen, a Harvard-educated lawyer, had served as the general counsel of the Department of Transportation, the general counsel at the White House Office of Management and Budget, and then as the deputy secretary of transportation. Rosen had also spent thirty years helping lead Kirkland & Ellis, one of the largest law firms in the world. Rosen and Barr had known each other personally for at least two decades. While Barr was outspoken and domineering, Rosen was known for being reserved and collaborative.

On December 15, Rosen and his deputy, Richard Donoghue, the former US attorney for the Eastern District of New York and now the acting deputy attorney general, arrived at the White House to meet with Trump, Cipollone, Acting DHS Deputy Secretary Ken Cuccinelli, and several other officials.

The previous day, members of the Electoral College had gathered in all fifty states and cast their official votes for the next president. Biden had decisively beaten Trump, 306 electoral college votes to 232. Rosen, noting that the Electoral College had formally voted the previous day, expected Trump to talk about securing his legacy. Instead, the president began the meeting with a long soliloquy about election fraud.

"The president started delivering remarks that, honestly, to me, seemed pretty consistent with the kinds of things that he was putting in the public domain; the election was unfair, there was fraud, bad things happened in Pennsylvania and Georgia," Rosen recalled in testimony to the Senate Judiciary Committee. "He sort of walked through 'People are telling me this, people are telling me that.'"

Rosen said that he and Donohue replied, "Well, people are telling you things that are not right. This is not accurate."

Trump, at one point, raised a claim about voter fraud in Atlanta. "Well, what about this? I saw it on the videotape, somebody delivering a suitcase of ballots," Rosen recalled Trump saying. "And we said, 'It wasn't a suitcase. It was a bin. That's what they use when they're counting ballots. It's benign.'" Rosen said that he and Donoghue "in a high-level way, we were not walking through each piece of evidence, but in a way of saying 'They're telling you things that are incorrect.'"

Rosen described the tone of the conversation as "even-keeled." "His tone was not angry. He wasn't raising his voice or something" and was "not belligerent."

As Trump continued speaking, Rosen tried to change the subject.

"I recall that at one point I said to the president, 'I really want to suggest to you, sir, respectfully, that it would be a better thing for everyone to use this last month to focus on some of the things that had been accomplished in the last four years—tax reform and the vaccine, Operation Warp Speed, and not go into this "the election was corrupt."'"

Trump dismissed Rosen's suggestion and focused on Antrim County, a rural area in Michigan where human error committed by an election clerk on election night had initially shown Biden winning the Republican stronghold. The error was corrected the following morning and Trump was declared the winner in the county. Despite that, claims that Dominion Voting Systems machines had been secretly programmed to switch Trump votes to Biden votes had spread widely on Twitter and Fox News.

Rosen and Donoghue told the president that the Antrim County claim had been dismissed by Department of Homeland Security investigators and other experts. Trump was unpersuaded. Eventually, the officials said that a hand recount was being conducted in the county. After nearly an hour, the meeting ended. Rosen and Donoghue assured Trump that they would continue to monitor the Antrim County results.

Days later, the recount found that the Dominion Voting Systems machines had counted the ballots correctly in Antrim County. Of the 15,700 votes cast in Antrim, Trump had retained his victory margin of roughly 3,800 votes. After the hand recount, Trump gained eleven votes and Biden lost one.

THOSE RESULTS MATCHED what dozens of federal and state judges had found across the country. In the roughly six weeks since the election, according to a *Washington Post* review, at least eighty-six federal and state judges, including thirty-eight judges appointed by Republicans, had dismissed lawsuits filed by Trump or his supporters alleging voter fraud. The rulings represented a remarkable show

of near unanimity by judges that ranged from Supreme Court justices to state jurists, from eighty-two to forty-two in age. Even judges
appointed by Trump weeks before the election ruled against him.

In Wisconsin, Federal Judge Brett Ludwig, a Trump appointee
who took the bench two months before the election, called the president's request "extraordinary." "A sitting president who did not prevail
in his bid for reelection has asked for federal court help in setting
aside the popular vote based on disputed issues of election administration," Ludwig wrote. "This Court has allowed plaintiff the chance
to make his case and he has lost."

In Pennsylvania, Federal Judge Matthew Brann, who served as
a county Republican chairman for a decade before serving on the
bench, called the Trump campaign's legal theories a "Frankenstein's
monster." "This Court has been presented with strained legal arguments without merit and speculative accusations, unpled in the oper-
ative complaint and unsupported by evidence," wrote Brann, days
after Giuliani personally argued the case before him.

In Arizona, Federal Judge Diane Humetewa flatly dismissed similar arguments from attorney Sidney Powell. "Allegations that find
favor in the public sphere of gossip and innuendo cannot be a sub-
stitute for earnest pleadings and procedure in federal court," wrote
Humetewa, a member of the Hopi Tribe who was named US attorney for the District of Arizona by George W. Bush and nominated to
the federal bench by Barack Obama. "Plaintiffs have not moved the
needle for their fraud theory from conceivable to plausible. "

In Wisconsin, State Supreme Court Justice Brian Hagedorn,
a longtime conservative, warned that American democracy itself
was at risk. "Something far more fundamental than the winner of
Wisconsin's electoral votes is implicated in this case," Hagedorn
wrote. "At stake, in some measure, is faith in our system of free
and fair elections, a feature central to the enduring strength of our
constitutional republic."

AFTER BARR'S TENURE formally ended and Rosen became acting attorney general on December 24, Rosen began receiving private phone calls from Trump, like James Comey, Jeff Sessions, Rod Rosenstein, and Barr before him.

Rosen estimated that during his five weeks as acting attorney general, Trump called him nearly every day. The president also forwarded him emails describing election fraud.

The initial call on December 23 was an exchange of pleasantries, Rosen said. "The first call was more of small talk," he said. "You know, it was "I understand that AG Barr is gone and you're in charge.""

A call the following day was cordial as well but then turned pointed. Trump said that the Justice Department was asleep at the switch and not really doing its job. Trump asked Rosen if he knew a DOJ official named Jeff Clark. Rosen replied yes, he knew him, and Trump quickly changed the subject. The fact that Trump knew Jeffrey Clark, a mid-level career DOJ official, struck Rosen as odd.

As he had done with others, Trump tried to charm Rosen on the calls and secure his loyalty. Rosen said that he sought to strike a balance during the phone conversations. He knew that he could not stop Trump from making claims.

"I can't control what he says," he said. "I can only control what I do from my position."

Rosen said his view of his role as acting attorney general was clear. "The Department of Justice is going to do its job, whether the president is happy, unhappy, measured, belligerent," Rosen recalled. "The Department of Justice is going to do what we think is right based on the facts and the law. We're going to be faithful to the rule of law, the Constitution, the system of government we have. And that's independent of anyone else, including the president of the United States."

ON SATURDAY, DECEMBER 26, Rosen's hopes that Trump might quietly accept his defeat abruptly ended. Jeffrey Clark, the obscure mid-level DOJ official Trump had mentioned, told Rosen and Dono-

ghue that he had attended a meeting with the president and Representative Scott Perry of Pennsylvania. Rosen, alarmed that one of his
subordinates had met with the president, tried to get a better sense of
what had happened.

At first, Clark minimized the meeting, saying that it had not been
planned. He also mentioned that he had been doing a lot of reading online, which startled Rosen and Donoghue, who feared he had
been researching election fraud conspiracy theories. They were even
more surprised when Clark then asked that the DOJ hold a press conference to announce that it was looking into significant allegations
of election fraud in Georgia and other states. Rosen and Donoghue
vetoed that suggestion immediately.

Clark, though, remained fixated on Georgia. On December 28,
Clark drafted a letter that he wanted Rosen to send to state legislators
in Georgia that wrongly stated that the Justice Department was investigating accusations of voter fraud in their state, and that the state legislature should move to void Biden's win there. Rosen and Donoghue
again rejected Clark's proposal.

THREE DAYS LATER, on New Year's Eve, Rosen, Donoghue, and
Clark met in person to discuss Clark's refusal to hew to the department's conclusion that the election results were valid. Donoghue
flatly told Clark that what he was doing was wrong. The next day,
January 1, Clark told Rosen that he was going to discuss his strategy
with the president early the next week, just before Congress was set
to certify Biden's electoral victory on January 6.

Without informing Rosen, Trump called state officials in Georgia
on Saturday, January 2. For a full hour, Trump pressured Secretary
of State Brad Raffensperger to "find" enough votes to declare Trump
the victor in Georgia. Raffensperger refused to do so. The following
day, the *Washington Post* broke the news of the call and posted the
recording of Trump pressuring Raffensperger.

Unbeknownst to Rosen, Clark was trying to take his job and

become acting attorney general. Clark had secretly met with Trump over the weekend and then told Rosen at midday on Sunday, January 3, that the president intended to fire Rosen and give Clark his job. And once Clark became acting attorney general he would try to stop Congress from certifying the Electoral College results. Clark told Rosen that he could stay on as his deputy attorney general, rendering the acting attorney general speechless.

"I thought that was preposterous," Rosen recalled in testimony to Congress. "I told him that was nonsensical, and that there is no universe where I was going to do that, to stay on and support someone else doing things that were not consistent with what I thought should be done."

Rosen, unwilling to step down, decided that he needed to hear from Trump directly that he wished to fire him. Rosen asked White House Chief of Staff Mark Meadows for a meeting with Trump that evening. He also asked the White House counsel, Pat Cipollone, to attend the meeting.

Rosen and Donoghue then informed Steven Engel, the head of the Justice Department's Office of Legal Counsel and Erica Newland's former boss, about Clark's latest maneuver. Donoghue convened a late-afternoon call with the department's remaining senior leaders, laying out Clark's efforts to replace Rosen and become the acting attorney general. Rosen, who was still in shock that Clark had betrayed him, requested the call, in part, because he feared others might also have secretly aligned with Trump.

The moment was unprecedented in the history of the Justice Department and the United States. For weeks, the sitting president, aided by Meadows, Giuliani, Clark, and Representative Scott Perry of Pennsylvania, among others, had been pushing baseless conspiracy theories that the election had been stolen from Trump. In one meeting, Trump had told them, "You guys may not be following the internet the way that I do."

At another point, Rosen and Donoghue were told to watch a YouTube video that Representative Perry had sent to Meadows. On the video, a man identified as a former CIA officer said that a State Department officer, the CIA, MI6, and an Italian defense company had secretly used Italian satellites to change votes from Trump to Biden in 2020. Donoghue dismissed the video as "pure insanity" and "patently absurd."

Because Rosen had refused the president's entreaties to embrace such claims, Trump was about to decide whether to fire Rosen and replace him with Clark. Rosen planned to head to the White House soon to learn his fate.

When Donoghue explained the situation on the conference call, a half dozen senior Justice Department officials listened in stunned silence. Clark, Donoghue told them, had secretly devised a plan with Trump to oust Rosen and use the department's power to force Georgia lawmakers to overturn the presidential election results.

"We got most, not all, but most of the AAGs on the phone," Donoghue later testified to Congress. "We very quickly explained to them what the situation was. I told them, 'I don't need an answer from you right now. I don't need an answer on this phone call. But if you have an answer, I need it in the next few minutes. So, call me, email, text me, whatever it is, if you know what you would do if Jeff Clark is put in charge of the Department.'"

Immediately Eric Dreiband, who was the head of the Civil Rights Division, said, "I don't need to think about it. There is no way I am staying," Donohue recalled. "Then the other AAGs began to chime in in turn and all essentially said they would leave. They would resign en masse if the president made that change in the department leadership."

The assistant attorneys general and other senior department officials who upheld their oath to protect and defend the constitution were Eric Dreiband, David Burns, Makan Delrahim, Claire Murray, Jeff Wall, and John Demers. One of the DOJ officials, who asked not to be named, recalled feeling that they had no other choice, given the stakes. They said they feared that "the public would lose confidence" in the Justice Department, "my biggest worry for the country."

The moment was reminiscent of the Saturday Night Massacre of the Nixon era, when Attorney General Elliot L. Richardson and his deputy resigned rather than carry out the president's order to fire the special prosecutor investigating him. The Clark plan, the officials concluded, would irrevocably harm the department, the government, and the rule of law.

For the next several hours, the officials who had agreed to resign together anxiously messaged and called one another as they awaited Rosen's fate.

JUST AFTER 6 P.M., Rosen, Donoghue, Engel, and Clark met at the White House with Trump, Cipollone, his deputy Patrick Philbin, and other lawyers. Trump had Rosen and Clark present their arguments to him in a bizarre meeting.

Cipollone advised the president not to fire Rosen and he reiterated, as he had for days, that he did not recommend sending the letter to Georgia lawmakers. Engel advised Trump that he and the department's remaining top officials would resign if he fired Rosen, leaving Clark alone at the department.

Trump seemed somewhat swayed by the idea that firing Rosen would trigger not only chaos at the Justice Department, but also congressional investigations and possibly recriminations from other Republicans and distract attention from his efforts to overturn the election results. Steve Engel, the OLC head and Newland's former boss, offered perhaps one of the most persuasive arguments. Appealing to Trump's ego, he told the president that if he fired Rosen no one would remember Trump's legacy or take him seriously again.

After nearly three hours, Trump ultimately decided that Clark's plan would fail, and he allowed Rosen to stay. Rosen felt that their decision to demand to immediately see Trump had prevented another constitutional crisis. He believed that if he had waited Trump would have publicly fired him and installed Clark. The United States had endured a near-coup without the public knowing about it.

In hindsight, Newland saw their actions as too little, too late. "What I can't shake is the feeling that the so-called adults in the room walked our democracy to the ledge and then walked away," she said. "They saved their own skins but American democracy? We're still teetering on that ledge."

Clark later categorically denied that he devised any plan to oust Rosen, or to formulate recommendations for action based on factual inaccuracies gleaned from the internet. "My practice is to rely on sworn testimony to assess disputed factual claims," Clark said in a statement to the *New York Times*. "There was a candid discussion of options and pros and cons with the president. It is unfortunate that those who were part of a privileged legal conversation would comment in public about such internal deliberations, while also distorting any discussions."

After Trump abandoned his DOJ plan, Rosen and his deputies concluded they had weathered the turmoil. Once Congress certified Biden's victory, there would be little for them to do until they left office.

They then made an enormous mistake. They decided that they would keep secret the president's failed attempt to seize control of the DOJ and use the department to reverse the election results. They reasoned that making it public would be the equivalent of "poking the bear" and potentially sparking another dangerous act by Trump. They presumed the lame-duck president had finally accepted the most basic—and central—norm of American democracy: the peaceful transfer of power. They were wrong.

AS SOON AS ERICA NEWLAND saw crowds of Trump supporters heading for the Capitol, the first thing she did was contact her husband.

"I called my husband and told him to be careful coming home from work," Newland recalled. "I said I thought this was the made-for-TV version of everything that had been going on in the Trump administration for the last three years."

On one level, Newland saw it as the physical manifestation of what she had felt in the DOJ. "I saw it as a continuation, not a break," she said. "There had been this destruction of our institutions quietly from the inside in ways that were very hard to communicate to the American people." She also hoped that Trump had finally overplayed his hand. "I said to multiple people I'm hopeful that the fever will break."

Nate Huber, the FBI instructor, watched the attack unfold on television from his home in Virginia. Now a supervisory intelligence analyst assigned to the FBI's Washington Field Office, he struggled to process what he saw unfolding. The idea of a violent mob storming the US Capitol was unimaginable to him.

"I was surprised by what I saw. I never thought that huge a group would storm the Capitol," he said. "And bring confederate flags into the Capitol. And damage the Capitol. I never thought I'd see that."

A FEW MILES AWAY from the Capitol, Merrick Garland sat in his home in Bethesda, Maryland, drafting a speech to reintroduce himself to the American people. When he saw television coverage of a mob overwhelming the police and entering the Capitol, he, too, was stunned. Trump supporters, many of whom appeared to sincerely believe the 2020 election had been stolen, stormed the Senate chamber and temporarily halted the certification of Biden's victory. Garland realized that he needed to completely rewrite the remarks he planned to give the following day. The attack made real the serious degree to which democracy was imperiled. It erased any misgivings Garland had about taking the job of attorney general.

In Wilmington, Delaware, the following day, president-elect Joe Biden introduced Garland as his nominee. After denouncing January 6 as "one of the darkest days in the history of our nation," Biden, who barely knew Garland, promised that he would restore trust in the independence of the Justice Department. "You are not the president or the vice president's lawyer," Biden said, referring to Garland. "Your loyalty is not to me. It's to the law, to the Constitution, to the people of this nation."

After being introduced, Garland thanked his family members for their support. He began his speech by quoting Edward Levi's words at his own swearing-in ceremony forty-six years earlier in the wake of Watergate. "Nothing can more weaken the quality of life, or more imperil the realization of the goals we all hold dear," Garland said, "than our failure to make clear by words and deed that our law is not the instrument of partisan purpose."

Garland then named Robert H. Jackson, the former prosecutor, attorney general, and Supreme Court justice, as his role model. Again, Garland emphasized the importance of prosecutors acting in measured and impartial ways. "The citizens' safety lies in the prosecutor who tempers zeal with human kindness," Garland said, quoting Jackson, "who seeks truth and not victims, who serves the law and not factional purposes, and who approaches his job with humility."

After describing his work as a judge, Garland briefly mentioned the violence the previous day—the first-ever attempt to reverse the results of a presidential election in American history. "As everyone who watched yesterday's events in Washington now understands, the rule of law is not just some lawyer's turn of phrase," Garland said. "It is the very foundation of our democracy." The future attorney general eloquently called for equal justice. "The essence of the rule of law is that like cases are treated alike. That there not be one rule for Democrats, and another for Republicans, one rule for friends, another for foes, one rule for the powerful, another for the powerless."

Lisa Monaco, who would serve as deputy attorney general, then spoke and invoked Levi as well. She recalled how, when asked by President Ford what the DOJ needed most in an era of flagging public trust in institutions, Levi responded, "A soul." Monaco said the department's mission was "To do justice without fear or favor, to keep the American people safe and to do so always consistent with the rule of law."

Vanita Gupta, who would serve as the department's number-three official, was more pointed in her remarks. Gupta, the daughter of immigrants from India, recalled how, when she was a child, a group

Merrick Garland, Lisa Monaco, and Vanita Gupta believed that encouraging civil servants to uphold norms would help prevent the DOJ and FBI from being used for political gain. (UPI / ALAMY STOCK PHOTO)

of skinheads had hurled food and racial epithets at her sister, mother, grandmother, and her as they sat in a McDonald's, eventually forcing them to flee for their safety. "Yesterday's horrific events at the Capitol reminded us that our democracy cannot be taken for granted, that our nation has a long history of disinformation, white supremacist violence, mob violence," Gupta said. "It also reminded us that our values and our constitution and our democracy, these do not protect themselves, it is people with courage who do that."

Press coverage of the speech focused on Garland's brief statement regarding January 6 and his failed Supreme Court nomination. At that point, Garland was an obscure figure to most Americans, a soft-spoken federal judge known primarily for the fact that his 2016 nomination to become a Supreme Court justice by President Obama had been blocked by Republican Senate Majority Leader Mitch McConnell and other Senate Republicans. No Senate majority leader in American history had taken such a step.

The unprecedented act of partisanship worked. McConnell and

Republicans refused to hold hearings or votes on Garland's nomination. After the resignation of Justice Anthony Kennedy and the death of Justice Ruth Bader Ginsburg, Trump appointed three deeply conservative justices. A once evenly divided Supreme Court, which largely matched the political divide in the country, now had a conservative super majority of six justices. McConnell later called blocking Garland's nomination "one of my proudest moments."

As Garland prepared to become attorney general, an urgent question was how the former judge, a lifelong centrist whose genial nature had made him a beloved figure in Washington legal circles, would respond to the challenge of Trumpism. Could the new attorney general show that non-partisan public service was still possible in a deeply polarized country? And could he restore public faith, particularly among Republicans, in the impartiality of the Justice Department?

Part II

BIDEN

CHAPTER 10

STOP THE STEAL

WHEN THRONGS OF PROTESTERS BEGAN WALKING toward the US Capitol on January 6, 2021, Steven D'Antuono monitored their movements from the FBI Washington field office a half dozen blocks away. He moved between the office's command post, where his deputies and members of other law enforcement agencies were gathered, and his office on a higher floor. "I was going up and down the stairs and checking," he recalled.

D'Antuono had ordered members of the office's tactical units—SWAT teams, hostage rescue teams, and its bomb squad—to be equipped, armed, and ready to deploy in case of violence. He and other law enforcement officials feared a repeat of the street brawls that had intermittently flared in a handful of cities during racial justice protests in the summer of 2020. Left-leaning anti-Trump protesters, including some members of antifa, had clashed with Trump supporters, including members of the Proud Boys militia. When Trump supporters had gathered in Washington in December, four people had been stabbed and thirty-nine had been arrested after melees erupted in various parts of the city.

Three days earlier, top officials from the DOJ, the Department of Homeland Security, and the Federal Emergency Management Agency had held a series of conference calls to discuss potential security threats on January 6. Robert O'Brien, Trump's national security advisor, participated in the calls as well. Officials discussed the possibility of protesters attacking federal buildings. But most of them considered the biggest risk to be what one called a repeat of the "same old" after-dark street brawling between anti-Trump and pro-Trump demonstrators.

O'Brien considered the counterprotesters—what Trump and Barr called antifa—to be the biggest danger. Christopher Miller, the acting defense secretary, was surprised that Jeffrey Rosen and other DOJ officials did not seem more concerned about the potential for violence.

Even though all of them had seen Trump bully officials in private and spread conspiracy theories in public, they assumed he would accept the certification of the election results.

Rosen and the other senior DOJ officials who had thwarted Trump's attempted takeover of the Justice Department did not warn other agencies about Trump's actions. As a result, most of the government officials in the meeting did not comprehend how determined Trump was to remain in power.

As D'Antuono monitored the pro-Trump demonstrators marching toward the Capitol, he, too, failed to foresee a worst-case scenario. He assumed that the Capitol Police, as well as the Metropolitan Police, would be able to contain the crowd. The number of demonstrators, which he estimated at 20,000–25,000 people, did not surprise him. What happened when they arrived at the Capitol did. "We believed that there was probably going to be something," D'Antuono recalled. "But a complete breach of the Capitol, in the violent manner it was done, was completely unfathomable."

D'Antuono and myriad other officials had not expected the unprecedented: an incumbent American president encouraging his supporters to storm the Capitol and prevent Congress from certifying his electoral defeat. As had occurred with the travel ban, the firing of James Comey, and numerous other DOJ clashes with Trump, Justice Department and FBI officials had underestimated Trump.

Over the course of the afternoon, D'Antuono dispatched roughly

250 FBI agents to the Capitol, including two SWAT teams, two hostage rescue teams, and a bomb squad. His supervisor, FBI Deputy Director David Bowdich, had personally gone to the Capitol after receiving frantic calls from furious lawmakers. As D'Antuono watched Trump supporters wander the halls of the Capitol for hours, he felt a sense of shock and shame. "Holy crap," he thought. "That shouldn't happen in this country."

ON PAPER, D'ANTUONO'S twenty-five-year career in the bureau should have prepared him for such a moment. A public corruption agent and CPA from Cranston, Rhode Island, D'Antuono had risen to one of the bureau's most coveted positions: leader of its flagship Washington field office. A well-regarded FBI veteran, D'Antuono oversaw 750 agents who investigated crimes ranging from public corruption by government officials to espionage and drug trafficking.

Earlier in his career, D'Antuono had overseen the bureau's white-collar crime programs in Washington, investigating money laundering, health care fraud, intellectual property theft, securities fraud, and running the bureau's forensic accountant programs. In St. Louis in 2014, D'Antuono had helped coordinate the response to demonstrations as a senior leader in the bureau field office following the fatal police shooting of Michael Brown, an unarmed Black teenager. Prior to that, D'Antuono was a public corruption supervisor in Washington and taught classes on white-collar crime at the FBI Academy in Quantico.

His time as head of the FBI's field office in Detroit should have made D'Antuono open to the idea that far-right militias were active in the country. Days before his new position in Washington was announced in 2020, agents from the Detroit office helped thwart one of the most dramatic kidnapping plots in the US in decades. FBI agents arrested fourteen men and accused them of plotting to kidnap

Michigan governor Gretchen Whitmer and put her on trial for implementing public health restrictions in response to the COVID-19
pandemic. Roughly half of the men were believed to have ties to a
local militia group called the Wolverine Watchmen.

In a live-streamed video to a private Facebook group, one of the
defendants had complained about state officials closing gyms during
the pandemic and called Whitmer "this tyrant bitch." "I don't know,
boys, we gotta do something," he said. "You guys link with me on our
other location system, give me some ideas of what we can do."

Nine of the men were convicted and five were acquitted at trial.
The convictions showed that some militia members believed the conspiracy theories spread by Trump. On January 6, they demonstrated it.

IN THE DAYS AFTER the January 6 attack, the FBI, the Capitol
Police, and other law enforcement agencies were assailed for not
deploying enough forces that day. Critics said they had missed multiple warnings, including statements on Trump's own Twitter feed.

A longtime FBI practice had failed. For decades, the bureau has
relied on its vast network of informants for tips and intelligence. That
strategy failed them in the days prior to January 6.

D'Antuono defended the FBI's performance. "We had two SWAT
teams already planned. We had HRT [Hostage Rescue Team] already
planned. We expected fights in the crowd," he recalled. "I think the
response that we provided was incredible, sending approximately two
hundred and fifty agents in the time frame that we did." He added,
"We were prepared for something to happen. We just weren't prepared for what the hell happened."

FBI Director Chris Wray, unlike James Comey, maintained a
low profile. Instead of publicly spearheading the FBI response to
the storming of the Capitol, Wray had D'Antuono and other deputies speak at press conferences. D'Antuono's first foray did not go
smoothly.

STOP THE STEAL 159

Just before D'Antuono was scheduled to speak, the *Washington Post* reported that the FBI's Norfolk field office had found an online thread on January 5 calling for an attack on the Capitol. "Congress needs to hear glass breaking, doors being kicked in, and blood from their BLM and antifa slave soldiers being spilled," the post said. "Get violent. Stop calling this a march or rally, or a protest. Go there ready for war. We get our President, or we die."

D'Antuono tried to explain why the FBI had not sounded the alarm after receiving the warning. "We have to separate the aspirational from the intentional and determine which of the individuals saying despicable things on the internet are practicing keyboard bravado, or intent to do harm," D'Antuono recalled. "In this case, we had no indication that information was linked to any specific person."

In fact, the FBI had received multiple warnings of violence, the *Washington Post* later found. On December 22, the social media platform Parler, which was popular with Trump supporters, sent the bureau three screenshots from a user who threatened to kill politicians. On January 2, Parler sent the FBI more posts, including one by a user who stated, "This is the final stand where we are drawing the red line at Capitol Hill. I trust the American people will take back the USA with force and many are ready to die," the person wrote, adding: "don't be surprised if we take the #capital building."

On Monday, January 4, two days prior to the attack, nearly three hundred Department of Homeland Security officials joined a conference call where officials from the department's regional security offices—known as fusion centers—shared what they were finding online. Extremist groups in the Northeast were sharing radio frequencies to use near the Capitol, one analyst said.

Men with violent criminal histories from the Midwest were discussing plans to travel to Washington with weapons, another added. The threats all focused on the same location, time, and date: the US

Capitol at 1:00 p.m. on January 6. Warnings were also issued by law-makers, former national security officials, local officials, researchers, FBI informants, and social media companies.

AFTER THE ATTACK, Democrats and Republicans lambasted the performance of the FBI. Liberals asked whether the FBI would have responded more aggressively if tens of thousands of Black people had marched on the Capitol. They also asked why so many of the rioters were allowed to leave the Capitol grounds instead of being immedi-ately arrested.

D'Antuono said that the FBI lacked the personnel to control such a large crowd. He also said that the Washington field office had shared the Norfolk intelligence report with the Capitol Police, Metropolitan Police, and multiple federal law enforcement agencies. D'Antuono argued that the report was "raw intelligence" and did not contain specific information. There was "no time, no place, and no idea who wrote it." D'Antuono said. "It could be a sixteen-year-old writing it from his mom's basement."

D'Antuono said that he had grown used to being publicly attacked over the course of his career. As a public integrity agent, he had inves-tigated Democratic and Republican politicians and been assailed by members of both parties. D'Antuono prided himself on being non-partisan. "The Left hates me. The Right hates me. But I can look in the mirror and know that I did the right thing," he said. "I'm a public corruption agent. I'm very balanced."

Congressional investigators, though, found that Trump's pres-sure had swayed the FBI. A report by the House select commit-tee that investigated the January 6 attack concluded that Barr and Trump's demands that the FBI consider antifa the country's larg-est public safety threat had influenced agents. The elevation of antifa, as well as the FBI's focus on attacks from "lone wolves," not large groups, limited the bureau's ability to see a "broad-right wing movement come together," according to the draft report. The document, obtained by the *New York Times,* said that focus on individuals created a cognitive bias that hampered critical thinking about other threats.

The draft report also found that the pressure fostered a false equivalency between far-right and far-left extremists. For years, DOJ and FBI officials had repeatedly stated that extremist white supremacists were the country's most serious domestic threat.

Republicans, after initially criticizing Trump, closed ranks behind the former president. Trump accused the DOJ and FBI of exaggerating the violence that occurred in the Capitol and persecuting conservatives. Baseless conspiracy theories spread online that the FBI had embedded undercover agents in the crowd and incited the riot as part of a secret operation to discredit Trump and his supporters.

When House Democrats impeached Trump for his role on January 6, only seven Republican senators voted to convict him, ten short of the number needed for him to be found guilty and banned from holding elected office. Before the vote, Trump and his allies had circulated a poll showing that 80 percent of Trump voters and 76 percent of Republicans were less likely to vote for a member of Congress who voted for his impeachment.

Even when Trump took an action more serious than Watergate— refusing to peacefully give up power—he paid little political price with his core supporters. The specter of political ruin and public shame that had prompted American presidents to obey democratic norms for more than two centuries had been exposed as a paper tiger.

AS THE FBI CONDUCTED the largest manhunt in its history and the public demanded answers about the first-ever attempt to block the certification of a presidential election, the Justice Department lacked key leaders. All the senior officials in the department—including Acting Attorney General Jeffrey Rosen, Acting Deputy Attorney General Richard Donoghue, and Acting US Attorney for the District of

Columbia Michael Sherwin—were in their positions until Biden administration officials replaced them. Based on past deadlock in the Senate, it would likely take weeks for the nominations of Merrick Garland and his top aides to wind their way through the Senate.

At the same time, many rank-and-file prosecutors in the US Attorney's Office in DC, which led the investigation, distrusted the holdover Trump administration officials supervising them. Some staffers remained critical of Barr's interventions in the Roger Stone case and his treatment of former US attorney Jessie Liu.

Trump appointees, in turn, didn't trust career civil servants, who they saw as liberal Democrats. Michael Sherwin said that he grew frustrated with what he viewed as the caution of DOJ and FBI leaders. "I had no leadership," he said. "No one was talking to me."

Fearing that rioters would carry out further attacks or try to disrupt Biden's inauguration, Sherwin urged federal prosecutors in Washington to find ways to work quickly. They charged defendants with misdemeanor crimes so they could be quickly arrested and face more serious charges later. Instead of formally indicting people, prosecutors filed criminal complaints.

D'Antuono and agents from the Washington field office took a similar approach. "Once it's over, we go into investigation mode," D'Antuono said. "That's our bread and butter." Relying on social media posts, cell phone records, and surveillance videos, they conducted what would become the largest criminal investigation in US history. "A lot of the first couple weeks was how are we going to manage this behemoth?" D'Antuono recalled. "There had never been a case like this. It was an unprecedented investigation that involved thousands and thousands of people."

Sherwin and D'Antuono had DOJ and FBI officials focus on identifying and arresting three types of rioters: members of militia groups, rioters who had attacked police officers, and rioters they could easily identify in photographs and video.

D'Antuono had agents scour images of the attack. "We had teams of people reviewing videos," he recalled. "People who assaulted officers were a priority." He added, "The mentality a lot of us had was to check off the stuff that you can do quickly. We need to pick off people that we can pick off right now."

Agents initially focused on "low-hanging fruit"—people who had posted images of themselves inside the Capitol. "It was the people you could identify quickly," D'Antuono recalled. "The Shaman and some of the more identifiable people on screen."

"The Shaman," Jacob Anthony Chansley, was a conspiracy theorist from Arizona who entered the Capitol shirtless, wearing a fur headdress with horns, and with his face painted red, white, and blue. He was arrested on January 9.

Richard Barnett, a sixty-year-old Trump supporter from Arkansas, was photographed sitting jubilantly with his feet on a desk in House Speaker Nancy Pelosi's office. "I wrote her a nasty note, put my feet up on her desk," Barnett bragged after leaving the Capitol. He carried an envelope with the Speaker's letterhead on it that he had taken from Pelosi's office. He argued that he had not stolen it, saying, "I put a quarter on her desk." Barnett was arrested on January 8 in Bentonville, Arkansas.

Lisa Eisenhart and Eric Gavelek Munchel, a mother and son, were photographed inside the Senate chamber together. Munchel, thirty, wore military-style clothing and held zip ties. Eisenhart was arrested on January 9 in Tennessee. Munchel was arrested the following day in Nashville.

Derrick Evans, a member of the West Virginia House of Delegates, filmed himself entering the Capitol. "We're in!" he said in his video. "We're in! Derrick Evans is in the Capitol!" Aaron Mostofsky, the son of a Brooklyn judge, entered the Capitol as well. So did Olympic gold medalist swimmer Klete Keller, who was captured on video wearing his Team USA jacket in the building. All three were arrested and Evans resigned from his post in the West Virginia legislature.

One of the many FBI officials involved in the investigation was Nate Huber, the supervisory intelligence analyst. He admitted that not anticipating the attack was an intelligence failure. "We knew there was an event scheduled but we didn't anticipate that level of violence."

But he said reforms enacted in the 1970s that were designed to prevent the bureau from interfering in politics limited their ability to track the planning for the January 6 rally. "We are always looking for any type of criminal or national security threats proactively but there are certain predication levels you need," he said, referring to evidence. "The bureau is very conscious of constitutionally protected free speech. The bureau has to be extremely careful about following that type of speech."

Instead of FBI personnel meddling in politics as Hoover had, he said, the bureau may have shifted too far in the opposite direction, becoming too hands-off with respect to groups that use violence to achieve their political goals. "When it comes to domestic terrorism, you may have a lot of people saying a lot of angry things online. But you have to be very careful," he said. "I think the bureau is overly cautious in not violating First Amendment–protected activities. So I think that played a role."

Huber also participated in the search for people who had committed crimes on January 6. He said that allegations that the bureau had shown political bias in the investigations and arrests were false. "Even after January 6 happened, I never saw politics happen," he said. "We just wanted to catch the people responsible for storming the US Capitol."

AS FBI AGENTS ROUNDED UP rioters, federal prosecutors in Washington devised a plan to broaden the investigation: pull together the names of people who may have known the assailants and investigate them for ties to the attack.

Those lists, the prosecutors proposed, should include the organizers of the rally where Trump spoke just before the assault, anyone who helped pay for rioters to travel to Washington, and any member of the far-right militia groups in the crowd that day.

In late February, two veteran prosecutors leading the riot inquiry, J. P. Cooney and Ken Kohl, presented a twenty-five-page proposal that laid out the strategy with a focus on uncovering possible conspiracies. Kohl had worked in the US Attorney's Office in Washington for nearly thirty years. He had been involved in the prosecution of Ahmed Abu Khatallah, a Libyan national accused of leading the attack on the US consulate in Benghazi that killed four Americans. And he had worked on the prosecution of four former Blackwater security guards accused of killing fourteen unarmed Iraqis in Nisour Square in Baghdad.

Cooney had worked in the US Attorney's Office for nearly a decade. In 2017, he argued the prosecution case against Democratic senator Robert Menendez of New Jersey on bribery charges. Jurors in the trial, though, deadlocked and a mistrial was declared. In 2019, Cooney had supervised the team of DOJ prosecutors in Washington who prosecuted Trump advisor and ally Roger Stone for lying to Congress and witness tampering. Cooney also signed and supported the sentencing memorandum calling for Stone to be sentenced to seven to nine years in prison, which Barr had overturned.

Kohl and Cooney's plan was in keeping with the Justice Department's public vow to charge all those who participated in the attack. At the same time, DOJ and FBI policies established after Hoover's abuses—as well as First Amendment free speech protections—barred the investigation of individuals because of their political activities. It is not against US law for individuals to join organizations, including extremist groups, or to participate in a protest, unless they are implicated in violence.

The prosecutors wanted to know who had been talking to Stewart Rhodes, the leader of the Oath Keepers, a militia whose members figured prominently in the attack. In a message on the Oath Keepers' website, Rhodes, a Yale Law School graduate, had urged members to come to Washington and "stand tall in support" of Trump. Rhodes was also part of an operation to provide security for Trump's close associates, including Roger Stone, who spoke at a rally the day before the attack.

Prosecutors hoped to obtain a search warrant for Rhodes. For years, investigators had suspected that the Oath Keepers and far-right nationalist groups had used to their advantage the reforms enacted in the 1970s. They said that all their activities—including events where their members were heavily armed—were political activities protected by the First and Second amendments.

In a meeting in late February, multiple senior Justice Department and FBI officials rejected Kohl and Cooney's proposal, citing concerns that it potentially involved investigating people without evidence that they had committed crimes. The DOJ officials who opposed the plan included Matthew Axelrod, who had served as a senior Justice Department official during the Obama administration and was helping run the department until Garland could be confirmed. Sherwin, the acting US attorney in Washington, DC, opposed it as well.

"There was a PowerPoint presentation and one of the things was subpoenaing the membership list of some of the organizations that founded the Stop the Steal rally," recalled one of the former DOJ officials who rejected the proposal. "That's not how the DOJ functions. You are subpoenaing the funders of a political rally." The official said that if evidence emerged implicating Trump or his aides in the violence, subpoenas could be issued. "If you get enough evidence saying that it was all coordinated by the Trump campaign, you act."

The decision by top Justice Department and FBI officials to overrule the two prosecutors came at a crucial time for the sprawling investigation. The public and Biden administration officials were demanding accountability for the riot, and Biden had vowed to confront and defeat domestic extremism in his inaugural address.

Kohl and Cooney also contacted the FBI's domestic terrorism section to brief investigators on their proposed strategy. They suggested that investigators look at rally organizers and organizations like militia groups. Senior FBI officials opposed that step as well, including Paul Abbate, the bureau's deputy director.

D'Antuono opposed Kohl and Cooney's proposal as well. He believed that collecting information about the guests at the Willard Hotel, where Roger Stone and other Trump allies had operated a "war room" on January 6, was improper and would spark a media firestorm. "If we subpoena the Willard records, it's going to be on the front page of the paper the next day," recalled D'Antuono. "They wanted to subpoena the whole hotel, of everyone who was staying there. There are privacy concerns. I would not want to be part of serving that. When I saw it, I said we just don't do that."

The FBI of 2021 was very different from the FBI of 2016. Five years earlier, bureau officials had opened a criminal investigation of whether Trump's campaign was coordinating with Russia on limited evidence. Now, they hesitated to investigate the "Stop the Steal" rally, an event that had attracted many of the people who had subsequently stormed the Capitol. Five years of Trump's attacks had reduced the bureau's appetite for risk.

CHAPTER 11

PROSECUTING VIOLENT EXTREMISTS

FOR DECADES, MERRICK GARLAND HAS WRESTLED WITH the Justice Department's role in prosecuting extremists and defending democracy. In 1979, at the age of twenty-six, after serving as a Supreme Court clerk for Justice William Brennan, Garland had become one of seven special assistants to Benjamin Civiletti, President Jimmy Carter's second attorney general. Civiletti, like his predecessor Griffin Bell, had worked to codify reforms implemented by Edward Levi during the Ford administration.

Garland, a baby boomer who had come of age during the Vietnam War and Watergate, shared the view of many young DOJ lawyers at the time. They were determined to prevent a repeat of Nixon's abuses when the president had used the DOJ to boost his reelection chances and attack his enemies.

Civiletti, the first Italian American to serve as attorney general, invited Garland and his other special assistants for lunch in his private dining room at the Justice Department to discuss legal issues. Garland exhibited qualities that would define his career: a tendency to silently listen, ask sharp questions, and keep his views largely to himself.

Garland also had a personal sense of how brutally state power could be used. His grandmother had fled western Russia, the site of myriad pogroms, in the early 1900s to escape anti-Semitism. Two of her siblings who remained behind died in the Holocaust. The fact that his grandmother had been welcomed in the United States and largely protected by American laws barring religious persecution had been a North Star of Garland's life. The lives of his parents and his own existence, he would later say, were due to the upholding of the rule of law in America.

"He literally cannot tell the story without choking up," said a senior DOJ official, referring to the attorney general's tendency to grow emotional when describing the debt he feels his family owes to the United States. "All he can think about is his family and what would have happened if this country didn't exist." Garland regularly tears up in interviews and speeches when he describes how the upholding of rule of law in the United States allowed his family to find safe haven and live with less fear of violent persecution.

Garland was raised in Lincolnwood, Illinois, a leafy suburb of Chicago, and his childhood focused on school and academics. His mother served on the town school board and his father ran a small advertising business out of the family's basement. His parents were Democrats but not active in politics. As a young man, he worked as a volunteer in the office of his local congressman, Abner Mikva, a liberal Democrat, for two summers but rarely talked about his own politics.

His sister later told journalists that she did not know his formal party affiliation. Instead, Garland used his gentility to excel academically and socially. In high school, he asked an exchange student to prom so she would have a date and performed in talent shows. A deft debater and top student, he graduated as class valedictorian, and secured a scholarship to Harvard.

At Harvard, he showed his tendency to seek consensus and served in student government. Graduating summa cum laude, Garland was accepted by Harvard Law School, where he thrived again, and became an articles editor of the prestigious law review. Former classmates, including Republicans, remembered him for his ability to get along with liberals and conservatives alike. Michael Chertoff, who worked on the review with Garland and later served as George W. Bush's homeland security secretary, said that Garland focused more on legal issues than political ones. "I don't think he was ever viewed in a particular camp," Mr. Chertoff said.

He came of age during the strife of the 1960s and 1970s. At one point, Garland lived a few blocks from a New York townhouse that was destroyed when members of the Weathermen, an American leftist group, accidentally set off a bomb they were making. When Garland worked as a young prosecutor in Washington, a fellow prosecutor was shot dead on the courthouse steps by a man he was prosecuting. Yet security was so lax on Capitol Hill that he was able to walk into Watergate, where a Nixon aide disclosed the existence of secret Oval Office tapes, and soak up the history.

After working at a law firm and getting married, Garland returned to the DOJ during the Clinton administration. Jamie Gorelick, the deputy attorney general, hired Garland as her own deputy. Gorelick was struck by Garland's perfectionism and sense of fairness. "Merrick Garland is meticulous to the *n*th degree," she later told journalists. "He is extraordinarily careful, extraordinarily thoughtful, and never self-aggrandizing, ever."

Under Gorelick, Garland oversaw multiple high-profile domestic terrorism cases in the late 1990s, including the investigation of Ted Kaczynski, known as the "Unabomber," and a bombing at the Atlanta Olympic games. But the case that would come to define Garland was the Oklahoma City bombing, the deadliest domestic terrorist attack in American history. On April 19, 1995, Timothy J. McVeigh, an Army veteran and far-right militia member, had parked a Ryder rental truck carrying a 5,000-pound ammonium nitrate bomb beside the Alfred P. Murrah Federal Building. After setting a timer, McVeigh walked away from the truck. The bomb killed 168 people, including nineteen children.

Garland, in an interview for an oral history of the bombing, recalled visiting the scene at night soon after the bombing. The day care center had been obliterated. "There was nothing there," he said. "It was just a big empty concave." Garland was also struck by the "stone cold" demeanor of McVeigh and his seeming lack of regret.

"There was just no indication from him that he had any feelings about what had just happened," Garland said.

During his time in Oklahoma City, Garland made a point of wearing a coat and tie whenever he surveyed the wreckage. He told DOJ colleagues that donning a coat and tie was a gesture of respect for the victims. "He has seen this hatred up close and in a very personal way," recalled Donna Bucella, an investigator who worked with Garland in Oklahoma City.

Overseeing the case from Washington, Garland was involved in every major decision in the case—including the decision to pursue the death penalty. McVeigh, who was found guilty of 160 state crimes and eleven federal offenses, was executed by lethal injection.

Frank Keating, then Republican governor of Oklahoma, praised Garland for his empathy. "Usually with prosecutors who are dealing with heartbreak and horror, there's a temptation to step away and put all the emotions off to the side," Keating said at the time. "That was never true with Merrick Garland."

After being nominated twice by Bill Clinton, Garland was confirmed by the Senate and became a federal judge on the US Court of Appeals in Washington in 1997. He sang Taylor Swift songs with his daughters in his car each day when he drove them to school.

Sixteen years later, Garland was named chief judge of the US Court of Appeals in Washington. Again, Garland displayed an embrace of consensus. During his twenty-four years on the appeals court, Garland wrote only sixteen dissenting opinions. Nina Totenberg, then NPR's legal correspondent, said that Garland's rulings showed him to be "a moderate liberal, with a definite pro-prosecution bent in criminal cases."

Twenty-seven years after Oklahoma City, Garland seemed to be uniquely qualified to take on the role of attorney general as Trump's four years in power came to an end. Trump opponents hoped that Garland would investigate and prosecute the January 6 attack as quickly as he had Oklahoma City. Instead, they would learn how difficult it can be to prosecute a former president.

ON GARLAND'S FIRST DAY as attorney general, the acting US attorney for DC, Michael Sherwin, and other officials briefed him on the status of the January 6 investigation. For the last three months, Sherwin, a Trump appointee and former federal prosecutor in Miami, had aggressively investigated the attack along with other interim officials. But they could not make major decisions until there was an attorney general in office.

In his presentation, Sherwin explained that investigators had organized their investigation in four tiers. The highest-level probes—known as "complex conspiracy investigations"—were focused on whether the attack was planned.

Four teams of prosecutors and FBI agents were investigating the specific areas. Team A probed "Links to Extremist & Hate Groups"; team B investigated "Public Influencers & Officials"; team C tried to trace any "Extremist Financing"; and team D examined whether "foreign influence" had played any role in the attack.

Garland was told that prosecutors had charged nineteen defendants with conspiracy charges, including nine members of the Proud Boys and ten members of the Oath Keepers. Sherwin said that prosecutors hoped to bring a more serious and rarely used charge, seditious conspiracy, against the group's leaders. The charge, in lay parlance, accused them of conducting an insurrection against the US government.

Prosecutors were also trying to identify the individual who had placed pipe bombs at the offices of the Democratic National Committee and the Republican National Committee and evaded arrest, the protesters who had attacked Capitol Police Officer Brian Sicknick, who died the day after the riot, and the fatal shooting of protester Ashli Babbitt by a law enforcement official inside the Capitol.

As the meeting ended, Garland was briefed on the prosecutors' long-term strategy. Sherwin said his office hoped to transition from a reactive intake mode to a proactive, long-term investigation that focused on the role of militias and any potential behind-the-scenes organizers of the attack. All the investigators agreed that the best way to approach the case was through a traditional "bottom-up" approach where low-level defendants, facing long potential prison sentences, would hopefully agree to cooperate and identify which organizations or leaders might have played a role.

Garland thanked Sherwin for the briefing. As was his custom, he had listened carefully but said little. Garland also thanked a group of line prosecutors who had been working on the January 6 cases nonstop since the attack. Garland had given no hint of how he would pursue the part of the January 6 investigation that would define his tenure as attorney general: the role of Donald Trump.

TRUMP AND BARR had left Garland with a minefield of politically sensitive cases. The attorney general was overseeing the investigation of the department's response to a Republican-led recount of 2020 election returns in Arizona; its response to Republican-led efforts to restrict voting; the reinstatement of consent decrees designed to prevent police abuses; the criminal investigation of Trump's lawyer and confidant Rudy Giuliani, for illegal lobbying; and a criminal investigation of Hunter Biden, the new president's son.

One Biden administration advisor recommended that the new attorney general immediately appoint a special counsel to investigate Hunter Biden. Garland did not do so and DOJ officials said he received no such recommendation. Garland, overall, remained convinced that DOJ employees, if they followed department norms, would be trusted by the American public to carry out thorough and fair investigations, as Levi had been.

Garland, though, faced a completely different political landscape than the one that existed in the 1970s. The GOP had wanted to push Nixon out of power. A half century later, the most powerful members of the GOP had acquitted Trump when he was impeached for January 6.

Garland's mission was also bedeviled by the fact that January 6 was not a singular event, but a crescendo point in Trump's yearslong, and ongoing, campaign to subvert the law for political and personal gain. Unlike Nixon, Trump faced no check on his actions from his own party. It was inevitable that any investigation of Trump by Garland's DOJ would be viewed by Trump supporters as a political attack on the GOP itself.

Garland was also operating in a completely different media landscape than the 1970s. Cable news commentators on the Right and to a lesser extent the Left vilified members of the opposing party. Social media had proven to be a supercharged disseminator of conspiracy theories. Trust in all institutions, including the DOJ, was declining. Four years of Trump being in power, espousing far-right ideologies and conspiracies, had made radicalism far more mainstream. Trump's constant attacks on law enforcement, particularly the FBI and Robert Mueller, had diminished public trust in the FBI. Many of his supporters appeared to trust no government authority. Without trust in the institutions, the rule of law would break down, whatever Garland's intentions.

CHAPTER 12

THE LOST YEAR

MERRICK GARLAND'S FIRST THREE MONTHS IN OFFICE produced a spate of decisions—some Trump-related and some not—that angered the Biden White House and liberal Democrats. They signaled that Garland's highest loyalty would be to the Justice Department ideals of the 1970s, not political considerations. Decisions that Garland was slow to make also raised questions about whether a former judge, who had just spent twenty-four years on the bench, could adroitly run a sprawling executive branch agency that is also the world's largest law office, employing 10,000 lawyers nationwide. The DOJ is also frequently, sometimes on a daily basis, at the center of a political firestorm.

In a series of decisions that angered Democrats, Garland opposed the full release of a classified department memo that William Barr had used to distort the findings of the Mueller investigation; had DOJ lawyers ask a judge to throw out civil lawsuits against Trump and Barr, which argued that the men were personally liable for the violent removal of protesters from Lafayette Square in 2020; and was continuing to defend several Barr-era DOJ legal positions that environmental groups had decried. The decision that sparked the most outrage from liberals was continuing to have DOJ lawyers defend Trump in a defamation suit filed by E. Jean Carroll, who had accused him of rape.

Garland had some successes. Career DOJ lawyers said they no longer felt they were being pressured to satisfy blatantly political demands from the president. The department brought charges in major cybercrime cases and established a domestic terrorism unit. Prosecutors won high-profile convictions in the brutal and racially-charged murders of George Floyd and Ahmaud Arbery.

Legal experts contended that Garland was simply trying to uphold past Justice Department precedents, such as government officials being immune from civil lawsuits involving law enforcement actions taken to protect a president. In a separate court filing, DOJ lawyers had said that Trump's remark that he would not have raped jour-nalist and author E. Jean Carroll because she was not his "type" were "crude and disrespectful," but his administration had correctly argued that he could not be sued over them.

Roberta Kaplan, Carroll's attorney, was dismayed by Garland's posi-tion. "It is truly shocking that the current Department of Justice would allow Donald Trump to get away with lying about it, thereby depriving our client of her day in court," Kaplan said. "The DOJ's position is not only legally wrong, it is morally wrong since it would give federal officials free license to cover up private sexual misconduct by publicly brutalizing any woman who has the courage to come forward."

Carroll, citing the MeToo movement, expressed astonishment of her own. "As women across the country are standing up and holding men accountable for assault—the DOJ is trying to stop me from having that same right," she said in a statement. "I am angry! I am offended!"

The DOJ's decision elicited the first in a series of private and pub-lic complaints from the Biden White House regarding Garland. A spokesperson publicly distanced Biden from the decision. "The White House was not consulted by DOJ on the decision to file this brief or its contents," a spokesperson said. "President Biden and his team have utterly different standards from their predecessors for what qualify as acceptable statements." The gulf between the Biden White House and Garland would steadily widen.

Trump and his allies in Congress, meanwhile, defiantly and falsely claimed that they were the victims of federal law enforcement abuse. At a House hearing on the January 6 riot, Representative Paul Gosar, Republican of Arizona, falsely claimed that supporters of the former president were being singled out for prosecution. "Outright propaganda and lies are being used to unleash the national security state against law-abiding US citizens, especially Trump voters," Gosar said. "The DOJ is harassing peaceful patriots across the country." Andrew Clyde, a House member from Georgia, professed that January 6 resembled a "normal tourist visit" to the Capitol.

Only three months after Garland took office, some progressives called for the new attorney general's ouster. Regardless of the merits of their arguments, they grasped something that the new attorney general apparently did not expect. Restoring "normal" order alone would not be enough to counter Trump's ceaseless and systematic efforts to discredit the DOJ and FBI as corrupt. They said that Garland's embrace of proper DOJ procedure was unwittingly causing him to underestimate the threat that Trump represented.

"Garland, in other words, is trying to treat Donald Trump as if he was a normal president, and his policies as if they were normal policies," Jeff Hauser and Max Moran, of the Revolving Door Project, which tracks executive-branch abuse, wrote in the *New Republic*. "We're seeing a scary example of how liberalism's belief in process itself, rather than the ideals that processes are supposed to help execute, can be easily manipulated by bad-faith, far-right actors."

They said that Trump's brazen willingness to weaponize the DOJ, use the legal system to delay investigations, and spread patently false conspiracy theories were a threat to democracy. "An attorney general who doesn't treat Trump like the unique threat he was and doesn't wake up every day raring to neutralize his influence on society, isn't an attorney general Biden can afford," Hauser and Moran wrote. "Every day Biden keeps Garland in charge of his legal agenda is a day Trumpism is normalized, and the inevitable battle against it in 2024 gets that much harder."

A senior DOJ official flatly rejected that claim. They said it was vital for the Justice Department to follow its practice of investigating specific crimes, such as the January 6 attacks, and not specific individuals, which can lead to bias. "I don't know who else in his position wouldn't reasonably be worried," said the official, referring to appearing partisan. "The department investigates crimes. It does not investigate individuals. The opposite of that is what happens in totalitarian regimes."

At the same time, Garland had limited time to investigate Trump's role in January 6. If the DOJ investigation—and any potential prosecution—of Trump unfolded too close to the 2024 election it would allow the former president to claim that he was being prosecuted for his political views, not his crimes. Months into Garland's tenure, the election clock was already ticking. The speed of the DOJ investigation of Trump would prove critical.

AGAINST THIS BACKDROP, Garland was concerned about misleading the public into believing that a prosecution of Trump was going to happen before the department had completed a thorough investigation. Some Democrats—and some people inside the department—argued that Garland's view was naïve. They felt it was unrealistic for him to think that he could somehow avoid publicly addressing whether Trump's actions on January 6 were criminal.

Garland also decided to not have his aides investigate just how much impropriety had occurred in the department under Trump, including what were believed to be multiple instances of abuse that the press did not discover. Garland said that this was a job for the department's inspector general, who only investigated transgressions after receiving formal reports of waste, fraud, and abuse.

Garland's top deputy, Deputy Attorney General Lisa Monaco, also revered the department's traditions and was known for caution. Monaco, a veteran DOJ and national security official, had worked as Janet Reno's counselor, Robert Mueller's FBI chief of staff, and Barack Obama's homeland security and counterterrorism advisor. Monaco was perceived by some as cautious and keenly aware that her ability to be confirmed by the Senate was her lifeline to higher-level positions.

In an effort to maintain the bipartisan support she would need to become attorney general or FBI director herself in the future, they said, Monaco stayed away from politically charged cases. Critics said that Monaco distanced herself from investigations that would make it hard for her to win Senate confirmation in the future. A senior DOJ official said that Monaco was decisive, not cautious, and suggested that the criticism was due to sexism. "She is a woman and a strong manager," said the official, who asked not to be named.

After two decades of working as a judge, Garland brought a judicial temperament to the office of the attorney general. At times, he ran his office like a judge's chambers. He peppered staff with questions and thoroughly tested the legal theories and evidence they presented in high-profile cases, including the investigation of Trump and other former senior officials regarding January 6.

"Yes, he went deep on big issues," said the senior DOJ official. Garland's goal, as a former federal appeals court judge, was to avoid mistakes that could result in prosecutions being delayed or dismissed, which would further undermine public confidence in the DOJ, the official said.

Garland knew that, because Trump was a former president, each case would likely be reviewed by the Supreme Court and receive exhaustive legal, media, and public scrutiny, the official continued. The New York Times later noted that, by trying to avoid even small mistakes, Garland risked making a large one: creating an opportunity for Trump to delay his federal trials until after the 2024 election.

Garland also preferred to maintain a low public profile. The senior DOJ official said that Garland believed that the department "is not a place to be performative." Officials should only speak publicly when it serves an "aim of the department."

Garland gave more speeches than his role models, Robert Jackson and Edward Levi, but Garland's speeches tended to be more understated. Levi, in particular, was famed for writing and delivering speeches that explained the rule of law to the American public. In an anthology of Levi's speeches, Anthony Lewis, the late New York Times columnist, praised Levi for directly confronting in his speeches the cynicism of Watergate.

"It was Edward J. Levi's first and overwhelming task as attorney general to end the cynicism of Watergate," Lewis wrote. "This wonderful collection of his speeches shows how he did it: with eloquent words that expressed his profound belief in American values. In our time of meanness, of strife, Levi reminds us what we should be."

Andrew Weissmann, the former Mueller investigator, noted that attorneys general can give speeches and television interviews but decline to give information about specific cases. He cited Watergate Special Counsel Archibold Cox's press conference when he announced that he was going to take his request for access to Richard Nixon's White House tapes to the US Supreme Court. He said that it was possible for Mueller and Garland to speak more often in public while respecting DOJ norms and not describing the details of criminal investigations.

"He said there are things I can't say but then he explained why he did it," Weissmann said, referring to Cox's tapes press conference. "The added component is that people get to take a measure of the man or woman making the statements. The demeanor and the substance of the person."

When Michael Sherwin, the outgoing, Trump-appointed US attorney in Washington, DC, spoke about the ongoing January 6 investigation in an interview with *60 Minutes*, Garland and his aides were frustrated. In the interview, Sherwin said that he felt that investigators had obtained enough evidence to charge some rioters with seditious conspiracy, a rarely used Civil War–era statute. "I personally believe the evidence is trending toward that, and probably meets those elements," he said.

Garland and his aides felt that Sherwin's statement potentially defamed the defendants and also described prosecutors' internal deliberations in detail. DOJ officials were upset that Sherwin had made that public. The judge in the case, Amit Mehta, held an urgent conference with lawyers from both sides of the case.

The judge said he was "surprised" that Sherwin had speculated about possible future charges on national television. Sherwin thought he had permission to do the interview, but he was referred to the department's office of professional responsibility for investigation. Sherwin's removal from the case, which he had helped to oversee since the day of the attack, created a leadership vacuum.

Garland was in many ways the opposite of Barr, who regularly used television interviews to air his views. While Garland was eager to avoid acting rashly or politically, Barr saw decisiveness, risk-taking, and publicly supporting the president's broad policy initiatives as part of being an effective attorney general.

Garland believed that his restraint, unpopular as it may have been with some Democrats, was the only way for the Justice Department to weather a future leader with authoritarian instincts who may treat the law as but another political tool, and election outcomes as mere formalities to wipe away. He needed to re-instill in the DOJ the sense that career lawyers could do their jobs apolitically without fear or favor and rebuild that culture. But one question remained unanswered: Was that culture ever there to the degree Garland thought it was?

Another challenge remained. It was unrealistic to think that the act of prosecuting a former president, one who said he had won the last election and remained a popular figure in his party, was not shot through with political implications. During Watergate, the public had trusted that institutions could be relatively impartial with a second-term president who could not be reelected. Not so in the Trump era, particularly after he chose to run for reelection in 2024.

Garland's goal, the senior DOJ official said, was to demonstrate to Americans that the department can act quietly, effectively, and impartially. To avoid any hint of political considerations impacting the department's prosecutions, "there has to be a wall," this person said in early 2021. "He has made that abundantly clear."

"He obviously understands what our country just went through," the official said. "Anyone who is attorney general and who is considering indicting a former president should be aware that the public needs to believe it was done by the book."

OVER THE COURSE OF 2021, Garland also focused his attention on issues not related to Trump and January 6. He closely monitored attempts to weaken voting rights in various states. During an interview with the *New York Times* about his first year in office, Garland said that defending civil rights, particularly voting, was a way to defend democracy and increase public trust in election results.

"The core purpose of the Justice Department is to protect civil rights and civil liberties, and the fundamental element of that is the right to vote," Garland said. "That's what makes this country a representative democracy." If those rights are curbed, he added, "inherently, people worry about whether elections are fair."

In his first year, Garland sued Texas and Georgia over their new restrictive voting laws, indicted people who had threatened election officials in Georgia and Nevada, and doubled the number of voting rights prosecutors in the department. He urged Congress to pass new voter protection laws and vowed to aggressively enforce them.

Garland also closely monitored attempts by states to ban abortions, which he considered a constitutional right. He personally worked on the DOJ's response to a Texas abortion law that all but banned the procedure, including the department's brief to the Supreme Court in opposition to the law and a DOJ lawsuit designed to prevent Texas from enforcing the statute. Both efforts failed.

Garland told the *New York Times* that the Texas law took away a right, and that it did so in a way that severely curbed the power of the courts. The result, he warned, was a road map for states seeking an "end run" around "any right in the Constitution."

The decision on whether to charge leaders of the Oath Keepers and Proud Boys with seditious conspiracy, meanwhile, remained in limbo. While the prosecution of low-level rioters was moving quickly, the investigation of potential January 6 organizers was slowed by a lack of key leaders fueled, in part, by the White House's desire to get liberal-leaning judges appointed to the bench to counter the record number appointed by Trump.

The senior DOJ official credited the Biden White House with obeying post-Watergate norms. The official said that the Biden White House discussed broad law enforcement and policy issues with the department but never pressured Garland or any DOJ official regarding any case—including the criminal investigations of Donald Trump or Hunter Biden, unlike what occurred under Trump. "They have never said a word," the senior DOJ official affirmed.

Biden White House officials, though, have privately expressed frustration to others regarding the slow pace of Garland's January 6 investigation and his appointment of special counsels to investigate Biden's handling of classified documents. The White House, at the same time, was slow to fill key DOJ posts that could help speed up its January 6 investigations. The White House did not nominate a new US attorney for Washington, DC—arguably the most important investigator in the January 6 probe—until July 26, four months after Garland became attorney general.

As Biden's nominee for US attorney in DC, Mathew Graves, slowly made his way through the Senate confirmation process, Channing D. Phillips, the acting US attorney, told staffers that he saw his role as a placeholder with limited power to make decisions about January 6 cases.

Prosecutors, meanwhile, began to complain about delays. They had decided that dozens of rioters should be offered plea deals but were unable to obtain approval from senior officials. Some prosecutors, according to press reports, considered the investigation "rudderless."

In DOJ headquarters, officials disagreed over whether to investigate individuals in Trump's orbit, a step that could lead investigators to the former president himself. "The notion of opening up on Trump and high-level political operatives was seen as fraught with peril," a former senior DOJ official told the Washington Post. "When Lisa and Garland came on board, they were fully onboard with that approach."

Over time, some DOJ officials began to think that even mentioning Trump by name had become taboo in DOJ headquarters. Aides who prepared briefings and updates for Garland and Monaco were told to avoid mentioning Trump and his allies, according to the *Post*.

Multiple senior DOJ officials flatly denied that they were discouraged from uttering Trump's name in meetings. "Not mentioning the name of Trump, that's false," said one official, adding of whoever made the allegation, "They weren't present in the meetings."

After Monaco was confirmed by the Senate and arrived in the department in April, she checked that the January 6 investigations were properly staffed. In June, six weeks after Monaco's arrival, a new unit was established to investigate the organizers of the January 6 rally, DOJ officials said. They acknowledged, though, that the unit was not staffed until the fall.

As the summer stretched into fall, prosecutors following the "bottom-up" approach to the investigation wanted to charge Oath Keeper leader Stewart Rhodes and several of the group's senior leaders with seditious conspiracy. But they had no answer from senior DOJ officials.

Some DOJ officials worried that seditious conspiracy charges could be overturned on appeal. Rhodes, a Yale Law School graduate, had been present on January 6, but had not set foot in the Capitol, a seemingly deliberate effort to dilute any case that prosecutors could bring.

In the fall of 2021, a senior prosecutor was quietly added to the January 6 investigation. Thomas Windom, career prosecutor in the US Attorney's Office in Maryland, had made a name for himself by successfully prosecuting members of "The Base," a white supremacist group, in 2020.

In 2019, Windom secured a guilty plea from Christopher Hasson, a former Coast Guard lieutenant and self-described white supremacist who had planned to assassinate Democratic politicians. Some Maryland defense lawyers, though, criticized Windom for being "inflexible," attacking witnesses and seeking excessive sentences.

After arriving in the Garland DOJ, Windom led the investigation by a grand jury in Washington of the speakers and organizers of the rally Trump addressed before the riot, as well as into whether any members of his administration or Congress tried to help obstruct the certification of the 2020 results. Windom also investigated the lawyers who helped to devise and promote the plan to create alternate slates of electors, including Rudy Giuliani, John Eastman, Jenna Ellis, and Kenneth Chesebro, who wrote memos supporting the elector scheme. Windom found no new evidence implicating Trump personally in a crime, but continued digging.

Several key senior positions, though, remained unfilled. The DOJ's National Security Division, an office charged with investigating domestic extremism that would normally review seditious conspiracy charges, was leaderless. The Biden administration had nominated Matthew Olsen, a former DOJ prosecutor who had helped create the National Security Division after the 9/11 attacks, in May, but he too was awaiting Senate confirmation. When Olsen's confirmation hearing was held on July 14, 2021, he shared it with five Biden administration nominees for federal judgeships.

A week later, the House Select Committee to Investigate the January 6th Attack on the United States Capitol held its first hearing. Four Capitol Police officers testified about their experience during the assault. They revealed no new bombshell details, but the committee—and its several dozen investigators—placed pressure on DOJ officials. The Democrat-dominated committee, along with its two Republicans, Liz Cheney of Wyoming and Adam Kinzinger of Illinois, were investigating the actions of Trump's inner circle and planning to subpoena Roger Stone, Steve Bannon, and others with potential ties to the Proud Boys and Oath Keepers.

Journalists, meanwhile, began uncovering evidence that Trump and his advisors had spent weeks after Biden was declared the winner of the 2020 race trying to find ways to reverse the outcome. In a book released in September, Bob Woodward of the *Washington Post* and Robert Costa of CBS News revealed that John Eastman, a conservative legal scholar, had written a memo to Trump arguing that Pence had the legal power to block the certification of Biden's win on

January 6 by citing the slate of fake pro-Trump electors and declaring the election outcome in dispute. White House counsel Pat Cipollone and multiple other White House lawyers had ridiculed Eastman's theory, which, in essence, said the vice president chooses the next president, not voters.

In October, the *Washington Post* reported that Bannon, Rudy Giuliani, Boris Epshteyn, and former New York City police commissioner Bernard Kerik operated a "command center" in the Willard Hotel during the week before the January 6 attack "with one goal in mind: overturning the results of the 2020 election." At the same time, the House January 6 committee recommended that the chamber vote to hold Bannon in contempt for refusing to testify before the panel. To the public, the House committee appeared to be investigating Trump's inner circle more aggressively than the Garland Justice Department.

ON OCTOBER 28, OLSEN and Graves were finally confirmed for their new posts in party-line votes in the Senate. Graves's nominations had been delayed by requests from Republican senator Ron Johnson of Wisconsin for more information about the DOJ's January 6 investigations. Trump and his far-right allies continued to claim, without citing evidence, that Trump supporters were being unfairly prosecuted and that the violence on January 6 was being exaggerated.

After formally joining the DOJ, Olsen and Graves both immediately worked to accelerate the DOJ investigation of who, if anyone, organized the violence on January 6. Olsen argued to Monaco that an attempt to use violence to reverse the outcome of an election was within the purview of the National Security Division. She approved his request. Soon after, Olsen and Graves received an hours-long briefing from Steven D'Antuono, the head of the FBI's Washington field office, about where the sprawling FBI investigation stood.

Olsen and Graves also began reviewing whether Rhodes and other members of the Oath Keepers could be prosecuted for seditious conspiracy. Roughly eight months had passed since Sherwin had told his deputies to discuss the potential charge with Monaco.

A core part of the process of advancing the Oath Keepers case was for senior DOJ officials to review a draft prosecution memo put together by lower-level prosecutors. Monaco, according to a senior DOJ official, did not see the draft memo until after Olsen arrived in the DOJ in November 2022. It is unclear why the draft prosecution memo did not reach Monaco for eight months.

When Graves and Olsen reviewed the seditious conspiracy charges, they concluded that charges "fit like a glove" in terms of Rhodes's actions before the attack, the *Washington Post* reported.

Rhodes, who had been careful not to enter the Capitol building, had also made a major error. He and his deputies had sent encrypted messages in the weeks before the attack that appeared to incriminate them in an effort to reverse the election results.

Graves, the US attorney in Washington, also tried to increase resources for the investigation. Prosecutors felt that too few resources were being put into investigating a potential conspiracy to reverse the results of the election. They also felt overwhelmed trying to prosecute hundreds of low-level rioters. Graves proposed to Monaco that he create a new unit that would examine the evidence of a plot to block the certification of the election results. Monaco approved the request and Graves approved a pre-existing request from Windom to join the January 6 probe. Graves assigned Windom to the group examining the fake electors scheme.

Soon after, Windom met with D'Antuono and told him that a grand jury would be investigating the fake electors scheme. Windom proposed issuing a subpoena for billing information at the Willard Hotel for the period around January 6.

D'Antuono opposed the request. He saw it as similar to Cooney's earlier proposal to subpoena the Willard records. He did not believe that the investigators had found enough evidence that a crime had been committed in the hotel to justify a subpoena. He also continued to worry that reckless investigative steps played into Trump's narrative that the FBI was a secret police organization spying on Trump supporters.

While DOJ and FBI officials argued, the House January 6 committee continued to aggressively investigate Trump's inner circle. In late November, the House issued subpoenas for Bannon, Stone, and three other Trump advisors. The individuals named suggested that the committee was investigating who had planned, organized, and financed the "Stop the Steal" rally that preceded the attack.

In early December, Ali Alexander, one of the people the committee had subpoenaed, agreed to voluntarily meet with investigators. Alexander, a right-wing provocateur who had organized rallies across the United States claiming that the 2020 election was stolen, promised to provide a trove of documents to the committee. But he said he played no role in the violence that unfolded. "Anyone who suggests I had anything to do with the unlawful activities on Jan. 6 is wrong," Alexander wrote in a memo to the committee. "They're either mistaken or lying."

In mid-December, three retired generals wrote an op-ed in the *Washington Post* imploring government officials to intensify their investigation. "Everything must be done to prevent another insurrection. Not a single leader who inspired it has been held to account," they wrote. "Our elected officials and those who enforce the law— including the Justice Department, the House select committee and the whole of Congress—must show more urgency."

AS THE ANNIVERSARY of January 6 approached, Garland came under increasing pressure to signal to the American public that the department was investigating the organizers of the attack. Windom, in fact, was examining the actions of Giuliani, Eastman, and other lawyers close to Trump, but Justice Department norms barred prosecutors from commenting on ongoing investigations.

Garland also didn't want to say anything false to the public or to give the impression that Trump was being targeted because of his political views. After a series of conversations, Garland agreed to use the department's traditional language regarding the pursuit of facts.

In an address in the Justice Department's Great Hall, Garland gave a lengthy speech that again tried to explain the department's norms. Garland began the address with three vows: "We will defend our democratic institutions from attack. We will protect those who serve the public from violence and threats of violence. We will protect the cornerstone of our democracy: the right to every eligible citizen to cast a vote that counts."

He then described the scope of the DOJ's January 6 investigation, saying that roughly 140 prosecutors had "issued over 5,000 subpoenas and search warrants, seized approximately 2,000 devices, pored through over 20,000 hours of video footage, and searched through an estimated 15 terabytes of data. We have received over 300,000 tips from ordinary citizens."

In all, the department had arrested and charged more than 725 defendants, in nearly all fifty states, including 325 charged with felonies. Garland then invoked Watergate.

"We follow the facts—not an agenda or an assumption. The facts tell us where to go next," he said. "Over forty years ago in the wake of the Watergate scandal, the Justice Department concluded that the best way to ensure the department's independence, integrity, and fair application of our laws—and, therefore, the best way to ensure the health of our democracy—is to have a set of norms to govern our work."

Garland went out of his way to explain that prosecutors were acting in a politically neutral manner. "The central norm is that, in our criminal investigations, there cannot be different rules depending on one's political party or affiliation. There cannot be different rules for friends and foes. And there cannot be different rules for the powerful and the powerless. There is only one rule: We follow the facts and enforce the law in a way that respects the Constitution and protects civil liberties."

He argued that the unprecedented nature of the January 6 attack made it more important than ever to stick to a traditional approach.

"We adhere to those norms even when, and especially when, the circumstances we face are not normal," he said. "Adhering to the department's long-standing norms is essential to our work in defending our democracy, particularly at a time when we are confronting a rise in violence and unlawful threats of violence in our shared public spaces and directed at those who serve the public."

Garland then made a statement that sparked intense media speculation that Trump would be indicted. "The actions we have taken thus far will not be our last," Garland vowed. "The Justice Department remains committed to holding all January 6 perpetrators, at any level, accountable under law—whether they were present that day or were otherwise criminally responsible for the assault on our democracy. We will follow the facts wherever they lead."

A week later, Rhodes and several other members of the Oath Keepers were indicted on charges of seditious conspiracy. The Michigan attorney general then announced that she had referred several Michigan residents to the DOJ for investigation for their role in a fake electors scheme in the state. The pressure on the DOJ—as well as the sense that it was on the verge of implicating Trump—soared.

In private, though, DOJ and FBI investigators were discovering what the Mueller team had learned as well. Multiple defendants who had been indicted by the DOJ declined to become cooperating witnesses against Trump. No explosive recordings or written evidence that would directly and definitively implicate Trump in a crime had emerged. The bottom-up approach had been followed over the course of the year, but it had produced no definitive links between the rioters, far-right groups, and Trump. Without that, prosecuting Trump would be a gamble.

CHAPTER **13**

A CLEAR AND
CONVINCING CASE

O N FEBRUARY 9, 2022, GARY STERN, THE GENERAL counsel of the National Archives, contacted the Justice Department and asked it to investigate Trump's handling of classified documents. By law, Stern was required to report any current or former government official who appeared to have mishandled classified information to the Justice Department for potential prosecution.

The former president's actions bewildered senior DOJ officials, who were surprised by Trump's apparent refusal to return the papers. The officials discussed the situation. Some assumed that he would quickly hand back the documents and resolve the case. Others predicted that Trump's recklessness would continue and they would be forced to criminally investigate the president. They knew that if they did so, they would be savaged by Trump.

What stuck out to some DOJ officials—lawyers long trained in caution and prudence—was how reckless and, more plainly, stupid it was for Trump to decline to simply return the documents. Many predicted that he would eventually do so. Others told them to prepare for a long legal battle.

After repeatedly asking Trump to return all official documents from his presidency over the course of 2021, the National Archives had finally received fifteen boxes of materials in early 2022 that contained—to the amazement of archivists—highly classified documents intermingled with other records and memorabilia. Archive officials found that the boxes contained 184 documents bearing classification markings,

192 WHERE TYRANNY BEGINS

including sixty-seven documents labeled "confidential," ninety-two documents marked "secret," and twenty-five documents labeled "top secret." The documents included correspondence between Trump and North Korean leader Kim Jong Un, and the letter that former president Obama had left for Trump in the Oval Office in 2017.

Under the Presidential Records Act of 1978, all records created or received by the president as part of their "constitutional, statutory, or ceremonial duties" are the property of the United States government. The law, one of the myriad reforms passed after Nixon initially refused to hand over recordings of White House meetings that he had made, was designed to increase transparency in the White House.

A week after asking the DOJ to investigate Trump, the archivist of the United States, David Ferriero, informed the chairwoman of the House Oversight and Reform Committee, Carolyn Maloney, that the transfer of the boxes had occurred after the National Archives and Records Administration had communicated with Trump's representatives throughout 2021. The letter's most explosive sentence stated that NARA had found "items marked as classified national security information" in the boxes and, as a result, had contacted the Department of Justice.

Ferriero was employing a tried-and-true Washington strategy: informing a member of Congress of a fact that will aid them politically is the equivalent of issuing a press release. Instantly, news broke that the DOJ had been notified that Trump may have mishandled classified documents—a crime. Maloney also opened up an investigation of her own.

Trump's Save America PAC posted a statement on behalf of the former president: "The National Archives did not find anything, they were given, upon request, Presidential Records in an ordinary and routine process to ensure the preservation of my legacy and in accordance with the Presidential Records Act."

The exchange fueled intensive speculation about whether the Justice Department was finally criminally investigating Trump's role on

January 6. Throughout 2021, the DOJ and FBI investigation of lower-level participants in the attack had continued, with more than seven hundred people charged.

TO THE DISMAY of many Trump opponents, it remained unclear if the former president himself was under scrutiny. After appearing to make little effort to investigate the former president for criminal activity, Garland and Monaco had taken a series of steps suggesting they could be investigating Trump.

A week after Garland delivered his January 6 anniversary speech promising to "follow the facts where they may lead," FBI agents arrested Stewart Rhodes, the fifty-six-year-old head of the Oath Keepers militia in Texas. DOJ prosecutors charged him with seditious conspiracy, the most serious charge filed against any January 6 defendant at the time. Soon after, the leader of the Proud Boys, Enrique Tarrio, and four of his top subordinates were indicted on seditious conspiracy charges as well. The case had played out as Michael Sherwin, the former US attorney for the District of Columbia, had said it would.

Inside the DOJ, though, it remained unclear that they were going to find enough evidence to put together a powerful case to prosecute Trump for January 6. Pressure on the DOJ to probe Trump's effort to reverse the outcome of the 2020 election continued to build.

A week later, on January 18, Michigan attorney general Dana Nessel delivered to the DOJ the results of her yearlong investigation into sixteen members of the Michigan GOP who had falsely claimed to be the state's presidential electors in 2020. Nessel said there was "absolutely" enough evidence to charge them with a crime. Two other prosecutors, Hector Balderas Jr., the attorney general of New Mexico, and a local prosecutor in Wisconsin, also asked the Justice Department to review the matter.

A week later, on January 25, Lisa Monaco told CNN that the

DOJ was investigating the fake slates of electors that falsely declared Trump the winner of the 2020 election in seven swing states: "Our prosecutors are looking at those," Monaco said. "And I can't say anything more on ongoing investigations."

Over the next four months, the House January 6 Committee ran public relations around both the Justice Department and the FBI. In a half dozen, tightly scripted hearings that combined carefully edited video clips with live testimony, the House Select Committee to Investigate the January 6th Attack on the United States Capitol painted a vivid picture of Trump's frantic effort to overturn the 2020 election and ultimately declared him personally responsible for the attack.

The panel obtained a thirty-eight-page presentation from former White House chief of staff Mark Meadows that recommended that Trump declare a national security emergency, invalidate all ballots cast by machine, and order the military to seize and recount all paper ballots. It obtained frantic texts from Fox News hosts Brian Kilmeade, Sean Hannity, and Laura Ingraham on January 6 asking Meadows to persuade Trump to immediately appear on television and quell the riot.

Bill Barr, in videotaped testimony, said that Trump had "become detached from reality" as he continued to promote stolen election conspiracy theories without "interest in what the actual facts were." Barr's successor, Acting Attorney General Jeff Rosen, testified before the committee about how Trump tried to replace him with Jeffrey Clark, the Trump loyalist who would spread Trump's false election claims.

Surprisingly, some of the most compelling testimony came from Cassidy Hutchinson, a little-known, twenty-seven-year-old aide to Meadows. In blunt, plainspoken language she described the chaos inside the White House, including how Trump had once hurled a plate of spaghetti at a wall.

Hutchinson testified that White House officials anticipated violence days before January 6; that Trump knew participants in the "Stop the Steal" rally were armed with weapons, including AR-15s, but still asked officials to relax security checks. In her most explosive testimony she said that Trump had planned to join the crowd at the Capitol and became irate when Secret Service agents refused to drive him there.

Seated a few feet behind Hutchinson throughout her testimony was a retired Justice Department official: Jody Hunt. After resigning from the Justice Department in 2020, Hunt began working as a lawyer at the law firm Alston & Bird. Weeks before her testimony, Hutchinson had fired Stefan Passantino, a lawyer paid for by the Trump campaign who she said coached her to give limited answers to the committee.

As soon as Hunt became Hutchinson's lawyer, he urged her to do the opposite. "I said to her, Cassidy, you have a subpoena, you are under oath, you have no claim of privilege so you have one job and only one job and that's to tell the truth no matter who it might hurt or help."

Hunt rejected a claim by Democratic strategist James Carville that Hunt was taking revenge on Trump by helping Hutchinson testify. He had never heard of Hutchinson when she asked his law firm about handling her representation. Hunt said that he was alarmed by Trump's system of providing witnesses with lawyers, such as Passantino, whose bills Trump paid. He feared that de facto hush money was at work.

"I think this is a huge problem," Hunt said, referring to the many witnesses represented by lawyers paid by Trump. "It appears that through this system they have found a way to keep things close hold, to learn about and navigate testimony by getting their lawyers to represent people."

A handful of Hunt's neighbors in Alabama shunned him after seeing him on television representing Hutchinson during the hearing. He continued to follow the code he had learned at the Justice Department: ethical lawyers engaging in nonpartisan public service. "I was honored to have the opportunity to represent her," Hunt said.

After Hunt met Hutchinson and learned that she had testified to the committee three times behind closed doors but had omitted key facts, he urged her to speak with the panel again. "You can't allow history, you can't allow the record to stand like this," Hunt recalled saying.

He then went to the committee, described what she had not mentioned previously, and they agreed to allow her to testify further. Soon after, they decided to have Hutchinson testify on national television.

While the January 6 committee made headlines, the DOJ investigation proceeded haltingly. Obtaining irrefutable evidence that Trump intentionally participated in a plot to reverse the results of the election was proving difficult. But prosecutors continued digging.

The classified documents case came to take up more and more time of the January 6 briefings given to Garland and Monaco. Garland displayed an old habit. When he faced a high-stakes legal decision, he studied it intently. Garland concentrated on how the documents could be recovered and how Trump could be treated like any other defendant.

WHEN THE DOJ SENT multiple letters about January 6 to Trump's lawyers in the spring of 2021, they stonewalled. In response, prosecutors had a federal grand jury in Washington issue subpoenas in February and March that made clear that the DOJ had moved beyond prosecuting those who stormed the Capitol.

They began to examine the possible culpability of a broad range of figures in efforts to overturn the 2020 election, including those who may have aided attempts to promote slates of fake electors. Prosecutors also began asking about the planning for the rallies that preceded the assault on the Capitol and sought information about VIPs who attended.

Trump, as he had in the past, made unforced errors that increased his legal jeopardy. In a political feud in March, the former president withdrew his endorsement of Republican House member Mo Brooks in the Republican primary for Sessions's former Alabama US Senate seat, undercutting the congressman's already slim chances in a crowded intraparty race. Brooks, in response, issued an extraordinary public statement that accused the former president of trying to illegally remain in power after the 2020 election.

"President Trump asked me to rescind the 2020 elections, immediately remove Joe Biden from the White House, immediately put President Trump back in the White House, and hold a new special election for the presidency," Brooks said. "As a lawyer, I've repeatedly advised President Trump that January 6 was the final election contest verdict and neither the US Constitution nor the US Code permit what President Trump asks. Period." Brooks also said that Trump had asked him to break the law on "multiple occasions" since September 1, 2021. He said the former president did not specify how exactly Congress would reinstall him as president, and Brooks repeatedly told him it was impossible.

On March 28, a federal judge in California issued a ruling that increased pressure on the Justice Department. In a civil suit against John Eastman, Judge David O. Carter ruled that Eastman and Trump most likely committed felonies when they tried to reverse the outcome of the election, including obstructing the work of Congress and conspiring to defraud the United States. In a major but unrelated development two days later, which was kept secret, the FBI formally opened a criminal investigation into the unlawful retention of classified documents in Mar-a-Lago.

In April, Ali Alexander began cooperating with the January 6 investigation after receiving a subpoena from prosecutors in Washington. Alexander was involved in efforts to challenge the election via political protests, and had contact with other protest organizers, extremist groups, members of Congress, and White House officials during the period after Election Day. The subpoena to Alexander sought information about members of the executive and legislative branches who were involved in the events or who may have helped to obstruct the certification of the 2020 election.

In May, DOJ prosecutors led by Windom subpoenaed multiple

lawyers close to Trump for information regarding the plan to create alternate slates of pro-Trump electors, including Rudy Giuliani, John Eastman, Jenna Ellis, and Kenneth Chesebro.

From May 16 to 18, 2022, FBI agents conducted a preliminary review of the fifteen boxes provided to the National Archives as part of the separate investigation of Trump's handling of classified documents. They identified documents with classification markings in fourteen of the boxes. FBI agents observed markings reflecting some of the highest levels of classification in the US government. Documents classified at these levels typically contain national defense information. Several of the documents also contained what appeared to be Trump's handwritten notes.

Yet prosecutors and FBI agents had still not unearthed specific evidence that would definitively make Trump personally responsible for the violence on January 6. Windom was also working with postal service investigators to examine whether sending fake electors to Congress was a form of fraud. Tensions on the team began to grow about what to do. "They were talking wire fraud. They were talking in generalities," D'Antuono recalled. "I said, 'Tom, we're not seeing anything in terms of a conspiracy.'"

In both the January 6 and classified documents cases, divisions were emerging between DOJ and FBI officials regarding how aggressive to be with Trump. New evidence would soon emerge that Trump had tried to obstruct the investigation into his handling of classified documents that would cause that case to be seen as the stronger of the two.

ON JUNE 3, JAY BRATT, the lead prosecutor in the classified documents investigation, traveled to Mar-a-Lago with two FBI agents from the Washington field office to pick up all remaining documents from Trump's lawyer. The night before the meeting, a worker at Mar-a-Lago called law enforcement officials with a tip. They had seen Trump's former White House valet and now personal assistant, Walt Nauta, move boxes into a storage room. The worker helped Nauta move some of the boxes but told investigators that he didn't know what was inside them.

When Bratt and the two FBI agents arrived at Mar-a-Lago, Bratt received an envelope from one of Trump's lawyers with thirty-eight documents in it—seventeen marked "top secret," sixteen marked "secret," and five marked "confidential." Bratt also received a signed certification from Trump attorney Christina Bobb attesting that a "diligent search" had been conducted and no additional classified documents were found at Mar-a-Lago.

After Bratt returned to Washington, DOJ and FBI officials disagreed on how to proceed. Abbate and Kohler agreed with D'Antuono and others in the FBI Washington field office that a search of Mar-a-Lago was premature. In a compromise, they decided to subpoena surveillance camera footage from inside Mar-a-Lago. In a development that stunned investigators, the footage showed Nauta moving large numbers of boxes the day before Bratt and the two FBI agents arrived. Trump's workers, Trump's lawyers, or Trump himself had lied to investigators.

As a Mar-a-Lago search grew more likely, Garland listened attentively at briefings and asked probing questions. Monaco listened as well but took no immediate position. The driving force and the official most at risk if no classified documents were found was Olsen, the head of the DOJ's National Security Division.

A similar dynamic played out across Pennsylvania Avenue in FBI headquarters. FBI Director Christopher Wray was briefed on the search, but took no formal position. Wray repeatedly told subordinates to treat the search of Trump's home "like any other case." Some FBI officials pushed back, pointing out that the case was not like any other, given Trump's status as a former president and long history of demonizing the bureau. Eventually, Wray signaled to the supervisors and agents involved in the search that he had their backs. After the contentious meeting in the FBI headquarters on August 1, Abbate agreed that the bureau had taken the steps needed to execute the search.

On August 5, DOJ officials obtained the search warrant from a federal judge. As FBI agents entered Mar-a-Lago at 9:00 a.m. on Monday, August 8, investigators nervously joked that they would all be fired if no classified documents were found. All told, that day agents recovered more than one hundred classified documents, and more than eleven thousand documents that were considered presidential records, that Trump had declined to hand over.

After Trump denounced the search that evening, FBI officials asked for more information to be released to the public. Their DOJ superiors refused, citing the department's tradition of only speaking in court. The decision exasperated FBI officials. "We had a generic press release prepared for the night of the search which would have explained that the FBI had conducted court-authorized activity," said a former senior FBI official, "but the DOJ decided not to put it out." FBI supervisors fielded calls from dozens of the bureau's fifty-six field offices. "We started getting questions," said the former official. "People were asking, 'What are you guys doing?'"

The former official said that the bureau should have been much more aggressive regarding communications, but DOJ policy generally prohibits disclosure of investigative information outside of court documents. "We couldn't tell anyone why we executed the search: there were top secret documents, sitting in unguarded rooms, where people go to parties on weekends."

Several days after the search, Trump's lawyers made a motion to release the search warrant, a step that prosecutors welcomed because it would allow them to make public the evidence they had before searching Mar-a-Lago. "After they filed the motion that opened the door, we had days to respond and we wanted to beef it up as much as possible," the former FBI official recalled.

After the morning briefing attended by senior DOJ and FBI officials, a small group stayed behind to discuss the Mar-a-Lago case. They decided to include a photo in the DOJ motion showing some of the classified documents that had been found.

FBI agents came up with a half dozen potential photos. Ultimately, prosecutors chose to include an image of classified documents lying on the flowered carpet in Trump's office. Agents had stacked them there as they searched the closet in Trump's office and found classified document after classified document. The photo—instantly circulated nationwide and worldwide—became iconic.

"We had more pictures but we didn't put them out. The take was that it was gratuitous. It was rubbing his face in it," recalled the former senior FBI official, who supports the bureau making more evidence public before trial in certain cases. "We told them, 'this is an exceptional case. We have people attacking offices.' To me, this is something that we need to reconsider in today's political climate."

On August 12, more court documents related to the case were released. They showed that eleven sets of classified documents were taken from Trump's property. A warrant also stated that the DOJ had probable cause to believe there were possible violations of the Espionage Act, which makes it a crime to release information that could harm national security.

"Adding that one picture of the documents spread on the floor, that is the most impactful thing that came out in our court filing," said the former senior FBI official. "In my mind, it put water on the fire. Even a lay person can look at it and say, 'Holy shit, that shouldn't be in his closet.'"

A current DOJ official agreed. "It's within appropriate norms but there aren't blinders on," said the official, referring to the realities of a 24/7 and highly partisan cable and social media environment. "That's why we put that picture in."

Current and former FBI officials said they were in favor of taking such steps because they believed that they could help the DOJ and FBI maintain the trust of some members of the public when false claims were made against them. "To me, one point of self-criticism is that we don't find a way to talk about the investigations that are critical for the country," said the former senior FBI official, who noted that law enforcement agencies often hold press conferences to update the public regarding other types of investigations, such as a missing child or a police-involved shooting. The former official called for the DOJ and FBI to loosen their policy of making little to no public

202 WHERE TYRANNY BEGINS

comment in certain high-profile cases. "Especially in times of low trust, silence is not helpful," the former official said. "It hurts us publicly and it hurts us internally. We're still struggling with it."

He said morale remained mixed at the FBI. "Awareness of the constant criticism is always there when decisions are being made and people are very aware of what the reactions will be" said the former official. "The concern is that people may become afraid to make the tough, yet correct, decisions for fear of the reaction."

Fatigue from relentless and systematic political attacks from Trump, Republicans, and a growing number of Democrats has risen in recent years. "It didn't happen in a vacuum. It's in the wake of the Hillary Clinton emails, Crossfire Hurricane, Carter Page FISA, and the profiling of Chinese nationals. And it's on and on. And now Biden has documents. And now Pence," the former senior FBI official said. "It's just one after the other after the other. You just know you're going to get yelled at by someone. And someone is going to defund you. There just doesn't seem to be enough stability left in Congress."

FOUR DAYS AFTER the release of the court-approved Mar-a-Lago search warrant, Steven D'Antuono, the former head of the Washington field office, was the focus of a conspiratorial monologue by Fox News host Tucker Carlson. Carlson falsely suggested that D'Antuono, who had tried to delay the Mar-a-Lago search internally, was part of a secret FBI plot to charge innocent Trump supporters with attempting to kidnap Michigan governor Gretchen Whitmer and to carry out the January 6 attack.

"The guy who made sure that FBI informants were active during a rally in the Michigan State House in 2020 as part of this concocted plot," Carlson said, referring to the Whitmer kidnap cases. "That same guy went on to become the guy who oversaw the investigation into—wait for it—January 6, the election justice protest they're calling an insurrection."

D'Antuono said that in DC and Detroit, and throughout his

twenty-seven years working as an FBI public corruption agent, he had been factual, ethical, and nonpartisan. He expressed bitterness about the impact of partisan cable news attacks on his family. "God and country for twenty-seven years and then you get blasted by Tucker Carlson and Jesse Watters and called corrupt," he said. "And my parents have been forced to see that. And my kids. That's not right. That's not right."

In his mind, D'Antuono's work for the FBI was akin to that of a baseball umpire trying to enforce the rules of the game fairly and consistently to prevent chaos. "All I was trying to do was call a good game," he said. "All I was trying to do was to keep both teams from killing each other."

CHAPTER 14

DELAY

THREE WEEKS AFTER THE RAID, DOJ AND FBI OFFICIALS found themselves facing an unexpected new challenge and adversary. On September 5, 2022, a federal judge in Florida issued a twenty-four-page decision that was a sweeping legal and political victory for Trump. Judge Aileen M. Cannon ordered that a neutral third party, or "special master," review the department's seizure of documents from Mar-a-Lago.

While the judge cited "the appearance of fairness" as her primary goal, the ruling served to bolster Trump's claim that he was the victim of a nefarious plot by FBI agents, whom he had started publicly calling "vicious monsters." Following a familiar playbook, Trump began spreading conspiracy theories, claiming that hidden forces—not his own refusal to return the documents—had forced the Justice Department and FBI officials to act. He warned in one social media post, "They are being pushed to do the wrong things by many sinister and evil outside sources."

Legal experts found the ruling alarming for other reasons. Cannon ordered Justice Department officials to immediately stop "reviewing and using the seized materials for investigative purposes" until the special master's review had been completed. Court battles over who should serve as special master and whether that person's review was fair could drag on for weeks. The ruling helped Trump employ a legal tactic from his days in New York: delay.

The ruling, in essence, froze the DOJ investigation in place. Normally, law enforcement officials would try to issue subpoenas, interview witnesses, and gather additional evidence. All those steps were delayed by Cannon's ruling.

In a separate finding, Cannon contended that Trump might have the power to block prosecutors from presenting certain documents in court because they were protected under executive privilege. Trump and his lawyers had floated that argument after the search, but legal experts had scoffed at it. They said past Supreme Court rulings had clearly established that the power to assert executive privilege lies only with the current president, not former ones.

Other experts noted a passage in Cannon's ruling where she said that Trump deserved special consideration because he is a former president. "As a function of Plaintiff's former position as president of the United States, the stigma associated with the subject seizure is in a league of its own," Cannon wrote. "A future indictment, based to any degree on property that ought to be returned, would result in reputational harm of a decidedly different order of magnitude."

Ryan Goodman, a New York University law professor, told the New York Times that Cannon had gone too far in defending the president who had appointed her. Halting the investigation was a drastic step that she did not have to take. "Judge Cannon had a reasonable path she could have taken—to appoint a special master to review documents for attorney-client privilege and allow the criminal investigation to continue otherwise. Instead, she chose a radical path."

Bill Barr, the former attorney general, criticized Cannon as well, but hedged. His reaction reflected how differently Republicans and Democrats continued to see Trump. Barr said that there was evidence that the former president had acted improperly but it was not clear if he had committed a crime. "The government has very strong evidence," Barr said. "Government documents were taken, classified information was taken and not handled appropriately." He added, "And there is some evidence to suggest—that they were deceived."

Barr argued, though, that Trump should not be charged, due to the impact that prosecuting a former president would have on the country. "I hope they don't do it," he said.

IN THE WAKE OF Cannon's ruling, Justice Department officials faced a decision. They had to decide whether to appeal Cannon's order to the Eleventh Circuit Court of Appeals, based in Atlanta. Six of that panel's eleven active judges were Trump appointees. If the DOJ lost there, it could appeal to the Supreme Court, where three of his appointees make up half of its six-justice conservative supermajority. If the DOJ lost in all those cases, legal precedent would be set that strengthened Trump's defense and could give former presidents new powers.

More broadly, legal experts feared that Cannon's ruling would further undermine the American public's trust in judges as neutral, nonpartisan arbiters. A series of Supreme Court rulings—particularly the overturn of *Roe v. Wade*—had driven down Democrat approval of the court. Trump, meanwhile, publicly categorized judges based on the president who had appointed them. He derided judges who ruled against him as "Obama judges" or "corrupt judges." Legal experts feared that Democratic anger at the Supreme Court and Trump's attacks would exacerbate public skepticism about the fairness of the court system.

What was pernicious about Trump's approach was that his systematic dismissal of judges as biased or on the take played on many Americans' long-standing, and often justifiable, distrust of government. Legal experts feared that Trump's long-term goal was to erode public trust in the courts: the branch of government that most aggressively and consistently rejected his false claims that the 2020 election was stolen. "Judges are in some ways, the last wall," Charles Gardner Geyh, a law professor at Indiana University, told the *Washington Post* after eighty-six federal and state judges rejected Trump's claims of election fraud in the 2020 election.

Geyh said that public support of the court system "remains precarious" in the United States. Gallup polls, for example, showed that public trust in the Supreme Court had declined from 58 percent in

2020 to 40 percent in 2023. "The Supreme Court is the flagship of the
federal judiciary," Geyh said. "If public confidence in the Supreme
Court is flagging, my fear is that support for the courts generally can
be dragged down with it."

Cannon's ruling also raised the possibility that judges in lower
federal courts would rule in a partisan fashion as well. Trump had
appointed a record number of federal judges, 245 of a total of roughly
800. Conservatives, meanwhile, feared the judicial activism of liberal
judges. Barr, an observant Catholic who opposes abortion, viewed
Roe v. Wade as liberal judicial activism where judges unilaterally
changed public policy instead of politicians elected by the majority
of voters doing so via new laws.

In his ruling rejecting Trump's claims of voter fraud in 2020, conservative Wisconsin State Supreme Court Justice Brian Hagedorn
warned other judges about using their power as jurists in a clearly
partisan fashion. The credibility of the courts as neutral, Hagedorn
argued, was a linchpin of American democracy. "The loss of public
trust in our constitutional order resulting from the exercise of this
kind of judicial power would be incalculable," he wrote.

TAKING A RISK and displaying faith in federal judges, DOJ officials
appealed Cannon's ruling to the Eleventh Circuit Court of Appeals
in Atlanta. Two weeks after Cannon's ruling, three Appeals Court
judges issued a twenty-nine-page ruling. Two Trump appointees,
Judges Britt C. Grant and Andrew L. Brasher, joined a Barack Obama
appointee, Judge Robin S. Rosenbaum, in unanimously reversing
Cannon's decision and allowing the DOJ to resume its investigation.

In a blistering opinion, the two Trump appointees rebuked Cannon, and Trump himself. They dismissed the former president's
claim that he had declassified the documents, writing that Trump
"suggests that he may have declassified these documents when he
was president," the appeals court wrote. "But the record contains no
evidence that any of these records were declassified." The judges also

flatly denied Trump's request that he and his lawyers, who did not have security clearances, be given access to 103 documents that the DOJ and FBI had identified as having the highest levels of classification due to the secrets they contained. The judges wrote that Trump "has not even attempted to show that he has a need to know the information contained in the classified documents."

Trump declared the ruling unfair and appealed to the US Supreme Court. Five weeks later, in a bland, single-sentence order, the nine justices unanimously rebuked Trump as well. The court rejected a request that the Supreme Court hear his argument that his lawyers should be given access to the 103 classified documents.

The former president's Supreme Court loss was no surprise to legal analysts who had predicted he would lose. "Trump is asking the Supreme Court for relief so small as to make it almost difficult to describe, and he's doing it based upon an incredibly technical legal argument," Steve Vladeck, a law professor at the University of Texas, wrote before the justices ruled. "Simply put, because his lawyers are (smartly) sticking to plausible legal arguments rather than the conspiratorial fantasies of their client and his supporters, the Supreme Court foray is likely to amount to very little."

After the ruling, Vladeck predicted that Trump would continue appealing to the nine Supreme Court justices, even though a majority of them had ruled against him in the documents case and the 2020 election cases. "I very much doubt it's the end," Vladeck said. "He has little incentive not to try to take each of his losses to the Supreme Court—not because his odds of winning are good but because it helps to both delay and obfuscate the adverse rulings against him in the lower courts."

Vladeck was right. Over time, Trump's Roy Cohn-inspired strategy of delay worked. In the classified documents case, Judge Cannon issued a series of rulings in 2024 that delayed Trump's trial. In the January 6 case, conservative Supreme Court Justices delayed Trump's trial. Led by Justice Samuel Alito, they seriously weighed a legal argument that liberal justices dismissed: that prosecuting Trump would weaken the presidency. America's hyper-partisanship—its two realities—appeared to be steadily infecting its judiciary as well.

Jake Grumbach, a professor of political science at the University of Washington, said that there was a logic to Trump's repeated court battles. Politically, court battles were a win-win for the former president as the DOJ investigation of him continued. If a judge ruled in his favor, Trump could say it showed that the DOJ was persecuting him. If Trump lost, he could say that a corrupt, partisan judge was persecuting him.

Grumbach said that Trump also appeared to be using a tactic embraced by a new generation of strongmen who had emerged in Hungary, Brazil, and several other countries in recent years. "There is also the political dynamic of a political strongman arguing that he is persecuted, and that the rule of law should not apply to him," Grumbach said. "This is a common historical feature of authoritarian leadership."

In Hungary, President Viktor Orbán had consolidated power not by shuttering the courts but by gradually discrediting them. Orban's government had dismissed judges who ruled against him as "traitors," and threatened to fire a judge overseeing investigations into corruption by members of his party.

Ilya Somin, a law professor at George Mason University, noted that the claims and legal positions adopted by Trump and his lawyers regarding the 2020 election and the Mar-a-Lago search have bordered on the legally ludicrous. "In some cases, Trump and his supporters make arguments that are so lame that almost any judge would turn them down," Somin said.

Yet Trump's court losses appeared to come with little political cost. Despite the rejection of Trump's false 2020 election claims by federal judges appointed by Republican and Democratic presidents, as well as the conservative-dominated US Supreme Court, opinion polls continued to show that a majority of Republicans believed that Joe Biden had not been legitimately elected president.

Aziz Huq, a law professor at the University of Chicago, said that the courts, no matter how they rule, cannot single-handedly ease the country's polarization: "In a world where over the last twenty-five years the national political scene has become more polarized, the court, no matter what it does, is going to be seen as biased on one side or the other," Huq said.

Nevertheless, Huq argued, the courts, more broadly, as well as universities and the news media, play a vital and constructive role in a democracy by determining basic facts needed for substantive political debate. "A standard view of democracy is that it's not just that you have elections," Huq said. "You also need a number of institutions that are providing ground truth so we can have a debate about fact."

CHAPTER 15

SILVER BULLETS

AS THE FEDERAL CRIMINAL INVESTIGATION OF TRUMP'S mishandling of classified documents intensified, the former president announced his candidacy for the 2024 Republican presidential nomination. Speaking yards from the bathroom, office closet, and storage space where he had stored dozens of classified documents, Trump declared in a rambling hour-long speech on November 15, 2022, that his run for reelection was about protecting the country.

"In order to make America great and glorious again, I am tonight announcing my candidacy for president of the United States," Trump said. "This will not be my campaign, this will be our campaign all together."

Analysts interpreted Trump's decision to announce his campaign nearly two years before the 2024 election as an effort to discredit the criminal investigation against him as politically motivated election interference. Trump's political standing at the time appeared weak. One week earlier, nearly all of the candidates he had endorsed in the 2022 midterm elections had lost their races—squandering what was widely seen as a golden opportunity for Republicans to gain large majorities in the House and a narrow control of the Senate amid the worst inflation in forty years.

Three days later, Merrick Garland walked onto the same stage that Bill Barr had occupied two and a half years earlier when he released the Mueller report to the public. Three officials, Deputy Attorney

General Lisa Monaco, US Attorney for the District of Columbia Matthew Graves, and Criminal Division Chief Kenneth Polite, stood where Rod Rosenstein and Ed O'Callaghan had. Like their predecessors, Monaco, Graves, and Polite were expressionless, in an effort to convince the public of their impartiality. Standing before a row of US and DOJ flags, Garland read prepared remarks in a monotone.

"Good afternoon. I am here today to announce the appointment of a special counsel in connection with two ongoing criminal investigations that have received significant public attention," Garland said. "The Department of Justice has long recognized that in certain extraordinary cases, it is in the public interest to appoint a special prosecutor to independently manage an investigation and prosecution."

The circumstances were, in fact, extraordinary. Trump—whose supporters stormed the Capitol to prevent Biden from taking office— had just announced that he was running again for president. And Biden had indicated that he, too, planned to seek reelection. Appointing a special counsel, Garland argued, "underscores the department's commitment to both independence and accountability in particularly sensitive matters." Garland was arguing that special counsels could be fair and impartial.

Calling the investigation "sensitive" was an understatement. Never before in US history had a federal prosecutor appointed by the current president criminally prosecuted a former president while they ran against one another. The investigation—and any subsequent trial of Trump—would be the most important prosecution in the roughly 150-year history of the Justice Department.

Whatever else Garland achieved during his tenure as attorney general, the Trump investigation would define his legacy. In his announcement, he continued his efforts to convince Americans that the judicial system was a place where fact, probity, and, most of all, nonpartisan public service still existed. Garland said that the new special counsel he had chosen embodied those very traits.

"Today, I signed an order appointing Jack Smith to serve as special counsel," Garland announced, adding that Smith would take over

Special Counsel Jack Smith's prosecutions of Donald Trump are the most important criminal trials in the history of the Justice Department. (AP PHOTO / JACQUELYN MARTIN, FILE)

two investigations: the January 6 and classified documents cases. "Throughout his career, Jack Smith has built a reputation as an impartial and determined prosecutor, who leads teams with energy and focus to follow the facts wherever they lead."

Garland immediately turned and walked out of the room without taking questions. His seven-minute statement, like so many other addresses in his tenure as attorney general, focused too little on explaining the working of the Justice Department, particularly to younger Americans who had minimal knowledge of the Watergate era.

Garland failed to explain the history of special counsels, the many rules that apply to their conduct, or past controversies regarding their work. He used DOJ catchphrases—"impartial" and "follow the facts wherever they lead"—that mean little to average Americans or, even worse, are dismissed by them as clichéd platitudes. In short, the nation's chief prosecutor failed to make his case to the public. Instead, he left the door open to Trump to define Smith, Garland, and the DOJ.

Within hours, Trump did just that. At a dinner event at Mar-a-

Lago that night, he said, "The corrupt and highly political Justice Department just appointed a super-radical-left, special counsel." He dismissed the ongoing investigations as part of the "never-ending witch hunt" and pointed a finger elsewhere. "If they are going to investigate me, they have to investigate all of these other presidents—and they have to start it right now," he said, claiming that Bill Clinton, George H. W. Bush, George W. Bush, Barack Obama, and Joe Biden should all be prosecuted without saying what crimes they committed. "We're living in a very corrupt country right now—never had anything like it," he said. "Our elections are rigged, tainted, and bad."

Instead of hurting Trump politically, the appointment of Smith strengthened him, a shocking reversal of fifty years of American political orthodoxy. Smith's appointment also unintentionally helped Trump and his allies to immediately shift the narrative away from the widespread defeat of their candidates in the midterms.

Representative Marjorie Taylor Greene, who rose to political power as a Trump acolyte, immediately tweeted "IMPEACH MER-RICK GARLAND!" She also called for Republicans, who had just narrowly won control of the House of Representatives, to cut off all funding to Smith's investigation and "defund any part of the DOJ acting on behalf of the Democrat party as a taxpayer funded campaign arm."

Trump supporters quickly discovered that Smith's wife, Katy Chevigny, a documentary filmmaker, had produced a movie based on former first lady Michelle Obama's *Becoming* book tour and donated $2,000 to President Biden's 2020 campaign. In 2010, she made $70 in donations to MoveOn.org, a progressive group, and ActBlue, a Democratic fundraising organization. The one campaign donation that Smith, a registered independent, appears to have made recently was $25 to Michael Dougherty, a Democrat who was elected district attorney in Boulder, Colorado, in 2018.

"You just can't make this stuff up," Andrew Clyde, a House Republican from Georgia, exulted on social media. "Katy Chevigny, wife of Jack Smith—the special counsel appointed by DOJ to go after President Trump, donated to Joe Biden's campaign and produced Michelle Obama's documentary." He added, "America cannot stand with a corrupt, two-tiered justice system."

Smith's appointment received little of the Republican support that Mueller's did in 2017. In four years in power, Trump's relentless—and effective—messaging had transformed the Republican political landscape when it came to special counsels.

Trump supporters appeared to fully embrace and believe his claims of being victimized by corrupt Democrats and a weaponized Garland Justice Department. And for moderate Republican politicians, supporting Smith was potentially politically fatal. Given Trump's continued hold of the Republican base and willingness to spread conspiracy theories, they feared being ousted by a Trump-backed challenger in a GOP primary.

The contrast to when Rosenstein announced Mueller's appointment was complete. In 2017, then House Speaker Paul Ryan had immediately hailed the new special counsel. "My priority has been to ensure thorough and independent investigations are allowed to follow the facts wherever they may lead," Ryan said at the time, using some of the DOJ's own language. "The addition of Robert Mueller as special counsel is consistent with this goal, and I welcome his role at the Department of Justice."

Senate Majority Leader Mitch McConnell supported Mueller as well and noted that the Republican-controlled Senate Intelligence Committee would "also continue its investigation into this matter."

Even ardent Trump supporters signaled to Americans that Mueller could be trusted. Mark Meadows, the future White House chief of staff and then pro-Trump House Republican, said. "I think he comes with more credibility on the Democrat side than the Republican side," he said. "But he has credibility on both sides."

In 2022, no major Republican endorsed Smith's appointment.

Instead, they echoed Trump's messaging, as they had since the Mar-a-Lago search. Former vice president Mike Pence, who risked his life and his political future by certifying the 2020 election results, criticized the appointment of a special counsel as well. "The timing of this decision—just a few short days after the president announced his intention to seek re-election," Pence said. "I think it is very troubling."

A former Justice Department official who worked during the Trump administration but broke with Trump over his refusal to concede the 2020 election said he saw Smith as an "attack dog" prosecutor. By choosing Smith, the official argued, Garland had preordained a prosecution of Trump, saying, "It's obvious."

UNLIKE MUELLER, SMITH was little known in Washington and completely unknown to Americans. Smith, fifty-four, had grown up in Liverpool, New York, a small upstate town of 2,500 near Syracuse. For college, he attended the State University of New York at Oneonta, studying political science. He was accepted by Harvard Law School, which he graduated from in 1994.

His first job as a prosecutor was with the US Attorney's Office in Brooklyn, where he handled violent crime and sex crime cases. He displayed an attribute that would define his career: doggedness. Smith once spent a weekend sleeping in the hallway of an apartment building so he could convince a woman to take the witness stand in a domestic violence case. After what Smith called a long talk, she did.

Smith also prosecuted cases that both punished and defended police officers. He was one of the federal prosecutors who prosecuted New York police officers who sodomized Abner Louima, a Haitian immigrant, with a broomstick.

From 2008 to 2010, Smith worked in the Netherlands as the investigation coordinator in the Office of the Prosecutor at the International Criminal Court in The Hague. Returning to the United States, Smith headed the Justice Department's Public Integrity Section from 2010 to 2015. One of the department's most fraught positions, the public integrity office investigates corruption by elected officials, voter fraud, and other highly politicized cases. During Smith's tenure, the office prosecuted Republican and Democratic elected officials alike. Smith's track record there was mixed.

In Smith's most high-profile case, he prosecuted former Democratic senator and vice-presidential nominee John Edwards for violating campaign finance laws. The case centered on payments that Edward had made to his mistress, which Smith argued were hush-money payments to keep the relationship secret. In a major setback for Smith, the jury acquitted Edwards of one of the charges and deadlocked on all the remaining charges. Eventually, all the charges were dropped. Under Smith, the unit also convicted Republican governor Bob McDonnell of Virginia of bribery charges but the US Supreme Court, in a unanimous verdict, threw out the verdict, finding that Smith's prosecutors had taken too broad an interpretation of federal bribery laws.

After briefly working as the head of litigation for the Hospital Corporation of America in 2017, one of the country's largest hospital chains, Smith returned to Europe the following year and worked as the chief prosecutor of a special court based in The Hague that investigated war crimes in Kosovo. Before being appointed special counsel in the Trump cases, Smith secretly flew from Europe to Washington, DC, for an in-person interview with Garland.

After Smith's appointment to lead the Trump investigation, he, like Garland, issued a perfunctory statement. "I intend to conduct the assigned investigations, and any prosecutions that may result from them, independently and in the best traditions of the Department of Justice," he wrote.

As Smith took over the most important case of his career, and the most important investigation in the history of the Justice Depart-

ment, little was known about him personally. The only recent photos of Smith showed a seemingly dour, bearded man dressed in the
purple judicial robe worn by officials at the International Criminal
Court. Few records of his private life existed online. Like many federal prosecutors of his age, he apparently shunned social media. In a
2018 interview posted by the Nashville Aquatic Club, Smith spoke in
a matter-of-fact tone about his long history of competing in triathlons
around the world.

"I have been racing since 2002 and did my 100th triathlon
in Miami last November," Smith said. "I had a good day and was
lucky enough to qualify for Team USA; as a result, I will be racing Long Course Triathlon Worlds in Denmark in July and Long
Course Duathlon Worlds in Switzerland in September, both for
Team USA. I have done 9 Ironmans including Kona and over twenty
half Ironmans."

Smith said one of his greatest challenges was recovering from
being hit by a truck while bicycling and fracturing his pelvis a decade
earlier. "While I came back from the injury (raced a triathlon 10
weeks later) it was too much too soon," he said. "The wreck took me
from doing Ironmans in the 10-hour range to doing them in the 12–
13 hour range."

He thanked a trainer for helping him fully recover but reserved his
strongest praise for his family, calling his wife "an amazing, award-
winning documentary filmmaker" and his daughter "a born story-
teller," adding, "I have no doubt she will also be winning awards
very soon."

Several people who Smith investigated as a prosecutor predicted that he would be relentless. James Risen, a former investigative reporter for the *New York Times* who won a Pulitzer Prize for
revealing the Bush administration's post-9/11 warrantless wiretap-
ping of Americans, said Smith repeatedly threatened to jail him if
he did not reveal the identity of his source. The legal siege, which
involved other prosecutors as well and lasted seven years, ended
when Attorney General Eric Holder told the prosecutors to stop

pressuring Risen to reveal his source. "Jack Smith came after me," Risen wrote soon after Garland appointed Smith. "If he goes after Donald Trump with the same unrelenting ferocity, Trump will be in trouble."

TWO WEEKS AFTER Smith was appointed, Stewart Rhodes, the leader of the Oath Keepers militia, was convicted of seditious conspiracy on November 29. The jury found that Rhodes was not guilty of two separate conspiracy charges and it also acquitted three other members of the militia of sedition. But the verdict represented a major victory for the Justice Department. It was the first of the roughly 900 January 6 criminal cases brought by prosecutors that showed that the attack on the Capitol was the product of an organized conspiracy.

Jeffrey Nestler, one of the federal prosecutors who brought the case, argued to jurors that Rhodes and Oath Keeper members "concocted a plan for an armed rebellion to shatter a bedrock of American democracy: the peaceful transfer of presidential power." In his closing arguments, Nestler argued that the men had ignored the will of the voters and federal law, because of their hatred of Trump's defeat. Weeks later, a federal judge sentenced Rhodes, fifty-eight at the time, to sixteen years in federal prison. It was the longest sentence handed down against any January 6 defendant. Conservative cable television hosts decried the sentence as unjust. Liberal cable television hosts cited Rhodes's case as an example of how Trump, too, might face justice.

Trump, though, was more careful than Rhodes, who had made multiple incriminating statements in texts and emails. And, under American law, even if Trump is convicted of a federal crime, he would not be disqualified for running for president. In past rulings, the Supreme Court has found that the requirements for serving as president are only those described in the Constitution: to be thirty-five years old, a natural-born US citizen, and resident of the country for fourteen years. Trump (or any other felon) is not banned from running for president. In 1920, the Socialist candidate for president, Eugene V. Debs, had run for the presidency from his federal prison cell in Atlanta. Two years earlier, Debs had been convicted under the Espionage Act for protesting against World War I and, in legal terms, intentionally obstructing the draft. He was sentenced to three concurrent ten-year sentences. Despite being imprisoned, Debs received nearly a million votes.

If Trump were to win the presidency in 2024, his legal advisors claimed, he could order his attorney general to drop the cases against him or even pardon himself.

A FINAL, UNEXPECTED legal development also aided Trump: Joe Biden became embroiled in a classified documents investigation of his own. Asked by reporters on August 29 about Trump's assertion that he had declassified all of the documents that he stored in Mar-a-Lago, Biden mocked the claim. "I just want you to know I've declassified everything in the world. I'm President, I can do—c'mon," Biden said as he was departing the White House.

But two months later, Biden found out that he, too, mishandled classified documents. On November 2, six days before the midterm elections, Biden's personal lawyers found several classified documents in a locked closet in the Penn Biden Center, a think tank in Washington where Biden had kept an office after leaving the vice presidency. The lawyers, who were in the process of closing Biden's office there, immediately notified the National Archives about the documents, which were from the Obama administration. But they did not contact the FBI.

On November 3, officials from the National Archives retrieved the documents. On November 4, they informed the Justice Department about the discovery. The Biden White House, meanwhile, kept the fact that Biden had mishandled classified documents secret.

Special Counsel Robert Hur lambasted Joe Biden's handling of classified documents. (AP Photo / Alex Brandon, File)

Four days later, on November 8, 2022, Biden and the Democratic party had one of the strongest midterm election showings by the party of an incumbent president in decades. The day after the midterms, the FBI began an assessment of whether classified information had been mishandled. On November 9, FBI agents searched the Penn Biden Center themselves.

Five weeks later, on December 20, Biden's personal lawyer informed the DOJ that a second batch of classified documents had been discovered in the garage of Biden's home in Wilmington. FBI agents retrieved the documents.

On January 9, 2023, CBS News finally broke the story that documents with classified markings had been found at the Penn Biden Center. For two months, the White House had managed to keep the story secret. In response to the CBS story, White House officials said "a small number" of Obama administration records, including some with classified markings, were discovered at the center. They did not reveal that additional classified documents had been found in Biden's Wilmington home.

Three days later, from the same stage where Garland announced Smith's appointment as special counsel, the attorney general appointed Robert Hur as special counsel to investigate Biden's handling of classified documents. "I am confident that Mr. Hur will carry out his responsibility in an even-handed and urgent manner, and in accordance with the highest traditions of this Department," said Garland.

Trump had mishandled more classified documents, roughly one hundred, compared to approximately ten mishandled by Biden. And while Trump was accused of obstructing attempts by National Archive officials to recover the documents, Biden had immediately handed them over. Trump had kept the case secret until the FBI searched his home. Biden had kept the case secret until the story leaked to the press. The Biden White House's decision weakened their claims that Trump was an outlier. Supporters of the former president said he was yet again being held to a higher standard.

Rosenstein, who had supervised Hur in the past, offered some advice to him. "I think the key when you're in this position is to just tune out all the media and all the politics and keep focus on the facts."

CHAPTER 16

UNINTENDED
CONSEQUENCES

T HROUGHOUT 2023, A MASSIVE BATTLE TO SWAY AMER-
ican public opinion played out on cable TV and online. Conservative TV pundits cast every indictment of Trump as devious.
Liberal pundits cast an indictment of Trump as a silver bullet for
Trumpism. Neither was true.

On April 4, Manhattan district attorney Alvin Bragg indicted
Trump on charges of falsifying business records as part of a hush-
money scheme. Bragg said that Trump, through his personal attorney
Michael Cohen, paid women he had affairs with to remain silent
during the 2016 election. While the allegations were titillating, they
had been widely reported in the press years earlier. The arrival and
arraignment of Trump in Manhattan sparked helicopter live shots,
but Bragg's case was seen as weak and playing into Trump's narrative
that he was being persecuted by Democratic prosecutors.

As the year progressed, though, the primary legal threat to Trump
remained Smith and his prosecutors. Smith assembled a small
team of prosecutors, many of whom had been working on the various Trump investigations. They included J. P. Cooney and Thomas
Windom, who had aggressively investigated the January 6 case. Jay
Bratt and George Toscas, the National Security Division prosecutors whose approach to the Mar-a-Lago search was criticized by FBI
agents, joined Smith's team as well.

On June 8, a federal grand jury in Miami handed down an indictment that charged the former president with thirty-seven criminal counts, including thirty-one counts of willfully retaining national defense information under the Espionage Act and one count of making false statements to federal investigators. Walt Nauta, a former White House valet to Trump who now worked as his assistant in Florida, was indicted on six counts and accused of trying to help Trump obstruct investigators.

Smith, perhaps learning from past mistakes, had been conservative in his charging decisions. Legal analysts said that the indictment was narrowly focused, and that Smith appeared to charge Trump only with crimes where strong evidence existed to make a case to a jury. Smith did not, for example, charge Trump with the crime FBI agents feared—violating Section 2071 of Title 18, which makes it a crime if someone who possesses government documents "willfully and unlawfully conceals, removes, mutilates, obliterates, falsifies or destroys" them. If a person is convicted of that charge, the statute states that they "shall . . . be disqualified from holding" any federal office.

One of the most surprising revelations in the indictment was an allegation that Trump had shown a classified document to a visitor in July 2021 at his golf resort in Bedminster, New Jersey. The visitor, who was reportedly writing a book about Mark Meadows, recorded the conversation with Trump. On the tape, Trump is heard showing off and describing a "plan of attack" against Iran that he said was prepared for him by the Department of Defense and a senior military official. Trump told the individuals that the plan was "highly confidential" and "secret." Trump then added, "As president I could have declassified it," he said. "Now I can't, you know, but this is still a secret."

Trump acknowledging—on tape—that a document was classified and that he lacked the power to declassify was a powerful piece of evidence for prosecutors, who could play the recording to the jury. Trump himself had undermined his long-running contention that he declassified all the documents he took to Mar-a-Lago before leaving office.

The forty-nine-page indictment also included multiple photos that showed boxes of documents stored in a bathroom, a ballroom, beneath a water pipe, and in a storage room. One image showed a box that had toppled over and spilled its contents on the floor.

The use of the photos in the indictment suggested that Smith and his team had seen the impact of the photo of classified documents strewn across the floor that prosecutors released after the search of Mar-a-Lago. A new DOJ approach where prosecutors made their cases to the broader public—not just in the courtroom during the trial—was gaining the upper hand inside the DOJ.

Smith made his first public appearance since being named special counsel. Unsmiling and stern, Smith delivered a somber three-minute address to television cameras. Dressed in a gray suit and blue tie, Smith was far less telegenic and entertaining than the former president he had just indicted.

Smith began his statement by saying that Trump's behavior had risked American lives. "The men and women of the United States intelligence community and our armed forces dedicate their lives to protecting our nation and its people," he said. "Our laws that protect national defense information are critical to the safety and security of the United States and they must be enforced."

Smith then spoke about the importance of accountability. "Adherence to the rule of law is a bedrock principle of the Department of Justice. And our nation's commitment to the rule of law sets an example for the world," Smith said. "We have one set of laws in this country, and they apply to everyone."

Five days later in Miami, Trump was booked and fingerprinted, and led to a courtroom in a federal courthouse for arraignment. As he sat nearby with a grim expression on his face and his arms crossed, his lawyer entered a not guilty plea on the former president's behalf. About twenty feet away in the courtroom, Smith, the special counsel, sat alongside other spectators in a rare public appearance. The two men did not exchange glances or speak to one another.

Two weeks later, new charges against Trump, Nauta, and a second Mar-a-Lago employee, Carlos De Oliveira, were added to the federal indictment in Florida. The allegations deepened Trump's legal jeopardy.

The new charges emerged after Yuscil Taveras, an information technology worker at Mar-a-Lago, agreed to become a cooperating witness for Smith's prosecutors. Taveras, who had declined to cooperate when he was represented by a lawyer paid by Trump, offered new testimony after changing lawyers.

Taveras told investigators that De Oliveira pushed him to find a way to delete Mar-a-Lago surveillance camera footage at the request of "the boss," a reference to Trump. The footage allegedly showed employees moving boxes before Bratt, the DOJ prosecutor, and two FBI agents arrived in Mar-a-Lago for a meeting with Trump's lawyers.

Taveras's account strengthened what was already one of the strongest charges in the indictment: that Trump had tried to obstruct the federal investigation into his retention of classified documents. Taveras's new testimony was further evidence that lawyers paid by Trump were apparently discouraging witnesses from cooperating with prosecutors. Jody Hunt, the former DOJ lawyer who represented Cassidy Hutchinson and warned that the system of legal representation could have the effect of silencing witnesses, was proven right.

TWO WEEKS LATER, on August 1, Smith indicted Trump on four counts related to the attempt to overturn the results of the 2020 presidential election. Smith charged Trump with conspiracy to defraud the United States, witness tampering, obstruction of an official proceeding, and conspiracy against the rights of citizens. The charges were the most serious, legally and politically, that the former president faced.

The final charge was in some ways the most telling. By citing a post–Civil War statute that makes it a federal crime to limit someone's right to vote, Smith, in the words of one former prosecutor, was creating a way to "tell jurors a story." The charge allowed Smith's prosecutors to argue that Trump's scheme to name fake electors in seven states was an effort to nullify the votes of tens of millions of voters who reside there.

"The attack on our nation's capital on January 6, 2021, was an unprecedented assault on the seat of American democracy," Smith said in a brief public statement. "It was fueled by lies. Lies by the defendant targeted at obstructing a bedrock function of the US government, the nation's process of collecting, counting, and certifying the results of the presidential election."

Legal experts noted that Smith did not file charges against Trump that would be difficult to prove, such as inciting an insurrection or seditious conspiracy, given that Trump did not enter the Capitol himself.

Smith also included flexibility in the indictment by including six of Trump's associates as co-conspirators, but not formally indicting them. Prosecutors could pressure the six to cooperate or face being charged. They could also choose not to indict the six and to only prosecute Trump, which would result in a streamlined, fast-moving trial with only one defendant: the former president.

Finally, observers praised the speed with which Smith brought charges. Past special counsels and independent counsels had been criticized for costly investigations that dragged on for years, casting shadows over presidencies.

Within months, however, the euphoria that Smith's long-awaited January 6 indictments brought to Trump opponents had faded. The US Supreme Court agreed in a one-page unsigned order to consider a request from Trump that Smith's charges be thrown out.

The former president claimed that he was immune from prosecution for any actions that he took while in office. The only process that could hold a president accountable, Trump argued, was being impeached by Congress.

The justices fast-tracked the case for oral arguments, but legal experts and Trump opponents feared that Trump's favorite legal tactic—delay—was working.

FIVE YEARS AFTER Donald Trump ousted him as attorney general, Jeff Sessions lives in a tastefully decorated home with his wife, Mary, in Mobile, Alabama. A few feet from a wall full of photos of his grandchildren sits the chair that Sessions occupied in the US Senate from 1997 to 2017.

During that twenty-year span, Sessions was Alabama's most powerful federal official, so popular in the deep-red state that Democrats didn't bother to run a candidate against him in 2014. A few feet away sits what Sessions calls his "cabinet chair," the seat he occupied during White House cabinet meetings when he served as Donald Trump's attorney general.

During our interview, Sessions pointed out the two chairs with a sense of pride. But my conversation with him over a homemade lunch of chicken salad and fresh lemonade revealed deeply partisan perceptions of reality that divide Americans.

At the beginning of the conversation, which took place the day after Jack Smith indicted Trump for trying to reverse the outcome of the 2020 election, Sessions stood by his decision to recuse himself from the Mueller investigation—a choice that infuriated Trump and ended Sessions's decades-long political career.

Trump, after leaving the White House, continued to publicly humiliate Sessions for not shutting down Mueller's special counsel investigation. When Sessions attempted to reclaim in 2020 the Senate seat he gave up in 2017, Trump backed his Republican rival, former Auburn University football coach Tommy Tuberville, and scorned Sessions.

Tuberville trounced Sessions in the Republican primary, winning by roughly 60 to 40 percent.

Despite the humiliations, Sessions continues to defend Trump. In the hyper-partisan landscape of American politics, he remained in Trump's camp. Cognitive dissonance seemed to dominate him when he spoke of the former president. "He did cross some lines on January 6," Sessions said, but he also contended that calling the events that day "an insurrection" was an exaggeration. Sessions dismissed the idea that Trump represented a serious threat to American democracy, describing him as a "blunderbuss."

He expressed disappointment in Garland and Smith, saying they were badly damaging the reputation of the DOJ by being politically biased in their investigations of Trump. Sessions saw the investigation of Hunter Biden as a more serious case. "It is the biggest public corruption case of my lifetime," Sessions maintained. "I could prosecute Hunter myself."

SESSIONS'S VIEWS REFLECTED how the criminal investigation of Donald Trump has unfolded in a way completely different from the criminal investigation of Richard Nixon. The country is so deeply polarized a half century after Watergate that many Americans seem to trust their political party more than the Justice Department, the FBI, or any prosecutor. Division and distrust threaten to gradually paralyze both organizations, where career law enforcement officials are increasingly suspicious of one another.

In the Hunter Biden case, two IRS agents, Gary Shapley and Joseph Ziegler, came forward as whistleblowers. They accused David Weiss, the US attorney in Delaware, and other DOJ officials of blocking them from pursuing investigative leads and slow-walking their investigation of the president's son. House Republicans seized on the two men's accounts and argued that Joe Biden himself was guilty of crimes. Garland denied that the Hunter Biden investigation was slowed in any way.

The same sense of distrust between agents and prosecutors that occurred in the Mar-a-Lago case unfolded in the Hunter Biden case. And even after Hunter Biden was criminally charged, partisans weren't satisfied. To Trump supporters, the Justice Department, by moving slowly, was going easy on Hunter Biden. To Trump opponents, the Justice Department, by moving slowly, was going easy on Trump.

The American criminal justice system has never been a perfect arbiter of fact. It has also never been a source of political unity. Large numbers of false convictions and confessions, particularly of Black and Latino Americans, have shown its systemic biases and failures. During Watergate, though, criminal charges and trials were seen as politically damaging, often fatally.

A confluence of factors—growing distrust in government and the mainstream media, a sense among working-class Americans that the wealthy have abandoned them, partisan gerrymandering, the rise of social media, inflammatory cable TV punditry, and Trump's willingness to win at all costs—have riven the country. Instead of Donald Trump and Hunter Biden being put on trial, the Justice Department, in many ways, was put on trial.

After weeks of riveting testimony in the New York hush-money case, a Manhattan jury found the former president guilty of thirty-four felony counts of falsifying business records in May 2024. Trump's conviction confirmed Trump supporters' views that the New York and DOJ prosecutors were politically biased.

Two weeks later, a Delaware jury found Hunter Biden guilty of three felony counts of violating federal gun laws. Defenders of the DOJ cited the prosecution by Weiss, who Garland had made a special counsel, as proof that the DOJ is not politically biased, no one is above the law, and Trump's claims of "rigged" trials were patently false.

Privately, prosecutors say that a criminal trial is not the best arena in which to resolve the country's political divisions. Prosecutions are not silver bullets and can have unintended consequences. "We are talking about the criminal justice system, which has certain requirements and rules, which are very exacting," said a DOJ official who asked not to be named. "We have to follow them."

"The critique of Trump is primarily a political one," the official added. "It is better addressed by the political system. It was not a good fit for the criminal justice system."

MANY OF THE CAREER civil servants in the DOJ and FBI who spoke with me for this book have given up on public service as a career. They fear that that the scorched-earth political wars of the Trump era will result in fewer and fewer Americans being willing to work as public servants.

Jody Hunt, Jeff Sessions's former chief of staff and the head of the DOJ's Civil Division, left Washington and moved back to Alabama, where he is the general counsel of his alma mater, Samford University in Birmingham. On April 25, 2024, Hunt attended in person the Supreme Court's oral arguments regarding Trump's claim that former presidents are immune from prosecution for any crime they commit in office.

"Sitting in the courtroom, I could not stop thinking about how remarkable it was that we were there listening to an argument about whether a former president, who once had been elected by the people, could now escape criminal responsibility for his efforts to undermine the will of the people in order to retain his position and power," Hunt said. "That has never happened in the history of our great nation—nor should it."

Bill Barr, the former attorney general, took the opposite approach. After three years of harshly criticizing Trump for refusing to accept that he lost the 2020 election, Barr reverted to the partisanship that marked his tenure and announced that he would vote for Trump in 2024.

"The real danger to the country—the real danger to democracy, as I say, is the progressive agenda," Barr said in an April 2024 Fox News interview. He added that supporting "Trump may be playing

Russian roulette, but a continuation of the Biden administration is national suicide."

Sarah Isgur, the spokesperson for the DOJ under Sessions, finds it heartbreaking to watch the leaders of the Justice Department, an institution she reveres, make decisions that make sense in legal terms but seem politically tone-deaf to her. She believes a core problem is the lack of political experience among the officials who run the DOJ, whom she described as "lawyers who read the news and think that they know politics." She sees the Trump and Biden years at the DOJ as a Greek tragedy. "You're watching this institution you love blunder over and over again," she said. "When they get attacked, the tendency is to huddle together and say nothing."

Ed O'Callaghan, the senior Rosenstein aide who helped over-see the Mueller investigation, believes that the rules regarding the appointment of a special counsel need to be tightened. To prevent special counsel investigations from dragging on indefinitely, O'Callaghan argues that a five-year limitation—the same statute of limitations on many federal cases—should be applied to them. O'Callaghan also suggested that the attorney general issue a new regulation that defines in greater detail what justifies the appointment of a special counsel.

O'Callaghan, now a partner at the white-shoe law firm Wilmer-Hale, worries that experienced people with good judgment will no longer be willing to work in the Justice Department. Whatever decision they make, he said, will be attacked by partisans who want to use the DOJ as a political punching bag. "It's going to be difficult to get people to serve in the right positions," O'Callaghan said.

Steven D'Antuono, the FBI agent who tried to slow the FBI search of Mar-a-Lago, retired from the bureau in the spring of 2023. Now working in the private sector, D'Antuono fears that the spread of false information and conspiracy theories online is eroding public trust in the FBI and other government institutions.

"I do believe we've become a shadow of where we were a decade ago," he said. "The more you continue to chip away at the foundation, the more there's a possibility of those foundations crumbling," he said. "I think the internet has ruined us as a society."

Nate Huber, the FBI intelligence instructor who flatly rejects Trump's claims of political bias in the bureau, left the FBI for a job in the private sector in 2022. His departure was caused in part by his embrace of remote work during the pandemic, which gave him more time with his family. Another factor caused him to leave as well: Trump's constant attacks on the FBI. "During the Trump years, it was just exhausting seeing the things said against the bureau, and the bashing of the bureau," he said.

Huber believes Congress should make it more difficult for presidents to fire FBI directors, suggesting that they only be removed for cause, or clear, verifiable misconduct. After departing from the FBI, he decided to fight the conspiracy theories he saw on social media. For the first time in his life, he was openly political, posting messages on X that attacked Trump, Elon Musk, and their supporters. In response, he received a torrent of attacks. "Boy, did that open up the floodgates," he said. "They said I was a Nazi." He gave up trying to defend the FBI on X but still tries to do so on other platforms.

The former senior FBI official involved in the Mar-a-Lago case who asked not to be named called for the FBI and DOJ to adapt to the times. The official said both organizations should communicate more openly with Americans to counter conspiracy theories.

"The only way they are going to trust us is through transparency. We need to do a better job of explaining to the American people—and internally to the FBI—why certain things are done," the former official said. "Our traditional way of communicating is struggling to keep up in an era of disinformation and an over-politicized climate," he told me. "In exceptional circumstances, you need to make exceptions."

Erica Newland, the former career DOJ lawyer in the Office of Legal Counsel, now works as counsel at Protect Democracy, a non-profit group where she focuses on creating guardrails that protect the rule of law and on secure accountability for abuses of power.

Newland said that she regrets her work in the Trump DOJ and she stands by what she wrote in the final passage of her op-ed in the *New York Times*. "We owe the country our honesty about that and about what we saw. We owe apologies. I offer mine here," she wrote, before concluding with a vow and a warning: "to lead by example and do everything in our power to ensure this never happens again. If we don't, it will."

EPILOGUE

EQUAL JUSTICE

RICHARD NIXON WAS REPUDIATED BY MEMBERS OF HIS own party, the Supreme Court, and the American public. When 57 percent of Americans polled supported his removal from office and Republican members of Congress told him that he would likely be impeached, Nixon resigned.

For the next fifty years, no president, Republican or Democrat, from Gerald Ford to Barack Obama, dared to interfere overtly in a federal criminal investigation, apparently fearing Nixon's fate. Donald Trump single-handedly rewrote American political orthodoxy, retaining deep political support in his party through two impeachments, the January 6 assault on the Capitol, and scores of criminal indictments. Criminal charges and felony convictions, in fact, helped him politically.

After Special Counsel Jack Smith indicted Trump twice in 2023, Republican political support for the former president increased. Public opinion polls found that 75 percent of Americans—and 87 percent of Republicans—had some, little, or no confidence in the Justice Department. Trump has discredited federal investigators in a way Nixon never dreamed.

Timothy Naftali, the founding director of the Nixon Presidential Library and Museum, said that Trump has survived because he is different from Nixon in one critical way. "Richard Nixon had not only a sense of history, but a sense of shame," said Naftali, now a senior research scholar at the Columbia School of International and Public Affairs. "Donald Trump has never been a student of history and has no sense of shame. He has no interest in protecting the honor of the presidency and clearly does not fear dishonor. It's honor and shame that has kept our system on the rails."

Naftali, who has studied multiple American presidencies, said that the drafters of the Constitution left some areas of governance poorly defined. "The founding generation thought that people could be restrained by shame and dishonor. We finally elected a president who was shameless and didn't care about presidential norms. That's the unique threat of the Trumpian personality."

Trump continues to maintain that he is the true defender of democracy and the victim of a vast plot by Democrats, judges, election workers, journalists, his own vice president, and his own Supreme Court nominees to steal the 2020 election from him. The former president and his allies have argued in court that a sitting president is immune from criminal prosecution—even if he assassinates a rival.

Trump said he would, if re-elected, implement Executive Order 13957, a measure that would strip hundreds of thousands of career federal workers of their civil service protections, allowing officials like Jody Hunt and Erica Newland to be quickly fired by the president. It would also expand the number of people the president personally appoints from roughly four thousand to hundreds of thousands, giving Trump one of the largest patronage machines in U.S. history.

Trump and his allies vowed to appoint special counsels to investigate Joe Biden, Jack Smith, Merrick Garland, Bill Barr, Chris Wray, Liz Cheney, and other rivals. He will establish a new "election integrity office" in the Justice Department to investigate his belief that the 2020 election was stolen. He has promised to free those convicted of storming the Capitol on January 6, whom he calls "hostages." Whatever Trump's motivations or mental state, his intentions are clear if he regains the presidency.

As I wrote in my last book, *In Deep*, the American presidency has grown ever more powerful since the 9/11 attacks, with both Republican and Democratic presidents embracing executive power when faced with national security threats or partisan gridlock. Trump took this to a new extreme, claiming far more executive branch power and privilege than any of his post-Watergate predecessors.

Many chapters of American history, such as the tenures of J. Edgar Hoover, A. Mitchell Palmer, and Richard Nixon, show that the concentration of power—combined with secrecy—is a recipe for abuse. The continued pursuit of executive power by presidents is a route to authoritarianism.

CAREER DOJ OFFICIALS were slow to recognize the dangers that Trump presented to public trust in the department they loved. From the travel ban to Sessions's recusal from the Trump-Russia investigation, they were unsure how to respond to him. Political appointees, such as Jeff Sessions and William Barr, saw Trump as a way to enact policies they long supported. They also appear to sincerely view Republicans, conservatives, and religiously observant Americans, in general, as under political and cultural siege from a dominant and dangerous American Left.

To their credit, many Trump political appointees eventually defied Trump. When Trump threatened core functions of the rule of law and American democracy—recusal from investigations and the peaceful transfer of power—Sessions, Barr, Rod Rosenstein, and other officials broke with him. When Trump then tried to seize control of the Justice Department on January 3 and install Jeffrey Clark as attorney general, the threat of a mass resignation by Jeff Rosen, Richard Donoghue, and multiple other senior officials stopped him. Days later, Trump struck again on January 6.

When Merrick Garland took office as attorney general in 2021, one of his most important missions was to use the singular fact-finding powers of the Justice Department to determine whether or not Trump had committed a crime during and after his time in office. Garland and many of his advisors, like so many of us, underestimated Trump and the need to rapidly investigate him.

The 1970s Justice Department norms that Garland wanted to reinforce also inadvertently helped Trump. The strict rules barring the DOJ and FBI from investigating any individual or group due to their political beliefs—measures designed to prevent a repeat of the abuses of J. Edgar Hoover and Nixon—unintentionally resulted in a slower, narrower, more cautious investigation of the organizers of the January 6 "Stop the Steal" rally and Trump himself.

Garland's determination to avoid even the smallest of legal mistakes, as the *New York Times* noted, may have resulted in Garland making one large error: failing to recognize that Trump could use delay to avoid being tried before election day. Despite his good intent, Garland may fail at one of his primary responsibilities as attorney general: the public fact-finding that comes from a trial and verdict.

At the same time, Democrats and liberal legal pundits relied too heavily on a belief that criminally indicting Trump would act as a political panacea and instantly reduce his popularity with voters. They also underestimated the complexity of prosecuting a former president. "These are the most complex, most important trials in American history," said Danny Cevallos, a criminal defense lawyer and legal analyst. "Delays are going to happen."

A 2021 statement by Democratic Congressman Jamie Raskin proved prophetic. Raskin said that Trump should be criminally investigated but cautioned that defeating him at the ballot box remained the central challenge. "We need to win this struggle politically," he said. Trump made the same point after his New York conviction, declaring, "the real verdict is gonna be November 5th by the people."

SWEEPING REFORMS LIKE the ones of the 1970s are needed in the FBI, DOJ, and the presidency. Jack Goldsmith, a former George W. Bush administration DOJ official, has proposed reforms that would help prevent presidents from abusing the vast powers of the DOJ and FBI.

Few of them, though, have been implemented since Biden took

office. Partisan gridlock in Congress makes enacting ambitious reforms, or even simple ones, trying. A bipartisan group of members of Congress made headway but failed to limit the sweeping emergency powers that presidents can unilaterally invoke and use indefinitely.

Congress did not clarify that the primary obstruction of justice statute applies to certain presidential actions. It failed to reform the president's sweeping pardon powers, which allowed Trump to signal to allies that if they declined to cooperate with criminal investigators, he would pardon them. It also failed to formally make using a presidential pardon to bribe, or to obstruct justice, a federal crime.

Significant loopholes in the law governing attempts by foreign powers to influence US elections—loopholes that were taken advantage of during the 2020 election—remain in place. Even one of Goldsmith's most anodyne recommendations remained unimplemented: Trump and other presidents are still not legally required to make their tax returns public.

AS THE 2024 ELECTION APPROACHED, senior officials in Merrick Garland's Justice Department held on to their belief that the department had to continue to adhere to its principle of being apolitical at all times. Some lamented that Garland had been dealt a bad hand as attorney general and that his legacy may be defined by the outcomes of the department's Trump investigations. Others lamented that the department was being unfairly asked to solve the country's political problems.

Those close to Garland say that the decision-making of the attorney general and his inner circle remains driven by his core belief in the ideals of the United States and the need to uphold the rule of law. Garland continues to feel enormous gratitude to the US for having provided a safe haven that allowed his grandmother to flee Europe before the Holocaust. Garland owes his very being, arguably, to the existence of the rule of law in the United States.

Garland and his aides fear that American democracy is under growing threat due to a lack of agreement regarding basic facts. In the 1970s, Americans agreed that actions like the Watergate break-in were improper. No such American consensus appears to exist today.

False information and threats of violence pile up more quickly due to the internet, Garland has told members of his inner circle. And the Attorney General has warned that threats to those who serve the public—teachers and election workers, judges and doctors—make Americans wary of being public servants and "not want to appear in public today."

That statement is correct, and it underlines the core—and extraordinarily alarming—finding of *Where Tyranny Begins*. In four years as president and three years as an ex-president, Trump has successfully used conspiracy theories, co-option, and threats to bend DOJ and FBI officials to his will to a greater extent than publicly known. Those who dared to defy him had their reputations damaged and their careers derailed. Current and former DOJ and FBI officials told me that they did not want to be named because they feared that Trump and his supporters would destroy their reputations, careers, and businesses and, potentially, physically harm them and their families. That is not the rule of law. That is not democracy.

Despite that threat, Garland remains adamant that the DOJ and FBI must remain scrupulously nonpartisan at all times, aides said. The attorney general acknowledges that the department's practice of not publicly commenting on investigations often leaves it defenseless in the face of partisan attacks from Trump and other politicians.

"Yes, the Justice Department has a hand tied behind its back compared to a political actor," Garland has told aides. But becoming a political actor is a line that Garland will never allow the Justice Department to cross. "We would not want to be a political actor," Garland has told aides. "That is the end of the rule of law."

ACKNOWLEDGMENTS

WHERE TYRANNY BEGINS WOULD NOT HAVE BEEN possible without the courage of the current and former FBI and DOJ officials who spoke with me. The fear of retaliation that some of them feel and their consequent wish to remain anonymous is justified. Out of respect for those fears, I have not identified those sources who wish not to be named either in the text or in the endnotes below in order to maintain their anonymity.

The work of numerous journalists also made this book possible. I am deeply indebted and grateful to them. Anakwa Dwamena, an amazing friend and former colleague at *The New Yorker*, thoroughly and patiently fact-checked this book, correcting my errors and ensuring its accuracy. Andrea Bernstein and Laura Jarrett provided incisive edits and thoughtful guidance as well. Any and all errors and omissions in this book are my own.

At W. W. Norton, John Glusman and Helen Thomaides put up with missed deadlines and turned rough drafts into coherent narrative and analysis. John, who published my first book, has been my champion for decades. This is my fifth book and it was by far the most challenging one to write. John and Helen's understanding, patience, and support were absolutely extraordinary. I will forever be grateful to them. Robert Byrne, the project editor, and Avery Hudson, the copy editor, were amazingly generous, skilled, and helpful, as was Jessica Friedman. I would also like to thank Julia Reidhead, Brendan Curry, Kyle Radler, Rebecca Homiski, Anna Oler, and Steve Colca.

My book agents, Sarah Chalfant and Rebecca Nagel of the Wylie Agency, fought for this book and encouraged, supported, and guided me every step of the way. I'm deeply grateful to them for decades of friendship, thoughtfulness, and kindness.

Karen Greenberg, the Director of the Center on National Security at Fordham Law, gave me a fellowship and was a constant source of insight, support, and encouragement. Sheila Foster and Julia Tedesco were enormously helpful as well.

My employers and colleagues at NBC News and *The New Yorker* showed enormous patience throughout the two years that it took me to write *Where Tyranny Begins*. My deepest thanks go to Rebecca Blumenstein, Catherine Kim, Peter Klein, Meghan Rafferty, Tom Namako, Ken Strickland, Chloe Arensberg, Mark Schone, Rich Schapiro, Adiel Kaplan, Kevin Monahan, Anna Schecter, Tom Winter, Jonathan Dienst, Andy Blankstein, Simone Weichselbaum, Hannah Rappleye, Courtney Kube, Dan De Luce, Julian Ainsley, Laura Strickler, Ken Dilanian, Didi Martinez, Yasmine Salam, Alex Chaidez, and many others at NBC for their support and patience.

I'm equally grateful to David Remnick, Deirdre Foley Mendelssohn, Mike Luo, Fabio Bertoni, Dorothy Wickenden, Virginia Cannon, Soo-jeong Kang, Jessica Winter, David Haglund, Josh Rothman, Rob Fischer, Micah Hauser, Nick Trautwein, Willing Davidson, Stephania Taladrid, Susan Glasser, Tammy Kim, Ronan Farrow, John Cassidy, Evan Osnos, Jelani Cobb, Sean Lavery, Fergus McIntosh, Maraithe Thomas, Monica Racic, Joanna Milter, Andrew Katz, Andrew Boynton, Whitney Holmes, Rachel Riederer, and many others at *The New Yorker*. Other former colleagues encouraged me as well, including Rich Greenberg, Eric Umansky, Mike Williams, John Blanton, Ned Parker, and Aram Roston.

The support, patience, and guidance of many friends kept me going, including Eric Wold, Ivan Obregon, Leigh Cheng, Lisa Ferrari, Kannan Sundaram, Don Nay, Shailesh Lal, John Bastian, Julian Borger, Jay Alan Erickson, Jay Brenchick, Jim Webb, Steve Cote, Billy Shore, and Andrew Curtis, among others.

I'm indebted to my parents, Carol and Harvey, siblings Laura, Erik, and Lee, stepparents, Andrea and George, stepbrothers Dan and Joel, in-laws Mary Jane, Jim, Chrissy, Jason, Karen, and Howard. Most of all, I owe my wife Kristen, and my daughters Ella and Julia, time. This book took me away from them for too long. Their love, patience, and support has been boundless, constant, and extraordinary. I thank them for being the loves of my life.

NOTES

PROLOGUE: A COME-TO-JESUS MEETING

xv   **relationship between the DOJ and the FBI:** David Rohde, *In Deep: The FBI, the CIA, and the Truth about America's "Deep State"* (New York: W. W. Norton, 2020), 5.

xvii   **his own planned presidential campaign:** Gregory Dehler, "Palmer Raids," in *Encyclopedia Britannica*, article published April 19, 2023.

xvii   **recalled a former senior FBI official:** Former senior FBI official, interview with the author, 2023.

xviii   **Steven D'Antuono . . . feared that the documents dispute:** Steven D'Antuono, interview with the author, 2023.

xviii   **According to public records, Bratt had donated $600:** Open Secrets (opensecrets.org).

xix   **official . . . said in an interview:** Senior DOJ official with knowledge of Bratt's work, interview with the author, 2023.

xxi   **DOJ prosecutors were seeking several years:** United States Attorney's Office, Western District of Missouri, "Former FBI Analyst Sentenced for Retaining Classified Documents," press release, June 21, 2023.

xxiii   **they shall "be disqualified from holding" any federal office:** Charlie Savage, "If Trump Illegally Removed Official Records, Would He Be Barred from Future Office?" *New York Times*, August 9, 2022.

xxiv   **scolded D'Antuono in an email:** Steven D'Antuono, multiple interviews with the author, 2023; senior Justice Department official, interview with the author, 2023.

xxiv   **an official known to few Americans ended the debate:** Interview with the author, 2023.

xxiv   **in polo shirts and khakis:** Carol Leonnig, Devlin Barrett, Perry Stein, and Aaron C. Davis, "Showdown before the Raid: FBI Agents and Prosecutors Argued over Trump," *Washington Post*, March 1, 2023.

xxv   **In an error- and exaggeration-laced 340-word statement:** "Trump: 'Mar-a-Lago Home under Siege, Raided by FBI,'" CBS Miami, August 8, 2022.

xxv   **House Republican leader Kevin McCarthy tweeted:** Kevin McCarthy (@ SpeakerMcCarthy), "Attorney General Garland: preserve your documents and clear your calendar," Twitter, August 8, 2022, 9:01 p.m.

xxv   **The Republican National Committee solicited money:** Republican National Committee, "Breaking News," August 8, 2022.

xxvi   **Some even asked about a conspiracy theory circulating online:** Former senior FBI official, interview with the author, 2023.

xxvi   **readying for armed revolution:** Andrew Welsh-Huggins and Patrick Orsagos, "Man Who Tried to Breach FBI Office Killed after Standoff," Associated Press, August 11, 2022.

xxvi   **Attorney General Merrick Garland held a press conference:** United States Department of Justice, Office of Public Affairs, "Attorney General Merrick Garland Delivers Remarks," speech, August 11, 2022.

xxvii   **Trump's goal during and after his presidency was clear:** Former senior DOJ official, multiple interviews with the author, 2023.

xxviii   **A five-word warning:** John Locke, *The Two Treatises of Civil Government* (Hollis ed.) (A. Millar et al., 1689). Online Library of Liberty (oll.libertyfund.org).

Chapter 1: LOL Nothing Matters Lawyering

3   **The order shocked civil liberties groups:** "Full Text of Trump's Executive Order on 7-Nation Ban, Refugee Suspension," CNN, January 28, 2017.

3   **barred refugees:** Executive Order 13769, January 27, 2017: Protecting the Nation from Foreign Terrorist Entry into the United States.

3   **Within days, federal judges blocked:** "Judge Blocks Trump Order on Refugees Amid Chaos and Outcry Worldwide," *New York Times*, January 28, 2017.

5   **Yates later recalled at the Aspen Ideas Festival:** David Choi, " 'What the Heck Is This Thing': Sally Yates Describes How She Found Out About Trump's Travel Ban," *Business Insider*, June 29, 2017.

6   **Hunt said in an interview:** Interviews with the author, 2023 and 2024.

8   **Newland recalled in an interview:** Interviews with the author, 2023 and 2024.

9   **an article in Lawfare:** Quinta Jurecic, Lawfare, "On Bullshit and the Oath of Office: The 'LOL Nothing Matters' Presidency," November 23, 2022 .

10   **On July 2, 1881, President James A. Garfield:** David Rohde, "How America Escapes Its Conspiracy-Theory Crisis," *The New Yorker*, October 29, 2020.

12   **the percentage of Americans who say that they trust the government:** Pew Research Center, "Public Trust in Government: 1958–2023," September 19, 2023.

12   **the percentage of Americans who say they trust the media:** Megan Brennan, "Media Confidence in U.S. Matches 2016 Record Low," Gallup, October 19, 2023.

12   **stirring art deco murals:** Ari Shapiro, "Murals Depict Power of Law and Justice," NPR, January 5, 2009.

13   **"an unprecedented experiment in peacetime political surveillance":** Beverly

Gage, *G-Man: J. Edgar Hoover and the Making of the American Century* (New York: Viking, 2022), 11.

14 **Webster vowed to depoliticize the bureau:** Rohde, *In Deep*, 32–33.

18 **Sessions as his nominee:** Phil Mattingly, Eric Bradner, and Tal Kopan, "Trump Picks Sessions for Attorney General," CNN, November 18, 2016.

18 **In an interview in his home in Mobile:** Jeff Sessions, interview with the author, 2023.

19 **Sessions was elected state attorney general:** John Sharp, "Courtrooms to Capitol: The Evolution of Jeff Sessions," AL.com, November 27, 2016.

20 **He derailed attempts:** Elaina Plott, "The Fall of Jeff Sessions, and What Came After," *New York Times*, July 2, 2020.

20 **Sessions had once called him "boy":** Plott, "The Fall of Jeff Sessions, and What Came After."

20 **Wayne Flynt . . . told the *New York Times*:** Sharon LaFraniere and Matt Apuzzo, "Jeff Sessions, a Lifelong Outsider, Finds the Inside Track," *New York Times*, January 8, 2017.

CHAPTER 2: DEMOLISH NORMS

24 **"We were both surprised":** Jody Hunt, interview with the author, 2023.

24 **"It was obvious since I had a role in the campaign":** Jeff Sessions, interview with the author, 2023.

24 **a copy of the regulation:** 28 U.S. Code § 528: Disqualification of Officers and Employees of the Department of Justice.

26 **Judge Donald Middlebrooks wrote:** United States District Court, Southern District of Florida, "Donald Trump v. Hillary R. Clinton, et al.," Donald Middlebooks, Order on Sanctions, January 19, 2023.

26 **the *Washington Post* broke the story:** Adam Entous, Ellen Nakashima, and Greg Miller, "Sessions Met with Russian Envoy Twice Last Year, Encounters He Later Did Not Disclose," *Washington Post*, March 1, 2017.

27 **he implored Sessions to intervene and stop Trump:** James Comey, *A Higher Loyalty: Truth, Lies, and Leadership* (New York: Flatiron Books, 2018), 256.

28 **Sessions left the meeting:** US Department of Justice, Special Counsel Robert S. Mueller, III, "Report on the Investigation into Russian Interference in the 2016 Presidential Election," March 2019, vol. II, 51.

30 **Sarah Isgur . . . said in an interview:** Interviews with the author, 2023.

30 **migrants caught crossing:** Kevin Sieff, "The Trump Administration Used an Early, Unreported Program to Separate Migrant Families along a Remote Stretch of the Border," *Washington Post*, July 9, 2012.

30 **agents referred all migrants caught crossing the border illegally:** US Department of Justice, Office of the Inspector General, "Review of the Department of Justice's Planning and Implementation of Its Zero Tolerance Policy and Its Coordination with the Departments of Homeland Security and Health and Human Services Evaluation and Inspection Division," January 2021.

32 **Sessions traveled to Nogales:** Jonathan Blitzer, "What Will Trump Do with Half a Million Backlogged Immigration Cases?" *The New Yorker*, June 20, 2017.

32 **Prosecutors would later tell the DOJ inspector general:** US Department of Justice, "Review of the Department of Justice's Planning and Implementation of Its Zero Tolerance Policy and Its Coordination with the Departments of Homeland Security and Health and Human Services," January 2021 (revised), 16.

33 **as many as one thousand children:** US Department of Homeland Security, Interagency Task Force on the Reunification of Families, Interim Progress Report, March 31, 2023, 9.

CHAPTER 3: TERMINATE AND REMOVE

34 **disclose that the FBI had launched a criminal investigation:** "Full Transcript: FBI Director James Comey Testifies on Russian Interference in 2016 Election," *Washington Post*, March 21, 2017.

35 **Attorney General Robert H. Jackson had famously warned:** US Department of Justice, Robert H. Jackson, Attorney General of the United States, The Second Annual Conference of United States Attorneys, "The Federal Prosecutor," April 1, 1940.

36 **facing a "five-hundred-year flood":** James B. Comey, "James Comey: This Report Says I Was Wrong. But That's Good for the F.B.I.," *New York Times*, June 14, 2018.

36 **said a retired senior FBI official close to Comey:** Interviews with the author, 2023 and 2024.

36 **In his surprise press conference, Comey announced:** Federal Bureau of Investigation, James B. Comey, "Statement by FBI Director James B. Comey on the Investigation of Secretary Hillary Clinton's Use of a Personal E-Mail System," July 5, 2016.

36 **without the permission of the attorney general:** Comey, *A Higher Loyalty*, p. 183.

37 **Comey again acted without the approval of the attorney general:** Comey, *A Higher Loyalty*, p. 197.

37 **Nate Silver later concluded:** Nate Silver, "The Comey Letter Probably Cost Clinton the Election," FiveThirtyEight, May 3, 2017.

38 **Strzok later wrote:** Peter Strzok, *Compromised: Counterintelligence and the Threat of Donald J. Trump* (Boston: Mariner Books, 2020), 185.

40 **angered federal prosecutors:** Anthony Noto, "Trump's Leading Pick to Replace New York's Top Federal Prosecutor Has Awkward Past in Illinois," Bizjournals.com, April 28, 2017.

42 **model federal prosecutor:** Daniel Hemel, "The Tragedy of Rod Rosenstein," Slate, March 27, 2019.

42 **his entire adult life:** "Former Deputy Attorney General Rod J. Rosenstein," US Department of Justice, staff profile, April 26, 2017.

43 the *Washington Post* said of Rosenstein: Editorial Board, "Democrats Are Holding Up One of Trump's Best Appointees," *Washington Post*, March 8, 2017.

43 Rosenstein did not express an opinion either way: Peter Strzok, *Compromised*, 242.

43 said that Comey never asked for his opinion: Rod Rosenstein, interview with the author, 2024.

43 Rosenstein claimed in a series of interviews: Rod Rosenstein, interviews with the author, 2023.

44 thousand-word memo: "Rod Rosenstein's Letter Recommending Comey Be Fired," BBC News, May 10, 2017.

44 terminated and removed: "White House Letters on Firing of FBI Director James Comey," Latimes.com, May 9, 2017.

45 [Huber] recalled in an interview: Interviews with the author, 2023 and 2024.

46 "show all my FBI people how much I love them": Andrew McCabe, *The Threat: How the FBI Protects America in the Age of Terror and Trump* (New York: St. Martin's Press, 2019), 221–23.

47 "shared the alarming call with the team": McCabe, *The Threat*, pp. 234–35.

47 wiping away his sterling reputation: Ruben Castaneda, "Profile of Rod Rosenstein, U.S. Attorney for Maryland," *Washington Post*, October 9, 2011.

CHAPTER 4: INVESTIGATE THE INVESTIGATORS

49 the new president told Lester Holt: "I Was Going to Fire Comey Anyway, Trump Tells Lester Holt in Interview," *NBC Nightly News*, May 11, 2017.

50 convicted Clinton's business partners: R. H. Melton and Michael Haddigan, "Three Guilty in Arkansas Fraud Trial," *Washington Post*, May 29, 1996, A01.

51 "I wanted the special counsel": Rod Rosenstein, multiple interviews with the author, 2023.

51 Rosenstein began secretly interviewing: Rosenstein, multiple interviews with the author, 2023.

52 Comey had memorialized each of his private encounters with Trump: Michael S. Schmidt, "Comey Memo Says Trump Asked Him to End Flynn Investigation," *New York Times*, May 16, 2017.

52 When Rosenstein spoke with Mueller: Rosenstein, multiple interviews with the author, 2023.

52 a full and thorough investigation: US Department of Justice, Office of the Deputy Attorney General. "Appointment of Special Counsel to Investigate Russian Interference with the 2016 Presidential Election and Related Matters," May 17, 2017.

53 "This is the end of my Presidency. I'm fucked": US Department of Justice, Special Counsel Robert S. Mueller, III., "Report on the Investigation into Russian Interference in the 2016 Presidential Election," March 2019. Vol. II, 78.

53 in a way that Hunt had never seen before: Jody Hunt, interview with the author, 2023.

55 **said Maryland's Democratic senator Ben Cardin:** Rebecca R. Ruiz and Mark Landler, "Robert Mueller, Former F.B.I. Director, Is Named Special Counsel for Russia Investigation," *New York Times*, May 17, 2017.

55 **A Pew survey found:** Pew Research Center, "Stark Partisan Divisions Over Russia Probe, Including Its Importance to the Nation," December 7, 2017.

56 **When Trump hired Ty Cobb:** Jeff Toobin, "Why the Mueller Investigation Failed," *The New Yorker*, June 27, 2020.

56 **Trump attacked Rod Rosenstein for appointing Mueller:** Donald J. Trump (@realDonaldTrump), "I am being investigated for firing the FBI Director by the man who told me to fire the FBI Director! Witch Hunt," Twitter, June 16, 2017, 9:07 a.m.

58 **Rosenstein . . . was delighted:** Rosenstein, interview with the author, 2023.

59 **the evidence was not sufficient to support criminal charges:** US Department of Justice, "Report on the Investigation into Russian Interference in the 2016 Presidential Election," Volume I, March 2019, 9.

62 **would later write in his memoir:** Andrew Weissmann, *Where Law Ends: Inside the Mueller Investigation* (New York: Random House, 2020), 109.

63 **"The idea that he had actually had some role":** US Department of Justice, Office of the Inspector General, "Review of Four FISA Applications and Other Aspects of the FBI's Crossfire Hurricane Investigation," December 2019, 302.

64 **You have these deeply held views:** Erica Newland, interview with the author, 2023.

65 **She later told George Packer:** George Packer, "The President Is Winning His War on American Institutions, *The Atlantic*, April 2020.

67 **Rosenstein declined to discuss it with Trump:** Rosenstein, interview with the author, 2023.

CHAPTER 5: DISPARAGE AND DISCREDIT

68 **Sessions said he did not recall playing any role in the decision:** Jeff Sessions, interview with the author, 2023.

70 **Weissmann . . . said in an interview:** Interview with the author, 2024.

70 **McCabe immediately released a lengthy statement:** Sarah N. Lynch, "Fired FBI Deputy Director McCabe's statement," Reuters, March 17, 2018.

71 **"The Mueller probe should never have been started":** Donald J. Trump (@realDonaldTrump), Twitter, March 17, 2018, 8:12 p.m.

72 **"Why does the Mueller team have 13 hardened Democrats":** Donald J. Trump (@realDonaldTrump), Twitter, March 18, 2018, 8:35 a.m.

72 **Brian Bennett later noted:** Brian Bennett, " 'This Is Very Good.' How Trump Beat the Mueller Investigation," *Time*, March 28, 2019.

73 **"a kind of destabilizing pull on our decision-making process":** Weissmann, *Where Law Ends*, 118.

74 **Barr recalled in a 2001 interview:** The Miller Center, "William P. Barr Oral History," University of Virginia, April 5, 2001.

75 **drove four visitors into the building's basement:** Philip Rucker and Carol Leonnig, *A Very Stable Genius: Donald J. Trump's Testing of America* (New York: Penguin, 2020).

76 **Mueller's team had identified numerous links:** US Department of Justice, "Report on the Investigation into Russian Interference in the 2016 Presidential Election," March 2019, vol. I, p. 9; Rod Rosenstein, multiple interviews with the author, 2023; O'Callaghan, multiple interviews with the author, 2023.

77 **Quarles's next statement surprised and puzzled:** Rosenstein, multiple interviews with the author, 2023; Ed O'Callaghan, multiple interviews with the author, 2023; William P. Barr, *One Damn Thing after Another: Memoirs of an Attorney General* (New York: William Morrow, 2022), 322.

77 **Rosenstein, and O'Callaghan:** Rosenstein, multiple interviews with the author, 2023; O'Callaghan, multiple interviews with the author, 2023.

77 **"the most confusing thing ever":** Former Justice Department official, multiple interviews with the author, 2023.

77 **Barr recalled asking:** Barr, *One Damn Thing after Another*, 240.

78 **"I do think he probably did some stuff":** Molly Ball, "These Ordinary Americans Discussed the Mueller Investigation. Here's Their Surprising Consensus," *Time*, March 26, 2019.

79 **indicted thirty-four people:** Andrew Prokop, "All of Robert Mueller's Indictments and Plea Deals in the Russia Investigation," Vox, December 17, 2019.

79 **"Trump's victory sent Democrats on a treasure hunt":** Barr, *One Damn Thing after Another*, 412.

79 **a once-commanding figure diminished by age:** Barr, *One Damn Thing after Another*, 239, 241.

79 **"a couple of people who were in this 'get Trump' mode":** Senior Justice Department official, multiple interviews with the author, 2023.

80 **"I shared his view that Mueller was a little shaky":** Rosenstein, interview with the author, 2023.

81 **Barr bluntly dismissed:** Barr, *One Damn Thing after Another*.

81 **fourteen instances:** Quinta Jurecic, "Obstruction of Justice in the Mueller Report: A Heat Map," Lawfare, April 21, 2019.

81 **impossible for Trump to obstruct justice:** David Rohde, "William Barr, Trump's Sword and Shield," *The New Yorker*, January 13, 2020.

81 **"The facts are clear":** Rosenstein, multiple interviews with the author, 2023.

81 **"He has advisors who told him where the line was":** O'Callaghan, multiple interviews with the author, 2023.

81 **compiled a four-page letter:** "Read Attorney General William Barr's Summary of the Mueller Report," *New York Times*, March 24, 2019.

81 **Mueller had not concluded:** Carrie Johnson, Philip Ewing, and Jessica Taylor, "Mueller Report Doesn't Find Russian Collusion, but Can't 'Exonerate' on Obstruction," NPR, March 24, 2019.

82 **didn't want to be seen as vouching for Barr's summary:** Jeff Toobin, "Why the Mueller Investigation Failed," *The New Yorker*, June 27, 2020.

82 **it was the job of the attorney general to write such a letter:** Andrew Weissmann, interview with the author, 2024.

82 **"an illegal takedown that failed":** Kaitlin Collins and Kevin Liptak, "Trump Claims Vindication after Mueller Does Not Establish Collusion," CNN, March 24, 2019.

83 **all grand jury material redacted:** Jeffrey Toobin, "Why the Mueller Investigation Failed," *The New Yorker*, June 27, 2020.

83 **Barr said he would consider it:** Barr, *One Damn Thing after Another*, 254.

84 **Barr painted the president sympathetically:** "Barr Full Press Conference on Mueller Report," streamed live on April 18, 2019, YouTube video.

85 **he felt Barr went too far in defending Trump:** O'Callaghan, multiple interviews with the author, 2023.

CHAPTER 6: SHIELD AND PROTECT

87 **supported Trump's policies:** David Rohde, "William Barr, Trump's Sword and Shield," *The New Yorker*, January 13, 2020.

87 **Barr and other officials convinced Trump:** William P. Barr, *One Damn Thing after Another: Memoirs of an Attorney General* (New York: William Morrow, 2022), 278.

87 **Legal experts widely dismissed:** Kevin Breuninger, "Watch: Trump Speaks at Census Event in Rose Garden," CNBC, July 11, 2019.

88 **largely declined to attack Barr:** Julie Hirschfeld Davis and Mark Mazzetti, "Highlights of Robert Mueller's Testimony to Congress," *New York Times*, July 24, 2019.

90 **"the view that conservatives are persecuted by the media":** Former Justice Department official, multiple interviews with the author, 2023.

90 **Twice during the call:** "The Trump-Zelensky Phone Call: Key Takeaways from Two New Documents," *New York Times*, September 25, 2019.

91 **Barr faced a decision:** David Rohde, "The Dangerous Position of William Barr," *The New Yorker*, September 29, 2019.

91 **Barr felt that the Ukraine call was idiotic and harebrained:** Barr, *One Damn Thing after Another*, 296, 300.

91 **Barr and White House Counsel Pat Cipollone both urged Trump:** Barr, *One Damn Thing after Another*, 297.

91 **Senate prepared to hold Trump's impeachment trial:** Former Justice Department official, interviews with the author, 2023.

91 **Barr and his aides told Liu to depart:** Carol Leonnig and Philip Rucker, *I Alone Can Fix It: Donald J. Trump's Catastrophic Final Year* (New York: Penguin, 2021), 55.

92 **the timing was suspicious:** Keith L. Alexander, Spencer S. Hsu, and Matt

Zapotosky, "Attorney General William P. Barr Names Timothy Shea, One of His Counselors, as the District's Interim U.S. Attorney," *Washington Post*, January 31, 2020.

92   **"We think he was bullshitting"**: Prosecutor who asked not to be named, multiple interviews with author, 2023.

93   **"He comes to conclusions and makes decisions very quickly"**: Former Justice Department official, multiple interviews with the author, 2023.

94   **"there is a way to rush through something"**: Another former Justice Department official, multiple interviews with the author, 2023.

94   **"The real crimes were on the other side"**: Donald J. Trump (@realDonaldTrump), Twitter, February 11, 2020, 1:48 a.m.

94   **After reading Trump's tweet, Barr cursed**: Leonnig and Rucker, *I Alone Can Fix It*, 56.

94   **Some of Barr's advisors described**: Former Justice Department official, multiple interviews with the author, 2023.

95   **subsequent testimony:** "Assistant U.S. Attorney Aaron Zelinsky Opening Statement," streamed live on June 24, 2020, C-SPAN.org.

95   **The president made his wishes known**: Jonathan Kravis, multiple interviews with the author, 2023.

96   **former DOJ official said Trump's threats caused prosecutors to fear**: former DOJ official, multiple interviews with the author, 2023.

96   **"time to stop the tweeting"**: Anne Flaherty, "Barr Blasts Trump's Tweets on Stone Case: 'Impossible for Me to Do My Job': ABC News Exclusive," ABC News, February 13, 2020.

96   **said that he had never told Barr what to do**: Barr, *One Damn Thing after Another*, 322.

97   **a memo calling Liu a member of the "deep state"**: Jonathan Swan, "Exclusive: Trump's 'Deep State' hit list," Axios, February 23, 2020.

98   **an Obama appointee, gave Stone the sentence Barr had recommended**: Darren Samuelsohn and Josh Gerstein, "Roger Stone sentenced to over 3 years in prison," Politico, February 20, 2020.

99   **a desire for revenge consumed Trump**: Former Justice Department official, multiple interviews with the author, 2023.

CHAPTER 7: STOKE CONSPIRACY THEORIES

100   **wanted to make sure that the DOJ was aggressively investigating**: William P. Barr, *One Damn Thing after Another: Memoirs of an Attorney General* (New York: William Morrow, 2022), 468.

100   **publicly supported the president's get-tough stance**: Barr, *One Damn Thing after Another*, 527.

101   **He blamed antifa**: Josh Gerstein and Evan Semones, "Barr Threatens to Bust 'Far-Left Extremist Groups' in Floyd Unrest," Politico, May 30, 2020.

101 **"Crossing State lines to incite violence is a FEDERAL CRIME!":** Donald J. Trump (@realDonaldTrump), Twitter, May 30, 2020, 2:20 p.m.

101 **A review of Minnesota court records:** Andy Mannix, "Court Records, FBI Contradict Trump's Claims of Organized 'Antifa-Led' Riots in Minneapolis after George Floyd's Death," *Star Tribune*, December 20, 2020.

101 **"designating ANTIFA as a Terrorist Organization":** Donald J. Trump (@realDonaldTrump), Twitter, May 31, 2020, 12:23 p.m.

101 **a statement that afternoon parroting Trump:** US Department of Justice, Office of Public Affairs, press release, "Attorney General William P. Barr's Statement on Riots and Domestic Terrorism," May 31, 2020.

102 **Barr noticed that small flecks of spit landed:** Barr, *One Damn Thing after Another*, 496.

102 **The outburst angered Barr:** Barr, *One Damn Thing after Another*, 496.

103 **Barr replied that he would look into it:** Barr, *One Damn Thing after Another*, 496.

104 **would not hesitate to recommend . . . the Insurrection Act:** Barr, *One Damn Thing after Another*, 497.

105 **he met privately with Esper and Milley:** Barr, *One Damn Thing after Another*, 497.

105 **to confirm that they opposed the use of the active-duty military:** Barr, *One Damn Thing after Another*, 497.

105 **"Are you freaking kidding me?":** US Department of the Interior, Office of the Inspector General, "Review of U.S. Park Police's Actions at Lafayette Park," June 2021, 14.

106 **he, Esper, and Milley were not thrilled with the idea:** Barr, *One Damn Thing after Another*, p. 499.

106 **clumsily brandishing the Bible:** David Rohde, "William Barr Is Going, but His Trumpian Legacy Remains," *The New Yorker*, December 16, 2020.

107 **"I should not have been there":** Helene Cooper, "Milley Apologizes for Role in Trump Photo Op: 'I Should Not Have Been There,'" *New York Times*, June 11, 2020.

107 **said that Barr had been used by Trump in Lafayette Park:** Former senior Justice Department official, multiple interviews with the author, 2023.

107 **In an interview on *Face the Nation*:** "Transcript: Attorney General William Barr on "Face the Nation," CBS News, June 7, 2020.

107 **"With tenacity and savvy, Geoff has done an excellent job":** US Department of Justice, Press Release, "Attorney General William P. Barr on the Nomination of Jay Clayton to Serve as U.S. Attorney for the Southern District of New York," June 19, 2020.

108 **Berman issued his own statement:** United States Attorney's Office, Southern District of New York, Press Release, "Statement of U.S. Attorney Geoffrey S. Berman on Announcement by Attorney General Barr," June 19, 2020.

109 **"opens the floodgates to fraud":** "Exclusive: Maria Bartiromo Interviews AG Barr on Police Reform, Big Tech Censorship, Durham Investigation," Fox News, transcript, June 21, 2020.

109 **"Mail-In Ballots will lead to a RIGGED ELECTION!":** Donald J. Trump (@ realDonaldTrump), Twitter, June 22, 2020, 7:10 a.m.

109 **several instances involving major companies in Turkey and China:** John Bolton, *The Room Where It Happened* (New York: Simon & Schuster, 2020), 458.

CHAPTER 8: MENACE

114 **"Domestic Terrorists have taken over Seattle":** Donald J. Trump (@realDonaldTrump), Twitter, June 10, 2020, 11:38 p.m.

114 **"Take back your city NOW. If you don't do it, I will":** Donald J. Trump (@ realDonaldTrump), Twitter, June 11, 2020, 2:08 p.m.

114 **"tell his Radical Left BOSSES":** Donald J. Trump (@realDonaldTrump), Twitter, June 11, 2020, 10:02 a.m.

114 **Fox News ran apocalyptic stories:** Jim Brunner, "Fox News Runs Digitally Altered Images in Coverage of Seattle's Protests, Capitol Hill Autonomous Zone," *Seattle Times*, June 12, 2020.

115 **the *Seattle Times* later reported:** Brunner, "Fox News Runs Digitally Altered Images."

115 **"He wanted to send the military into Seattle":** Former senior Justice Department official, multiple interviews with the author, 2023.

116 **Barr regarded progressives as "Maoist":** William P. Barr, *One Damn Thing after Another: Memoirs of an Attorney General* (New York: William Morrow, 2022), 163–65.

117 **DOJ official said the journalists assumed:** Former Justice Department official, multiple interviews with the author, 2023.

118 **"The White House put a lot of pressure on us":** Former senior Justice Department official, multiple interviews with the author, 2023.

118 **"Vice President Biden, as dumb as he may be, knew everything":** Brooke Singman, "Trump Lays Down Gauntlet for Barr on Durham Probe: Either 'Greatest Attorney General' or 'Average Guy,'" Fox News, August 13, 2020.

119 **The interview infuriated Barr:** Barr, *One Damn Thing after Another*, 524.

119 **the president had no business prejudging an investigation:** Barr, *One Damn Thing after Another*, 524.

120 **"You buy that bullshit, Bill?":** Barr, *One Damn Thing after Another*, 526.

121 **The *New York Times* later reported:** Adam Goldman, Katie Benner, and Zolan Kanno-Youngs, "How Trump's Focus on Antifa Distracted Attention from the Far-Right Threat," *New York Times*, January 30, 2021.

121 **growing increasingly frustrated with the investigation:** Charlie Savage, Adam Goldman, and Katie Benner, "How Barr's Quest to Find Flaws in the Russia Inquiry Unraveled," *New York Times*, January 26, 2023.

121 **She also denounced the draft:** Savage, Goldman, and Benner, "How Barr's Quest to Find Flaws in the Russia Inquiry Unraveled."

121 **suggested . . . that officials could be prosecuted:** Charles Creitz, "Barr Says

Trump Was Right to Fire Intel Watchdog, Calls Russia Probe 'One of the Great-est Travesties,'" Fox News, April 9, 2020.

122 **"we are not dealing with just mistakes or sloppiness":** Creitz, "Barr Says Trump Was Right to Fire Intel Watchdog, Calls Russia Probe 'One of the Great-est Travesties.'"

122 **Durham was unwilling to challenge Barr:** Savage, Goldman, and Benner, "How Barr's Quest to Find Flaws in the Russia Inquiry Unraveled."

122 **Two people close to Barr said he had pressed:** Savage, Goldman, and Benner, "How Barr's Quest to Find Flaws in the Russia Inquiry Unraveled."

123 **demanded that his attorney general bring criminal charges:** Peter Baker and Maggie Haberman, "Trump Lashes Out at His Cabinet with Calls to Indict Political Rivals," *New York Times*, October 8, 2020.

124 **Gilliar . . . told the *Wall Street Journal*:** Andrew Duehern and James T. Areddy, "Hunter Biden's Ex-Business Partner Alleges Father Knew about Venture," *Wall Street Journal*, October 23, 2020.

124 **Barr cut him off twice:** Barr, *One Damn Thing after Another*, 530–31.

124 **"The real October surprise is Bill Barr":** Aide to Bill Barr, multiple interviews with the author, 2020.

CHAPTER 9: FRAUD

127 **gut feeling that Biden would prevail:** William P. Barr, *One Damn Thing after Another: Memoirs of an Attorney General* (New York: William Morrow, 2022), 537.

128 **Barr quickly concluded that Biden had, in fact, won:** Barr, *One Damn Thing after Another*, 540.

129 **70 percent of Republicans did not think the 2020 election:** Catherine Kim, "Poll: 70 Percent of Republicans Don't Think the Election Was Free and Fair," Politico, November 9, 2020.

129 **a memorandum authorizing US attorneys to investigate:** US Department of Justice, Office of the Attorney General, "Post-voting Election Irregularity Inqui-ries," November 9, 2020.

130 **Barr himself did not believe that the election was stolen:** Aide to Bill Barr, multiple interviews with the author, 2020.

130 **Richard Pilger, the head of the DOJ's Election Crimes Branch:** David Rohde, "William Barr Can Stop Donald Trump's Attempted Coup," *The New Yorker*, November 11, 2020.

131 **Barr later told journalist Jonathan Karl:** Jonathan D. Karl, "Inside William Barr's Breakup with Trump," *The Atlantic*, June 27, 2021.

131 **In a final interview with the *Military Times*:** Meghann Myers, "Exclusive: Esper, on His Way Out, Says He Was No Yes Man," *Military Times*, November 9, 2020.

133 **Barr met with Trump in person to discuss the fraud allegations:** Barr, *One Damn Thing after Another*, 545.

133 appeared to have little impact on Trump: Barr, *One Damn Thing after Another*, 545.

133   **would prompt Trump to undermine Republican chances:** Robert Costa, Paul Kane, and Erika Warner, "Fear of Losing Senate Majority in Georgia Runoffs Drives GOP Embrace of Trump's Unfounded Claims of Election Fraud," *Washington Post*, November 10, 2020.

134   **Trump said they were both "missing in action":** Talia Kaplan, "Trump: DOJ 'Missing in Action' on Alleged Election Fraud," Fox News, November 29, 2020.

134   **Justice Department had uncovered no evidence:** Michael Balsamo, "Disputing Trump, Barr Says No Widespread Election Fraud," Associated Press, December 2, 2020.

134   **"Did you say this?":** William P. Barr, *One Damn Thing after Another: Memoirs of an Attorney General* (New York: William Morrow, 2022), 5.

134   **an aide told Barr that Trump wanted to speak with him:** Barr, *One Damn Thing after Another*, p. 4.

135   **wrote that Barr had destroyed "his name for all eternity":** Joe Hoft, "AG Barr Destroys His Name for All Eternity—His Actions Today Confirm He Is Just Another Card-Carrying Swamp Rat," Gateway Pundit, December 1, 2020.

135   **Fox News host Lou Dobbs denounced Barr on his nightly show:** David Rohde, "William Barr's Break with Donald Trump," *The New Yorker*, December 5, 2020.

136   **"Why didn't the Fake News Media, the FBI and the DOJ":** Donald J. Trump (@realDonaldTrump), Twitter, December 10, 2020, 9:21 p.m.

136   **"Just had a very nice meeting with Attorney General Bill Barr":** Donald J. Trump (@realDonaldTrump), Twitter, December 14, 2020, 5:39 p.m.

137   **"He leaves a wounded department":** Rohde, "William Barr Is Going, but His Trumpian Legacy Remains."

137   **Stephen Gillers, an expert in legal ethics:** David Rohde, "William Barr Is Going, but His Trumpian Legacy Remains," *The New Yorker*, December 16, 2020.

137   **David Laufman, a former Justice Department official:** Rohde, "William Barr Is Going, but His Trumpian Legacy Remains."

139   **the *New York Times* published an op-ed by her:** Erica Newland, "I'm Haunted by What I Did as a Lawyer in the Trump Justice Department," *New York Times*, December 20, 2020.

139   **Trump asked to speak with Deputy Attorney General Jeff Rosen:** US Department of Justice, "Former Deputy Attorney General Jeffrey A. Rosen," May 22, 2019.

140   **On December 15, Rosen and his deputy, Richard Donoghue:** United States House of Representatives, Select Committee to Investigate the January 6th Attack on the United States Capitol, "Hearing on the January 6th Investigation," June 23, 2022.

140   **The president started delivering remarks:** United States Senate, Committee on the Judiciary, "Interview of Jeffrey Rosen," August 7, 2021.

141   **The error was corrected:** Angelo Fichero, "Audit in Michigan County Refutes Dominion Conspiracy Theory," FactCheck.org, December 19, 2020.

141   **according to a *Washington Post* review:** Rosalind S. Helderman and Elise Viebeck, "'The Last Wall': How Dozens of Judges across the Political Spectrum

Rejected Trump's Efforts to Overturn the Election," *Washington Post*, December 12, 2020.

142 **ruled against him:** Helderman and Viebeck, "'The Last Wall.'"

142 **called the president's request "extraordinary":** Patrick Marley, "Federal Court Judge Dismisses 'Extraordinary' Trump Lawsuit Seeking to Overturn Wisconsin Election," *Milwaukee Journal Sentinel*, December 12, 2020.

142 **called the Trump campaign's legal theories "Frankenstein's monster":** Josh Gerstein, Kyle Cheney, and Zach Montellaro, "'This Is Simply Not How the Constitution Works': Federal Judge Eviscerates Trump Lawsuit," Politico, November 21, 2022.

142 **Federal Judge Diane Humetewa flatly dismissed:** Helderman and Viebeck, "'The Last Wall.'"

142 **warned that American democracy itself was at risk:** Helderman and Viebeck, "'The Last Wall.'"

143 **Rosen began receiving private phone calls:** US House of Representatives, "Hearing on the January 6th Investigation."

143 **A call the following day was cordial as well:** United States Senate, Committee on the Judiciary, "Interview of Jeffrey Rosen," August 7, 2021.

143 **Rosen said that he sought to strike a balance:** US Senate, "Interview of Jeffrey Rosen."

144 **Clark minimized the meeting:** Katie Benner, "Trump and Justice Dept. Lawyer Said to Have Plotted to Oust Acting Attorney General," *New York Times*, January 22, 2021.

144 **Clark told Rosen that he was going to discuss his strategy:** US House of Representatives, "Hearing on the January 6th Investigation."

145 **"I thought that was preposterous":** US House of Representatives, "Hearing on the January 6th Investigation."

146 **dismissed the video as "pure insanity" and "patently absurd":** US House of Representatives, Select Committee to Investigate the January 6th Attack on the United States Capitol, "Hearing on the January 6th Investigation," June 23, 2022.

146 **a half dozen senior Justice Department officials listened:** US House of Representatives, "Hearing on the January 6th Investigation."

146 **"There is no way I am staying":** US House of Representatives, "Hearing on the January 6th Investigation."

147 **Trump had Rosen and Clark present their arguments to him:** US House of Representatives, "Hearing on the January 6th Investigation."

147 **if he fired Rosen no one would remember Trump's legacy:** US House of Representatives, "Hearing on the January 6th Investigation."

148 **Clark later categorically denied that he devised any plan to oust Rosen:** Katie Benner, "Trump and Justice Dept. Lawyer Said to Have Plotted to Oust Acting Attorney General," *New York Times*, January 22, 2021.

148 **the president's failed attempt to seize control of the DOJ:** US House of Representatives, "Hearing on the January 6th Investigation."

148 **"I called my husband and told him to be careful":** Erica Newland, multiple interviews with the author, 2023–24.

149 **"I was surprised by what I saw":** Nathan Huber, multiple interviews with the author, 2023–24.

149 **Garland sat in his home in Bethesda, Maryland:** Current senior Justice Department official, multiple interviews with the author, 2023 and 2024; and Katie Benner, "After a Rocky First Year, a Cautious Garland Finds His Footing," *New York Times*, April 25, 2022.

149 **"Your loyalty is not to me":** Lauren Gambino, "Biden Introduces Merrick Garland as Attorney General Pick," *The Guardian*, January 7, 2021.

Chapter 10: Stop the Steal

155 **Trump supporters had gathered:** Tom Jackman, Paul Duggan, Ann E. Marimow, and Spencer S. Hsu, "Proud Boys Sparked Clashes during Pro-Trump Rally, D.C. Officials Say," *Washington Post*, December 14, 2020.

155 **top officials from the DOJ:** Aaron C. Davis, "The Attack: Before, During and After," *Washington Post*, October 31, 2021.

156 **"same old" after-dark:** Davis, "The Attack: Before, During and After."

156 **street brawling between anti-Trump and pro-Trump:** Jackman, Duggan, Marimow, and Hsu, "Proud Boys Sparked Clashes during Pro-Trump Rally, D.C. Officials Say."

157 **receiving frantic calls from furious lawmakers:** Select Committee to Investigate the January 6th Attack on the US Capitol, "Interview of David Bowdich," December 16, 2021.

158 **the *Washington Post* reported:** Devlin Barrett and Matt Zapotosky, "FBI Report Warned of 'War' at Capitol, Contradicting Claims There Was No Indication of Looming Violence," *Washington Post*, January 12, 2021.

159 **"We have to separate the aspirational from the intentional":** Steven D'Antuono, multiple interviews with the author, 2023.

159 **D'Antuono recalled:** Interviews with the author, 2023.

159 **three hundred Department of Homeland Security officials:** Davis, "The Attack: Before, During and After."

161 **most serious domestic threat:** Adam Goldman and Alan Feuer, "Bias and Human Error Played Parts in F.B.I.'s Jan. 6 Failure, Documents Suggest," *New York Times*, February 1, 2023.

163 **Agents initially focused on "low-hanging fruit":** Steven D'Antuono, multiple interviews with the author, 2023.

163 **a conspiracy theorist from Arizona:** Marie Fazio, "Notable Arrests after the Riot at the Capitol," *New York Times*, January 10, 2021.

165 **J. P. Cooney and Ken Kohl, presented a twenty-five-page proposal:** Carol Leonnig and Aaron C. Davis, "FBI Resisted Opening Probe into Trump's Role in Jan. 6 for More Than a Year," *Washington Post*, June 19, 2023.

166 **The DOJ officials who opposed the plan:** Former Justice Department official, multiple interviews with the author, 2023.

166 **"There was a PowerPoint presentation":** Former Justice Department official, multiple interviews with author, 2023.

Chapter 11: Prosecuting Violent Extremists

170 **"I don't think he was ever viewed in a particular camp":** Sheryl Gay Stolberg, Matt Apuzzo, and Katherine Q. Seelye, "Merrick Garland Is a Deft Navigator of Washington Legal Circles," *New York Times*, March 26, 2016.

170 **"Merrick Garland is meticulous to the *n*th degree":** Ari Shapiro, "Attorney Jamie Gorelick: Merrick Garland Is at Heart a Public Servant," NPR, March 16, 2016.

171 **"He has seen this hatred up close":** Mark Leibovich, "Merrick Garland Faces Resurgent Peril after Years Fighting Extremism," *New York Times*, February 20, 2021.

171 **Frank Keating, then Republican governor:** Mark Leibovich, "Merrick Garland Faces Resurgent Peril after Years Fighting Extremism," *New York Times*, February 20, 2021.

171 **"moderate liberal, with a definite pro-prosecution bent":** Nina Totenberg and Carrie Johnson, "Merrick Garland has a reputation of collegiality, record of Republican support," NPR, March 16, 2016.

172 **investigators had organized their investigation in four tiers:** Former DOJ official, multiple interviews with the author, 2023–24.

173 **and DOJ officials said he received no such recommendation:** Justice Department officials, multiple interviews with the author, 2023–24.

Chapter 12: The Lost Year

175 **a spate of decisions:** Katie Benner, "Garland Defends Justice Dept. Moves Upholding Trump-Era Positions," *New York Times*, June 9, 2021.

175 **no longer felt they were being pressured:** "After a Rocky First Year, a Cautious Garland Finds His Footing," *New York Times*, April 25, 2022.

176 **"It is truly shocking . . . I am angry! I am offended!":** Jeff Hauser, Max Moran, Matt Ford, Ankush Khardori, et al., "Why Is Merrick Garland Defending Donald Trump?" *New Republic*, June 8, 2021.

177 **Hauser and Moran wrote:** Jeff Hauser et al., "Why Is Merrick Garland Defending Donald Trump?"

177 **A senior DOJ official flatly rejected that claim:** Interviews with the author, 2022 and 2023.

178 **this was a job for the department's inspector general:** Justice Department officials, multiple interviews with the author, 2023–24.

179 **Monaco stayed away from politically charged cases:** Current and former Justice Department officials, multiple interviews with the author, 2023–24.

179 **"Yes, he went deep on big issues"**: Justice Department official, multiple interviews with the author, 2023–24.

179 **the department "is not a place to be performative"**: David Rohde, "The Political, Legal, and Moral Minefield That Donald Trump Left for Merrick Garland," *The New Yorker*, June 15, 2021.

180 **"Levi reminds us what we should be"**: Anthony Lewis, review of Edward H. Levi, *Restoring Justice: The Speeches of Attorney General Edward H. Levi*, Jack Fuller, ed. (University of Chicago Press, 2013).

180 **noted that attorneys general can give speeches**: Andrew Weissmann, interview with the author, 2024.

180 **referring to Cox's tapes press conference**: Andrew Weissmann, interview with the author, 2023.

180 **In the interview, Sherwin said**: Scott Pelley, "Inside the Prosecution of the Capitol Rioters," *60 Minutes*, March 22, 2021.

180 **Sherwin thought he had permission to do the interview**: Former DOJ official, multiple interviews with the author, 2024.

181 **"the public needs to believe it was done by the book"**: senior Justice Department official, multiple interviews with the author, 2023–24.

182 **During an interview with the *New York Times***: Katie Benner, "After a Rocky First Year, a Cautious Garland Finds His Footing," *New York Times*, April 25, 2022.

183 **The official said that the Biden White House**: Justice Department official, multiple interviews with the author, 2023–24.

183 **White House officials, though, have privately expressed frustration**: Perry Stein and Devlin Barrett: "Garland Comes before Congress with his Record in the Spotlight," *Washington Post*, September 19, 2023.

183 **Channing D. Phillips, the acting US attorney, told staffers**: Carol Leonnig and Aaron C. Davis, "FBI Resisted Opening Probe into Trump's Role in Jan. 6 for More Than a Year," *Washington Post*, June 19, 2023.

183 **Prosecutors, meanwhile, began to complain about their superiors**: Leonnig and Davis, "FBI Resisted Opening Probe into Trump's Role in Jan. 6 for More Than a Year."

183 **a former senior DOJ official told the *Washington Post***: Leonnig and Davis, "FBI Resisted Opening Probe into Trump's Role in Jan. 6 for More Than a Year."

184 **Multiple senior DOJ officials flatly denied**: Justice Department officials, multiple interviews with the author, 2023–24.

184 **the unit was not staffed until the fall**: Justice Department officials, multiple interviews with the author, 2023–24.

184 **wanted to charge Oath Keeper leader Stewart Rhodes**: Leonnig and Davis, "FBI Resisted Opening Probe into Trump's Role in Jan. 6 for More Than a Year."

184 **Some DOJ officials worried**: Justice Department officials, multiple interviews with the author, 2023–24.

184 **criticized Windom for being "inflexible"**: Glenn Thrush, Alan Feuer, Michael

S. Schmidt, "The Man Helping Drive the Investigation into Trump's Push to Keep Power," *New York Times*, June 28, 2022.

185 **awaiting Senate confirmation:** Dylan Tokar, "White House to Nominate National Security Veteran for DOJ Post," *Wall Street Journal*, May 17, 2021.

185 **In a book released in September:** Bob Woodward and Robert Costa, *Peril* (New York: Simon & Schuster, 2021), 209–10.

186 **In October, the *Washington Post* reported:** Jacqueline Alemany, Emma Brown, Tom Hamburger, and Jon Swaine, "Ahead of Jan. 6, Willard Hotel in Downtown D.C. Was a Trump Team 'Command Center' for Effort to Deny Biden the Presidency," *Washington Post*, October 23, 2021.

186 **Olsen and Graves were finally confirmed:** "On the Nomination PN610: Matthew G. Olsen, of Maryland, to Be an Assistant Attorney General," Roll Call Votes, Senate Vote #443 in 2021 (117th Congress), govtrack.us, October 28, 2021.

187 **discuss the potential charge:** Leonnig and Davis, "FBI Resisted Opening Probe into Trump's Role in Jan. 6 for More than a Year."

187 **Graves proposed to Monaco that he create a new unit:** Leonnig and Davis, "FBI Resisted Opening Probe into Trump's Role in Jan. 6 for More than a Year"; Justice Department officials, multiple interviews with the author, 2023–24.

187 **fake electors scheme:** Mike Giglio, "What the Conviction of Stewart Rhodes Means for Right-Wing Militancy," *The New Yorker*, December 7, 2022.

187 **D'Antuono opposed the request:** Stephen D'Antuono, multiple interviews with the author, 2023.

188 **financed the "Stop the Steal" rally:** Luke Broadwater, "House Panel Subpoenas Roger Stone and Alex Jones in Capitol Riot Inquiry," *New York Times*, November 22, 2021.

188 **three retired generals wrote an op-ed:** Paul D. Eaton, Antonio M. Taguba, and Steven M. Anderson, "3 Retired Generals: The Military Must Prepare Now for a 2024 Insurrection," *Washington Post*, December 17, 2021.

189 **Garland gave a lengthy speech:** Department of Justice, Office of Public Affairs, "Attorney General Merrick B. Garland Delivers Remarks on the First Anniversary of the Attack on the Capitol," Department of Justice, January 5, 2022.

190 **indicted on charges of seditious conspiracy:** Alan Feuer and Adam Goldman, "Oath Keepers Leader Charged with Seditious Conspiracy in Jan. 6 Investigation," *New York Times*, January 13, 2022.

Chapter 13: A Clear and Convincing Case

193 **Pressure on the DOJ to probe Trump's effort:** Edward-Isaac Dovere, "Democrats Fret as Garland's January 6 Investigation Creeps Closer to Pre-midterm Deadline," CNN, June 8, 2022.

193 **Lisa Monaco told CNN that the DOJ was investigating:** Evan Perez and Tierney Sneed, "Exclusive: Federal Prosecutors Looking at 2020 Fake Elector Certifications, Deputy Attorney General Tells CNN," January 26, 2022.

195 **Hunt rejected a claim by Democratic strategist James Carville:** Jody Hunt, multiple interviews with the author, 2023–24.

195 **Hunt said, referring to the many witnesses:** Hunt, multiple interviews with the author, 2023–24.

196 **Garland concentrated on how the documents could be recovered:** Justice Department officials, multiple interviews with the author, 2023–24.

196 **they stonewalled:** Justice Department officials, multiple interviews with the author, 2023–24.

198 **Windom was also working with postal service investigators:** Glenn Thrush and Adam Goldman, "Inside Garland's Effort to Prosecute Trump," *New York Times*, March 22, 2024.

199 **they decided to subpoena surveillance camera footage:** Steven D'Antuono, multiple interviews with the author, 2023.

199 **As a Mar-a-Lago search grew more likely:** FBI and DOJ officials, multiple interviews with the author, 2023–24.

200 **The former official said that the bureau should have been much more aggressive:** Former senior FBI official, multiple interviews with the author, 2023–24.

201 **"In my mind, it put water on the fire":** Former senior FBI official, multiple interviews with the author, 2023–24.

201 **when false claims were made against it by Trump:** David Rohde, "After the Trump Raid, Silence Is Not an Option for Merrick Garland," *The New Yorker*, August 9, 2022.

202 **The guy who made sure that FBI informants were active:** Tucker Carlson, "There's a Reason the Public's Confidence in the FBI Has Plummeted," Fox News, August 16, 2022.

203 **"All I was trying to do was call a good game":** Steven D'Antuono, interview with the author, 2023.

CHAPTER 14: DELAY

204 **the ruling served to bolster Trump's claim:** David Rohde, "The Mar-a-Lago Raid and the Trumpification of the Judiciary," *The New Yorker*, September 7, 2022.

204 **"many sinister and evil outside sources":** Donald J. Trump (@realDonaldTrump), Truth Social, September 5, 2022, 1:23 p.m.

205 **Ryan Goodman . . . told the *New York Times*:** Charlie Savage, "'Deeply Problematic': Experts Question Judge's Intervention in Trump Inquiry," *New York Times*, September 5, 2022.

205 **"The government has very strong evidence":** Martha McCallum, "Bill Barr on 'Deeply Flawed' Special Master Ruling," Fox News, September 6, 2022.

206 **"Judges are in some ways, the last wall":** Rosalind S. Helderman and Elise Viebeck, "'The Last Wall': How Dozens of Judges across the Political Spectrum Rejected Trump's Efforts to Overturn the Election," *Washington Post*, December 12, 2020.

207 **"The loss of public trust in our constitutional order"**: Helderman and Viebeck, " 'The Last Wall.' "

208 **Steve Vladeck, a law professor at the University of Texas**: Steve Vladeck,
"Trump's Supreme Court Gambit Isn't Frivolous. Why It Will Likely Fail Anyway," MSNBC.com, October 10, 2022.

209 **there was a logic to Trump's repeated court battles**: Jake Grumbach, interview
with the author, 2023.

209 **Ilya Somin, a law professor at George Mason University**: Interview with the
author, 2023.

210 **Aziz Huq, a law professor at the University of Chicago**: Interview with the
author, 2023.

Chapter 15: Silver Bullets

211 **"In order to make America great and glorious again"**: Gabby Orr, Kristen
Holmes, and Veronica Stracqualursi, "Former President Donald Trump
Announces a White House Bid for 2024," CNN, November 16, 2022.

212 **"I am here today to announce the appointment of a special counsel"**: US Department of Justice, Office of Public Affairs, "Attorney General Merrick B. Garland
Delivers Remarks on the Appointment of a Special Counsel," November 18, 2022.

214 **"IMPEACH MERRICK GARLAND!"**: Marjorie Taylor Greene (@repMTG),
Twitter, November 18, 2022, 2:52 p.m.

214 **"You just can't make this stuff up"**: Andrew Clyde (@Rep_Clyde), Twitter,
November 21, 2022, 5:34 p.m.

216 **he saw Smith as an "attack dog"**: Former Justice Department official who asked
not to be named, multiple interviews with the author, 2023.

216 **In a 2018 interview posted by the Nashville Aquatic Club**: "Masters/TRI
Q&A: Jack Smith," Nashville Aquatic Club (swimnac.com), January 31, 2018.

219 **"Jack Smith came after me"**: James Risen, "I Experienced Jack Smith's Zeal
Firsthand. Will Trump Get the Same Treatment?," The Intercept, November 23, 2022.

222 **Rosenstein . . . offered some advice**: Rosenstein, multiple interviews with the
author, 2023.

Chapter 16: Unintended Consequences

223 **Smith assembled a small team of prosecutors**: Justice Department officials,
multiple interviews with the author, 2023–24.

225 **forty-nine-page indictment**: Scott Simon and Deepa Shivaram, "What We
Know about the Trump Indictment So Far," NPR, June 10, 2023.

226 **Taveras told investigators that De Oliveira pushed him**: Katherine Faulders,
Alexander Mallin, and Mike Levine, "Recent Obstruction Charges against

Trump, Others Followed Cooperation from Mar-a-Lago IT Worker: Sources," *ABC News*, August 22, 2023.

229 **in the Hunter Biden case:** Devlin Barrett and Jacqueline Alemany, "Backroom Battles between IRS Agents, Prosecutors in Hunter Biden Tax Case," *Washington Post*, October 2, 2023.

230 **We are talking about the criminal justice system:** Justice Department official, multiple interviews with the author, 2023–24.

231 **Jody Hunt, Jeff Sessions's former chief of staff:** Interviews with the author, 2023.

232 **Sarah Isgur, the spokesperson for the DOJ under Sessions:** Interviews with the author, 2023.

232 **Ed O'Callaghan, the senior Rosenstein aide:** Interviews with the author, 2023.

232 **Steven D'Antuono, the FBI agent who tried to slow the FBI search:** Interviews with the author, 2023.

233 **Nate Huber, the FBI intelligence instructor who flatly rejects:** Interviews with the author, 2023.

233 **the former senior FBI official involved in the Mar-a-Lago case:** Interviews with the author, 2023.

233 **Erica Newland, the former career DOJ lawyer:** Interviews with the author, 2023 and 2024.

Epilogue: Equal Justice

235 **When 57 percent of Americans polled supported his removal:** Andrew Kohut, "From the Archives: How the Watergate Crisis Eroded Public Support for Richard Nixon," Pew Research Center, September 25, 2019.

235 **some, little, or no confidence in the Justice Department:** Charles Franklin, "New Marquette Law School National Survey Finds Biden Trailing Three GOP Opponents, Trump Dominating GOP Primary," Marquette University Law School Poll, October 4, 2023.

235 **"has never been a student of history and has no sense of shame":** Interview with the author, 2024.

238 **Jack Goldsmith . . . has proposed reforms:** Jack Goldsmith, "The Failure of Presidential Reform for a Second Trump Presidency," *Lawfare*, May 15, 2023.

ABOUT THE AUTHOR

David Rohde is a two-time winner of the Pulitzer Prize and the author of *In Deep: The FBI, the CIA, and the Truth about America's "Deep State"* and three other books. He is the national security editor at NBC News and a former executive editor of the *New Yorker* website, where he wrote about the Justice Department, democracy, and disinformation. He is also a former *New York Times*, Reuters, and *Christian Science Monitor* reporter. He lives in New York with his family.